HEATHER GOODALL grew up at Padstow near Salt Pan Creek on the Georges River and has worked closely with Aboriginal people in numerous innovative social histories. She is the author of *Invasion to Embassy: Land in Aboriginal Politics in NSW*, which won the NSW Premier's Prize for Australian History in 1997 and, with Isabel Flick, a senior Aboriginal activist from north-western NSW, *Isabel Flick: The Many Lives of an Extraordinary Aboriginal Woman*, which was awarded the Magarey Medal for Australian women's biography in 2005. Heather is co-editor of two international volumes on environmental history: *Echoes from the Poisoned Well: Global Memories of Environmental Injustice* (2006) and *Waters, Sovereignty and Borders in Asia and Oceania* (2008). She is currently Professor of History at UTS where she is researching the relations between Australia's people and environments with those around the Indian Ocean region.

ALLISON CADZOW has been senior researcher on the UTS/DECC's Georges River parklands and cultural diversity project, and co-authored the website *Gold and Silver: Vietnamese Migration and Relationships with Environments in Vietnam and Sydney* (2006). She is currently co-editing an HSC Aboriginal Studies teachers' resource book with Professor John Maynard. She has been an assistant curator at the National Museum of Australia. Allison received the 2009 Library Council of NSW Honorary Fellowship to research the State Library of NSW's collections on traveller, environmentalist, Buddhist, feminist and solicitor Marie Byles.

Rivers and Resilience

Aboriginal people on Sydney's Georges River

Heather Goodall and Allison Cadzow

UNSW
PRESS

A UNSW Press book

Published by
University of New South Wales Press Ltd
University of New South Wales
Sydney NSW 2052
AUSTRALIA
www.unswpress.com.au

National Library of Australia
Cataloguing-in-Publication entry
Author: Goodall, Heather.
Title: Rivers and resilience: Aboriginal people on Sydney's Georges River/
Heather Goodall, Allison Cadzow.
ISBN: 978 1 92141 074 1 (pbk.)
Notes: Includes index.
Subjects: Aboriginal Australians – New South Wales –
    Georges River – History.
    Aboriginal Australians, Treatment of – New South Wales –
    Georges River – History.
    First contact of aboriginal peoples with Westerners –
    New South Wales – Georges River.
Other Authors/Contributors: Cadzow, Allison.
Dewey Number: 305.89915099441

Design Di Quick
Front cover photomontage Di Quick *Georges River National Park*
Back cover L-R Joe Anderson (courtesy *Cinesound Review*, no.100, 29 September,
1933: reproduced with permission of Thought Equity Motion, Ellen James née
Williams and Judy Chester née Smith

Contents

To Kevin Cook
who has been inspirational in linking the city river
communities to wider communities in country areas,
across the nation and around the world.

To the reader

Warning: This book contains some stories and photos of Aboriginal people who have passed away. Including their names and their images allows an accurate record to be kept. However, we understand that in some Aboriginal communities, seeing the names and photographs of the deceased may cause sadness and distress, particularly to relatives of those people. So we ask you to proceed with caution, and to accept our apologies for any sadness caused through these necessary inclusions.

Spelling: There is some variation in the spelling of many Aboriginal names and words, due largely to the inconsistent practices of white observers and recorders over the years. We have used the most generally accepted forms, which are either those indicated in J Kohen and R Lampert, *Australians to 1788*, or *Barani*, the City of Sydney Aboriginal History website, although some Local Land Councils have chosen a different spelling. We appreciate that the spellings we have used will not always be the forms some people prefer.

All reasonable efforts were taken to obtain permission to use copyright material reproduced in this book, but in some cases copyright holders could not be traced. The authors welcome information in this regard.

Acknowledgments

Many people have been involved in the writing of this book. In particular, a history of Aboriginal people on the Georges River could not have been written without the generous support, encouragement and feedback of the many Aboriginal people who have a connection with the river. We hope this book will be just the start of many more of their stories being heard by a wider audience and across the years. A special thank you to all the participants who are listed throughout the book, but especially to those who have shared their family stories with us: Shayne Williams, Ellen James, Judy Chester, Janny Ely, Kevin Cook, Lewis Solberg, Allan Carriage, Wayne Dargan, Dean Kelly, Denis Foley, Robyn Williams, Cliff Foley, John Lennis, Jason Groves, Kerry Toomey, Karen Maber, Tony Pearce, Brad Steadman, Robyn Young, Fran Bodkin, Lesley Yasso and to many others.

Funding support has been essential for our research, and we would like to thank the institutions which have offered it: the NSW

Department of Environment and Climate Change, the Australian Research Council and the University of Technology, Sydney. This book has been written as one part of the wider ARC-funded Linkage research project, *Parklands, Culture and Communities*, led by Heather Goodall and Stephen Wearing (UTS) and Denis Byrne (DECC).

The artist Ken Searle has made a great contribution to the book through his evocative hand-drawn local maps and shoreline images. The valuable overview map of the river has been lucidly drawn by cartographer Ian Faulkner. Our publisher Phillipa McGuiness has given us sustained support and encouragement from the book's conception, and we appreciate the guidance of Heather Cam, Di Quick and Chantal Gibbs at UNSW Press, and James Drown's careful editing in bringing it to fruition.

Peter Read has played an important role in reading sections of the book and offering excellent advice from its earliest stages, with his enthusiastic support along the way, and most recently in his role in organising explorations by boat to the many places along the river.

Historical records, photos and newspapers have been an important source for this book. Some are in the care of Aboriginal organisations and others are held in the major libraries or local studies collections. We are grateful for the assistance of the staff of State Records NSW, where a range of government records are kept. The State Library of NSW, with its specialist manuscript and picture holdings in the Mitchell library, holds important records and is assisted by its Aboriginal staff, Melissa Jackson and Ronald Briggs. On particular themes, we have been greatly assisted by the staff of the National Archives of Australia, National Library of Australia, the Australian War Memorial, the Australian Institute of Aboriginal and Torres Strait Islander Studies, the National Film and Sound Archive, the Powerhouse Museum, the archivists at the Department of Environment and Climate Change, and the Local Studies librarians in Hurstville, Rockdale, Sutherland, Liverpool, Bankstown and Kogarah.

Tranby Aboriginal Cooperative College has been a particularly important source of collaboration and energy in the Aboriginal and wider Australian communities. It is also an extensive source of images and archives, and the Tranby staff have been unfailingly helpful in supporting this book. Our thanks as well to the staff and organisations of the Gandangara and Tharawal Local Aboriginal Land Councils and to the Northern Illawarra Aboriginal Collective. The DECC staff, and particularly Vanessa Cavanagh, Pam Young, Jody Orcher, Christine Hopkins, Georgina Eldershaw and Damian Lucas, have all been constantly supportive. The River Keeper for the Georges River, Simon Annabel, and the Georges River Combined Councils Committee were also helpful. We would especially like to thank Vandana Ram, at Bankstown Council, and Jo Morris at Liverpool City Library for their sustained and creative encouragement.

In order to write a history about a long length of a city river, covering many different local areas and over a long period of time, we have been greatly assisted by many generous researchers, educators and activists. They have offered resources, references and time; they have read drafts to give wonderful feedback and have asked penetrating, challenging and useful questions. We would particularly like to thank Dr Jo Kijas and Dr Stephen Gapps for their thorough, tenacious and innovative research. We have been greatly assisted by the generous support and long experience of Terry Kass, Sharyn Cullis, Bob Haworth, David Morrisey, Keith Vincent Smith, Grace Karskens, David Hollinsworth, Chris Illert, Ted Trainer, Pauline Curby, Beverly Earnshaw, Michael Organ, Suzanne Kenney and Brian Shaw. Above all, we would like to thank Denis Byrne for his sustained, thoughtful feedback.

Finally, each of us would like to say thank you as well to the people close to us who have kept us going while we worked on this book: From Allison, thanks to my ever-supportive family, especially my mother Jan and my father Jim. Your love, support and encouragement have flowed constantly from the very beginning and mean so much to me. My sister Fiona and brother Stuart have also been a source of strength. Thanks to my friends Miranda Cook, Suzie Oneeglio, Amanda Sutton, Collette Vella and Alisa Duff for numerous discussions. Special thanks to Ali Jaffee who has listened patiently, advised and questioned thoughtfully – and helped keep me afloat in so many ways.

From Heather, thanks to my friends Val, Elliott and Chris Goodacre, and my brothers Craig and Mark Goodall for wonderful memories; to Barbara Flick and Judy Chester for hard advice and good humour; to my mother-in-law Judy Torzillo for warm support and brilliant editing; to my daughters Judith and Emma, for their enthusiasm for the past and their hopes for the future, and to my husband Paul, for his perceptive insights, endless patience and unfailing love.

ONE

Aboriginal people and city rivers: an introduction

In 1933 an Aboriginal man, Joe Anderson, appeared on a Cinesound newsreel in cinemas around Australia. Speaking from a bushland setting, and demanding respect with his first words, he said:

> Before the white man set foot in Australia, my ancestors had kings in their own right, and I, Aboriginal King Burraga, am a direct descendant of the royal line ... There is plenty fish in the river for us all, and land to grow all we want ... The black man owned Australia, and now he demands more than charity. He wants the right to LIVE![1]

Where was he when he spoke? Not in the remote desert of Australia or on the tradition-rich Darling or Clarence Rivers in rural New South Wales, places where white Australians were then more used to seeing Aboriginal people.

Joe Anderson said this on the banks of Salt Pan Creek, a tributary

Joe Anderson speaking
near his home at Salt Pan
Creek in 1933.

of the Georges River near Bankstown. Even in 1933, this river was right in the middle of Sydney's fastest growing population. On its banks had been built most of the city's new factories, and its waters were carrying the worst of their pollution.

How did Joe Anderson come to say this in the middle of the city, when Aboriginal people are not 'supposed' to have a history in city landscapes? Why was he standing on Salt Pan Creek in particular, and what did that place mean to him? Why did he want to say it at all? And how on earth did his speech make it into the cinemas all around Australia?

Joe Anderson had pushed his way on to the new film industry's newsreels to get his message heard. He was facing an urgent threat. His family – Dharawal people – had lived on their country on the Georges River for generations, and he had dwelt on Salt Pan Creek for over 20 years. For much of Joe's lifetime, Aboriginal people had lived in relative peace with their white neighbours on this part of the river, but from the early 1930s the pressure to evict them had escalated as it never had before. Now describing the Aboriginal people who lived there as 'newcomers', the local white population argued that they, not the Aboriginal people at Salt Pan, should decide the river's future.

It was also no accident that he made his appeal from this Salt Pan Creek camp. The role that the riverbank camp had played in sheltering political refugees and in nurturing future activists from all over the state and beyond was even more remarkable than Joe's ability to reach the public eye. Jack Patten, Bert Groves, Bill Onus, Ted Thomas, Charlie Leon, Jacko Campbell and Tom Williams were each to become iconic names in later decades, and they had all lived in this camp on this river through the 1930s. Their future directions were shaped by their vigorous discussions around the camp fires, and by the fearless Friday night public speeches that Joe and other older camp members delivered to white passers-by in the city markets.

How had this happened? How had Salt Pan Creek become a place which generated so much energy and built so many connections beyond its own small area?

All these questions become even more puzzling when we learn just a bit about Joe's very long history on the river. He was directly descended from the northern Dharawal people who had always owned the Georges River area. Yet this was no simple community. Joe was also related to the southern Dharawal people from the Five Islands near Wollongong, while his stepfather was from the Murray River and his brothers and sisters were related or married to people from different places again, right across the state. His community then was not one which had endured by staying the same. It had continued to exist on the river because it had engaged with the traumas and stresses of more than a century of living in a colonised city, and had adapted and developed so it could come out fighting like Joe did in 1933.

This capacity to engage actively with traumatic change is close to the current uses in psychology of the word 'resilience', implying not only the capacity to absorb stress but to transform in order to cope with it.[2] This is different from the way the word is used in economics and ecology, where it suggests a return to a steady state after stresses; a restorative rather than a transformative process.[3] The Aboriginal experiences on the river have not allowed a return to the past, but they have drawn on the past to make a new future. The way Joe Anderson phrased his speech is a demonstration: building from the authority conferred by the past, he was looking to the present and future to demand justice.

The film of Joe standing at the camp on the bank of Salt Pan Creek also points us to the Georges River itself. Just a few more inquiries make it clear that Aboriginal people were not scattered over the geography of the whole city. Instead, they were living on or near the city's rivers. So the wider question which this book examines is what role have rivers played in the resilience demonstrated by Joe's presence and his words?

Rediscovering
the river

This book came about because in the 1970s Jacko Campbell challenged one of us, Heather Goodall, to learn more about the place that Jacko and I both shared – Salt Pan Creek. Jacko had been campaigning for justice for Aboriginal people all his life. Born at Burnt Bridge in Kempsey early in the 1920s, he had travelled with his family to live some of his childhood at that busy, exciting camp on the eastern side of Salt Pan Creek, before later becoming a senior figure in the Jerinja community at Roseby Park. I had been born in the 1950s and had grown up in Padstow on the western side of Salt Pan Creek. Jacko and I had gone to the same school, although not at the same time. Jacko wanted to know why I hadn't heard about all these extraordinary people living just a few miles away from my house. And he wasn't only talking about the 1930s: he was still talking and planning the future with the Aboriginal communities on the Georges River.

Many Aboriginal people have been involved and interested in the making of this book, and their stories begin to be told in it. Both of us, Heather and Allison, are from non-Aboriginal backgrounds, but our lives have been entangled with the Georges River as well. Heather, as Jacko had pointed out, grew up there and really should have known about this rich history. My ignorance demonstrated just how painfully little local white people know about this continuing story. Allison was born in the 1970s, and like many other people had moved to the river suburbs after living elsewhere. She visited popular places on the river like the Carrs Park bushland with her family on weekends.

As historians, our work has led us to the archives, but most importantly it has led to the Aboriginal communities who continue to be connected by the river. Talking with people about how they have remembered life on the Georges River has opened up some new ways to think about Aboriginal history in the city. It turns out that there are many

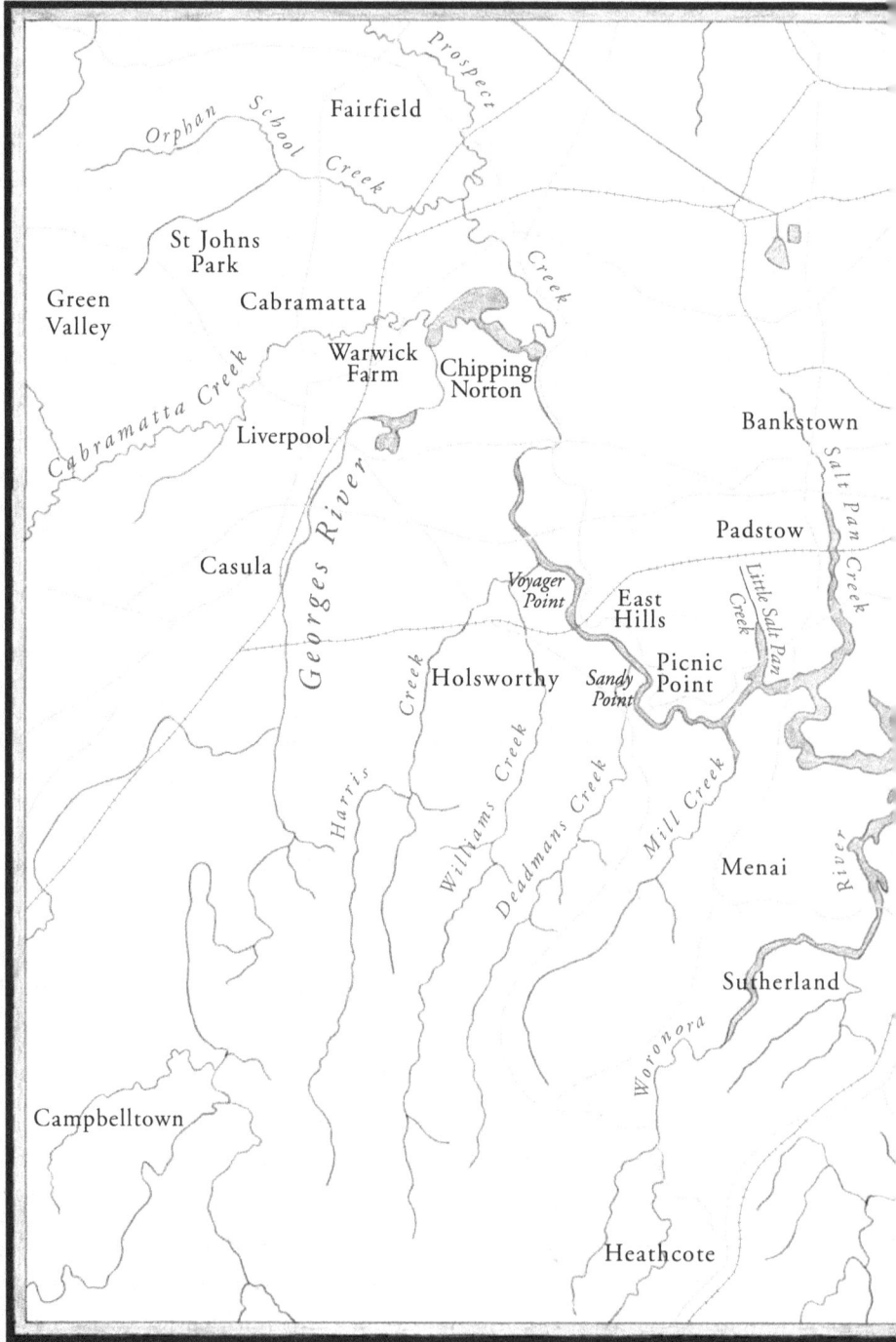

Orphan School Creek

Fairfield

Prospect Creek

St Johns Park

Green Valley

Cabramatta

Warwick Farm

Chipping Norton

Cabramatta Creek

Liverpool

Bankstown

Georges River

Padstow

Salt Pan Creek

Casula

Voyager Point

East Hills

Little Salt Pan Creek

Holsworthy

Sandy Point

Picnic Point

Harris Creek

Williams Creek

Deadmans Creek

Mill Creek

Menai

River

Sutherland

Campbelltown

Woronora

Heathcote

Ian Faulkner

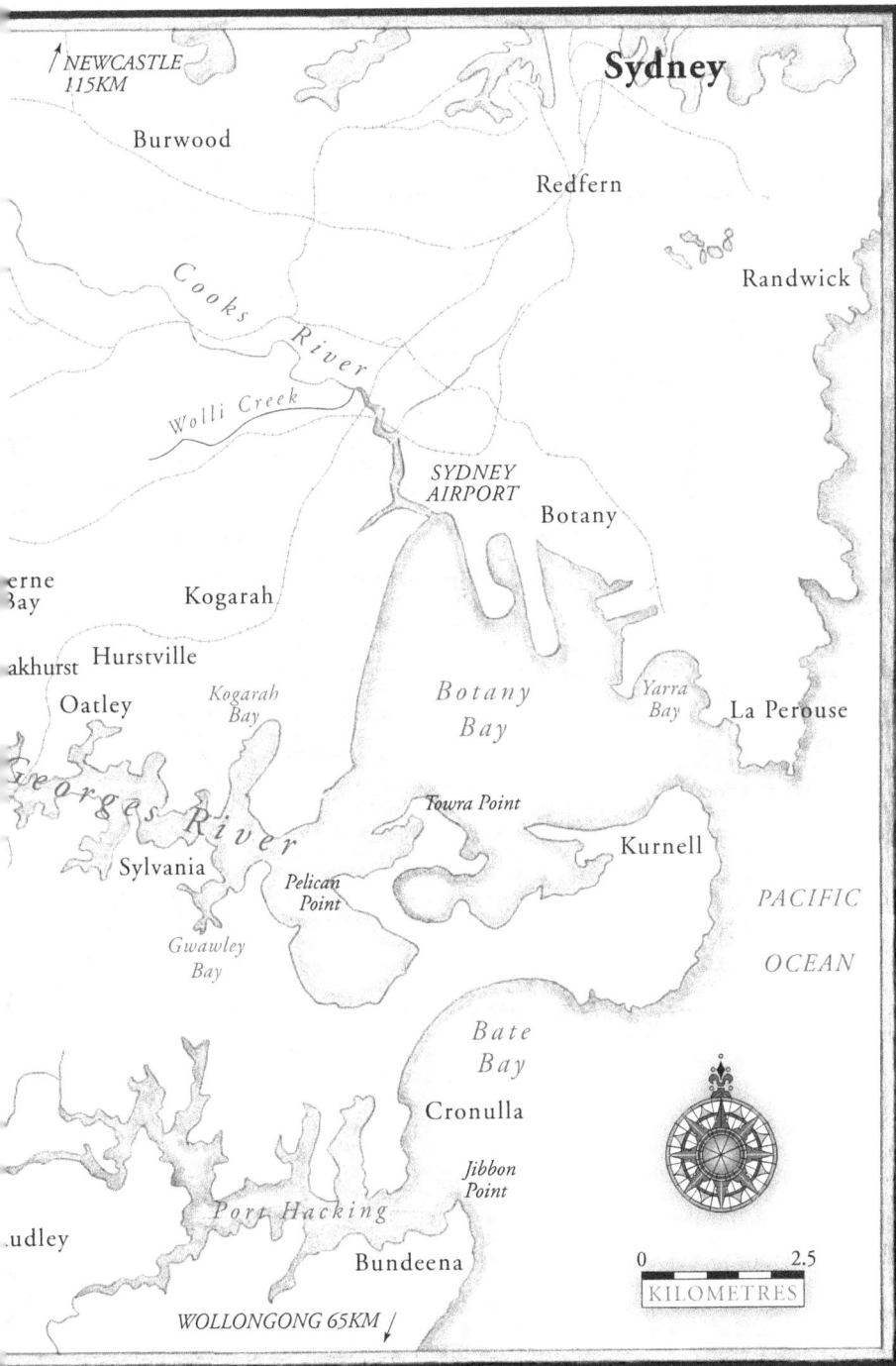

NEWCASTLE 115KM

Sydney

Burwood

Redfern

Randwick

Cooks River

Wolli Creek

SYDNEY AIRPORT

Botany

erne Bay

Kogarah

akhurst

Hurstville

Oatley

Kogarah Bay

Botany Bay

Yarra Bay

La Perouse

Georges River

Sylvania

Towra Point

Pelican Point

Kurnell

PACIFIC OCEAN

Gwawley Bay

Bate Bay

Cronulla

Jibbon Point

udley

Port Hacking

Bundeena

WOLLONGONG 65KM

0   2.5
KILOMETRES

stories as compelling as Joe Anderson's, but to find them it has been important to refocus our research and take some different approaches.

Firstly, this book focuses on the river itself, and on the mobility it allowed, as a key way to understand Indigenous people's continued presence. While this is a history of the Aboriginal people and the land along the Georges River, it does not concentrate on the surveyed boundaries of properties, Aboriginal reserves or National Parks. This story emphasises the relationship *between* sites and places, rather than thinking only about the patches of land inside any one set of fences. To do this, it stresses the waterways which formed the shape of the land in the first place and the rich environments of which, both before and after colonisation, have provided an intensively harvested economic source, a rapid transport and communication system, and a source of cultural symbol and narrative. If we concentrate only on spots and sites on the land – especially the well-known Aboriginal reserve at La Perouse – we lose sight of the way people have moved along and around the river, not only before settlement but ever since. They have used its full length, and the flexibility it gives, to communicate and to rebuild their sense of cultural responsibility to both kin and country.

Secondly, it will make links, both across time and between the different points of view that come from focusing on local issues or looking more broadly across a region or a country. Across time, we link the accounts of early conflict between settlers and Aboriginal owners and the present day experience of Indigenous people in Sydney. Much published work has focused on one or the other, but it has given little indication of how the distant past and the present have been directly linked, nor does it show how change has occurred over time. Such change involved both people and places – and the impacts of urbanisation have been powerful on land and waterways along the Georges River. Logging, grazing, agriculture and fishing had all caused great changes by the early twentieth century, not dissimilar to those faced by Aboriginal people in rural areas. After 1940, however, the intensification of the city economy, with more factories and more population, put unprecedented pressure on the city's environment, quite unlike those known in the bush. Most of the new factories and most of the incoming people were placed on the Georges River and its sister the Cooks, which also flows into Botany Bay. These two rivers paid the heaviest price for Sydney's growth.

This book links the Aboriginal history and local stories of this one small area with the wider changes and policy shifts which have occurred across the state. Did these policies work out differently in city areas than in rural areas? Did local conditions reflect the overall policy, or was something different happening when policies were implemented on the ground and in different areas? And did policies that claimed to be for everyone affect everyone in the same way? The book will show as well how Aboriginal history was linked to the wider currents of Australian history like industrialisation and warfare. And it will link the stories of the local people in each chapter with environmental changes in the rivers, the city and the region.

Thirdly, this book will trace the histories of the complex Sydney Aboriginal communities which have existed from these very early days. It is not only about Aboriginal people who were on the Georges River at the time of the British invasion. The histories of the people or the language groups who lived on the river at that time are the subject of rich and important continuing work.[4] The debate about who can and who cannot be considered as 'traditional owners' in any area has become more heated because of the demands of the 1993 Native Title Act, which requires a proven 'traditional' relationship to a place before a claim can be lodged. Given the adversarial nature of these cases, this question continues to be discussed throughout the state and the nation. Yet this reflects only one strand in the broader history in any area. The tracing of traditional owners is not, therefore, the focus of this study.

The evidence we have found about the Georges River demonstrates that, from the earliest days of British settlement, there was frequent movement into and out of the Sydney township and the whole Georges River valley by Aboriginal people who had come from right across the state and beyond. They have all helped to form Aboriginal Sydney as it is today. Together they have created families which were a mixture of traditional owners and incoming Aboriginal peoples who lived with, married into and worked with the survivors from earlier groups of river communities. Some of them also lived with, married and worked with non-Aboriginal people in relationships which varied widely. Some were exploitative and some conflictual but sometimes they were deeply affectionate and mutually supportive. The question is not whether there were families built across racial and geographic lines – because there undoubtedly were. Rather, the real questions are about what the qualities of those relationships were. Why did some allow the Aboriginal partners to express their Aboriginal identity strongly, while others meant that Aboriginal family backgrounds were ignored or denied? The book will consider the experiences of both women and men, to understand why the stories of some might be missing from the records, even though they were very important to how Aboriginal families survived. Over time, all of these people have formed the Sydney Aboriginal communities which have challenged racial segregation and discrimination, and have forced recognition of Aboriginal people's rights to full citizenship. They have demanded acknowledgement of the role of Aboriginal people to exercise cultural responsibility to protect the lands and waters of their city homes.

We use these approaches to answer our questions about how Salt Pan Creek became a place which could generate Joe Anderson's speech. In doing so, we will be exploring some of the major ideas which are circulating in debates in Australia – and around the world – about land, indigeneity and change, about environment and about cities. Some of these ideas are not usually considered in relation to Aboriginal people, or are not used in discussions about cities. We plan to do both because they help us understand the resilience of Aboriginal cultures on the river. These ideas are about: 'tradition' in Aboriginal Australian and global Indigenous societies (including environmental knowledge) and its relationship to change over time; the ongoing cultural and social work which is done by all societies to create meaning in places, to 'make locality'; the relationship of mobility to the attachment to single or bounded places; and the nature of 'nature', and what it stands for in human societies, large and small, rural and urban.

'Traditional' knowledge and change

Ideas about Aboriginal traditions and their cultural and social relations to land have been dominated by research into communities living in remote or rural areas. Aboriginal people in cites today are often assumed to be from some other place, which is where their 'real' attachment must continue to be sustained. Or they are assumed to have lost any direct relationship to the landscape because the city environment has changed so much since the initial European invasion or since urbanisation began. Both these assumptions are based on the mistaken idea that Aboriginal 'traditional' cultures were unchanging and static, consisting of a closed and fully formed parcel of knowledge or stories which could be handed down intact across generations for thousands of years – and which therefore could not cope with changes.

Like all human cultures, Aboriginal philosophies, values and environmental knowledge have been dynamic, shaped by both conservative and creative forces within Aboriginal societies. There are many dimensions to tradition which involve process rather than content. The ways in which people acquire custodial responsibilities for land, for example, are known to involve far more than simple inheritance from a parent. Instead multiple events, such as the place of one's conception and birth, confer potential responsibility. Each of these circumstances demand that mothers and families are acutely aware of locations and the changes in them, to ensure the growing child is well informed. The outcome is that people are encouraged to pay close attention to the land in which they are living and for which they have responsibilities – which will in turn continually refresh the details of the environmental relationships within the story. Traditional narratives can, in such ways, embody details about both past and changing environments. Alterations in environmental details can be folded into the patterns of the existing oral medium, just as extra stanzas about new events can be included in traditional songs at the geographically correct points, identifying where (rather than when) the new event occurred.[5]

So in Australian Aboriginal societies, as Indigenous and non-Indigenous researchers have explained, ceremonies and oral traditions have always involved an interaction between established, existing knowledge and the ongoing changes in the natural and human environment which inevitably faced any society which has survived so well for so long.[6] Aboriginal traditional societies were the custodians of flexible, responsive cultures which allowed Aboriginal people both to keep the best and richest of their traditions and yet still record and cope with changes.

The differences can be seen by considering the very common idea among natural resource managers today that 'traditional environmental knowledge' can be listed and laid out in a database because it consists of a set of separate, itemised 'facts' or data. This might record the valuable details of traditional stories, but it will miss the moral of such stories about life principles which will form the plot or the overall values of the story.[7] This was the sort of argument used against the Yorta Yorta people in their Native Title claim in 1998, when Federal Court judge Justice Olney told them he would not grant their claim on the Murray River and the surrounding area because 'the tide of history has indeed washed away any real acknowledgment of their traditional laws and any real observance of their traditional customs'.[8] In making 'tradition' sound like a collection of unchanging items, Olney took this database view that traditional culture could not change or adapt or engage with challenging new environments. The demands of present-day political campaigns have often pushed Aboriginal people and their supporters into a similar position of ignoring cultural change. Ironically, what have seemed victories, such as land rights laws, have often locked people into similar, inflexible constraints on the way that evidence from the past, always fragmentary at best, is collected, interpreted and disputed as if it could not engage with change.[9]

A strong body of international research concludes that the fixed, 'database' view of traditional environmental knowledge is not adequate. The work of Firket Berkes in Canada and elsewhere shows that, on the contrary, traditional indigenous knowledges are shaped in constant interaction with changing environments. Close attention and constant feedback between the material conditions and the people who live close to them informs indigenous knowledges.[10] Traditional societies, Berkes shows, are able to respond to seasonal and to longer-term changes because their knowledge is dynamic and develops to fit changing environments, rather than remaining static and so losing connections to the environment as it changes around them.

This capacity to engage with changing environments in a pre-colonial setting must have been severely challenged by the greatly accelerated changes occurring after the sudden arrival of colonisers. The British brought with them new methods of land-use, rapidly changing the landscape. They brought new diseases, which just as rapidly reduced Aboriginal populations. The changes to landscapes and waterways have been greatest of all in areas where cities have developed. Yet because Aboriginal cultures have always had the capacity to engage with changing environments and conditions, they may not have been 'broken' or 'washed away'. Instead, Aboriginal cultural principles and processes may have survived, even if the details of day-to-day practice had to be greatly changed. Such processes of cultural life may have been used as strategies to make sense of new conditions. A number of researchers have begun investigating how Aboriginal societies and cultures might have coped with change in remote and rural Australia, where a very large proportion of Aboriginal people lived until the mid-twentieth century.[11]

This book will ask those questions of a city environment, and in particular that of a river. Sydney, though often thought of as a harbour city, is a city where river valleys penetrate right into the heart of the central business district and run through every type of residential and commercial development. These rivers offer variable and unstable geographies which have ensured that settler developments – right up to the present day – have not been able to proceed evenly. How would Aboriginal cultural processes have been maintained on a river like the Georges River, which flows through the most dense populations and the heaviest industrial development in the whole of the city? We argue that close study of river history can show how this has worked.

One example of this is Guragurang, which is the only river in our study area for which the local language name has survived British colonisation. Guragurang is the Dharawal name for Mill Creek, which runs into the Georges River from the south near what is now Menai. The presence of a number of Aboriginal people at this junction who were prepared to talk with the botanist explorer Robert Brown in 1803 led to the name being recorded in the first place.[12] Later it was the qualities of the river bank and bushland along the western bank of Guragurang/Mill Creek which made it a key site for Aboriginal survival in the mid-nineteenth century. We know about this story, once again, because the Aboriginal people living independently there were also active in their interaction with white travellers. Finally, Guragurang

returns to view once more when it becomes a key site in the transformative strategies of late twentieth-century Aboriginal people as
they remake cultural responsibility for country with a defence of the
land along its eastern escarpments.

The meaning of place:
'making locality'

The second important cluster of ideas concerns cultural relationships
to land. These have been discussed most usefully by Arjun Appadurai, an anthropologist who has worked on the comparison between
modern small-scale societies, like Aboriginal kinship networks, and
large-scale societies, like those which exist in cities.[13] Appadurai looks
at the things such societies have in common in how they relate to
places. He points out that no relationship to place is ever inevitable or
'natural', no matter how small-scale the society is. Each culture has to
put a lot of cultural effort, through ceremonies, rituals, conventions
and rules, into encouraging people to feel that their relationship to
places is so 'natural' that they barely notice it. This work of 'making
locality' – which involves constantly building and renewing the relationships between places and people – is done through the patterns
and expectations of the society, that is, through its culture. Hugh Raffles, observing how people go about 'making places' in the Amazon,
argued that locality was more than simple location. He explained that
the 'the hard, often deliberate work of place making' resulted in a
meaningful environment which was more than the physical elements
of a place: it included the meanings people had developed about it and
the wider connections they brought to it.[14]

People have to keep on 'making locality' all the time, they do not
just 'inherit' it fully made and finished like an artefact to be displayed
as required. 'Making locality' allows for historical change because

it does not suggest that relationships to country are fixed once and for all. Instead they are in constant interaction with changing environments (as Birkes points out) and with changing populations (as Raffles and Cederloff have discussed in expansions of Appadurai's work).[15] This idea of 'place making' or 'making locality' means that ceremonies can be understood not just as ways to remember or teach *about* country, but also as the ways to stimulate and intensify the emotional attachment *to* country. Since place-making is more about the people than the physical ground, it is equally helpful in understanding changing relationships to land in heavily settled rural areas in Brewarrina on the Barwon River, around Taree on the mid north coast of New South Wales or in the suburbs of Sydney on the Georges River.

While these places are changing, and when ceremonies might no longer be performed, one of the ways in which people with traditional affiliation might 'make locality' in these places is through everyday ways of living. This might be done by tactics like walking around a city, as de Certeau suggests in his *Practice of Everyday Life* and as Byrne and Nugent have described to Aboriginal people doing through the way they move across country in Taree.[16] Yet another everyday way to 'make locality' might be through fishing on the rivers – a productive activity which often leads to yarning and talking over memories, which strengthen attachments.[17] All these are ways to make relationships to places both 'everyday' and taken for granted but at the same time emotionally strong and very real. Yet there is no reason to think this would only apply to people with a traditional affiliation to that place. It is the process which makes the place meaningful, not the material of the place itself. So this will be a way to understand how people who originally came from another locality, as so many people living on the Georges River have, can still 'make a place' in an area to which they have only recently arrived.

Mobility and
attachment to place

The third cluster of ideas is around mobility and how it relates to the concept of 'place attachment'. This is usually considered in terms of bonding with fixed and bounded spaces, making 'local studies' a static concept. It is also a normative one – meaning that it implies that all people seek and maintain affiliation to a single bounded 'place'.

One important contribution to this cluster of ideas has been the wider discussion about immigration, a body of research in Australia which is usually conducted very separately from that about Aboriginal experience. Yet this is directly relevant for Aboriginal people who have chosen or been forced to move away from the place to which they had their earliest affiliation. This might have been where they or their parents were born and so it might be the place that they may have the most detailed knowledge about and where they might seem to have the most legitimate affiliation and responsibility. However, if a ceremony or ritual, or even just talking and reminiscing, can evoke and strengthen vivid emotional connections to country, then doing the same for a distant place will also strengthen relationships to it, even among people who are seldom able to visit. People can continue to 'make locality' long after they have left it.

At the same time, the cultural processes of making locality in one place can also be applied to a new place. For example, carefully noticing the environment in order to remember (or choose) conception and birth places is a cultural process which knits future generations into responsibilities for country. Such processes will be meaningful so far as they fulfil those central principles of Aboriginal society that are enabled by relationships to country: that is, to take on a mature role in the social network by fulfilling responsibilities to look after land.[18] These continuities have been described by Francesca Merlan in her study of Aboriginal migrants into the Northern Territory town of Katherine. These people tried to restore relationships to their more distant country by the same sort of observation of landscape in their new home as they would have carried out in their old home. In this way they were able to recognise signs of mythic energy and narrative which showed continuity with ceremonial stories from their own heritage.[19]

Despite many Aboriginal people having been displaced by choice or force from their original homelands, Australian analysts almost never consider Aboriginal people along with non-Indigenous migrants or refugees, no matter how similar their experiences of movement and dislocation may be. Recent research into migration is especially important for considering urban Aboriginal situations, particularly Iain Chambers' work on what he calls 'migrancy'.[20] He argues that migration is not a simple, one-way movement which is completed when the migrant lands in the new country, or even completed after a period of 'adjustment'. There are continuing effects as people seek to both maintain a relationship to their home country and at the same time secure their place in the new home. These experiences can be considered in relation to Aboriginal people living in Sydney but born in Wellington, just as much as for Vietnamese people living in Sydney but born in Hanoi. Both will have continuing connections to each place, and their lives will continue to be shaped by relationships to both and by their strategies to manage their sense of multiple affiliations and continuing displacement.

From her work with Roma (or Gypsies) in Europe, Liisa Malkki goes further, and her conclusions are particularly relevant for Aboriginal cultures. She argues that it has tended to be the bureaucratic officials of nation states as well as refugees who have wanted to define the normal condition as one of fixed abode, of 'rootedness' in place. This makes mobility look like a state of distress or abnormality. Malkki argues that for Roma, it is the expectation of mobility that is normal. They do not see it as either normal or functional to have a sedentary and confined geographic home base. She argues that the concept of fixed 'home' is not a universally shared one but instead a projection of particular class, cultural and historical values.[21] While Aboriginal people may share something like this view, it has been hard to express it against the relentless attacks they have faced because the British branded them as 'nomads' and used a misrepresentation of their mobility to obstruct the recognition of their rights to land.

A final but important body of research about mobility is the work of geographer Doreen Massey. She argues that 'places' are not limited to their physical borders and material conditions, but are creations of movements in both space and time. They are nodes in the networks of meaning which are created by the people who live in and move through these places.[22] So a place like Riverwood on the Georges River, for example, is 'made' through the social relationships of the people who live there, who may be simultaneously in communication with homelands in Wellington as well as with histories which stretch back decades into campsites along the riverbank in Sydney. The place where they currently live is made more meaningful because of these connections over time as well as the movement into and out of that place by the people who live there but also travel backwards and forwards to other places. So there are many 'Riverwoods', not just what is visible on the map. Although the nature of the physical landscape and river is important in shaping the activities in the area at any one time, and something in which all of its residents will share, they will each bring to it a rich web of past places and knowledges (links through time) and continuing connections (links through space). These bonds shape the way they see and value the focal 'place', the way they create meaning in this space to 'make locality'.

This merging of the ideas about locality and mobility allows us to see the river and its landscape as being created though the actions and attitudes of the people who come to it with their many networks of histories and cultures, all interacting with the changing physical environment of the river itself.[23]

Internationally, this recognition of mobility as part of a normal way to understand places is critically important in the approaches to land and water for many societies around the world. This is most evident for those which have become identified as pastoral herders or as harvesters (or 'hunter-gatherers', 'kumri' harvesters or as 'kin-ordered' societies). Pastoral herders have challenged the fixed 'rooted' orientation of the peak international bodies such as International Union for the Conservation of Nature and its working group on Indigenous and Local Communities, Equity, and Protected Areas which are now developing guidelines for the managing the relationships between indigenous peoples and parklands designated as protected areas.[24] The word 'indigenous' has been qualified into longer terms like 'mobile indigenous peoples' to recognise herders like the Sami in arctic Europe and some African pastoral groups. In Australia, such a recognition has already been demanded by Aboriginal Australians from at least 1975, when they expressed their frustrations with the Northern Territory Land Rights Act. Even from 1967 in New South Wales, Aboriginal people had been concerned when the National Parks and Wildlife Service was given charge of protecting 'Aboriginal heritage sites' but not the pathways and journeys in which these sites were often intimately embedded. The focus on fixed and bounded sites, always inherent in the settler view of landscape, has been intensified by today's political and legal context, in which Aboriginal land claims are only recognised if they can be surveyed, fenced and incorporated into some form of legal land tenure.

Mobility is a marked characteristic of Aboriginal people's experiences over the whole period of colonisation, not just from 1945 (as is often presumed) but from 1788 and even earlier. Anthropology of the most sedentary groups across the continent in Australia has shown that prior to the invasion, huge ceremonial gatherings and traditional long trade journeys were regular if not frequent occurrences. Mobility was and is as much a defining characteristic of Aboriginal cultures as affiliations with meaningful bounded places. Both are entwined and both are important. The technologies of mobility have changed and will continue to change: from canoes to rowboats and tinnies, from trains to motorcars. In the Georges River area, even the land vehicles are all still moving on routes shaped by the river valleys. Mobility was and still is crucial in people's lives.

Consolidating the links through space and time which this movement creates, the rivers have also actively drawn people to them. They have offered threads of familiarity and allowed people to feel linked to the non-urban places they remembered or to the spiritual worlds which they might have sought out for contemplation, refuge or recreation. This study will explore the recognition of the river as an important corridor of mobility which was sustained and used actively for economic and cultural Aboriginal life throughout the whole period of settlement to the present.

The nature of 'nature'

Ideas about the river's environmental history – the changing hydrology, geology, botany and zoology of the river and its landscape – are important contributors to thinking about how Salt Pan Creek came to be a significant place for Aboriginal people. It was not only a refuge but had the natural, economic and cultural resources to foster such political activity as that of Joe Anderson and the many other events which followed.[25]

There are valuable studies of the native botany and zoology of the Sydney region – including of the Georges River estuary and its surrounding region – which chart the way the environment looked before Europeans arrived.[26] Since the invasion, the major narrative of environmental history on the Georges River has been the impact of intensifying settlement and then industrialisation on the riverine ecologies. Yet as Noel Butlin discovered in the 1970s, these environmental changes had not been well recorded and there was little data from which his team could learn about the impact of long-term industrialisation.[27] The most helpful scientific analysis has often emerged from tracing a particular species, such as the mangrove plant. This plant is an important example because it has been valued by both Aboriginal and non-Aboriginal users who have harvested it for different reasons and have appreciated it in ways which changed over time. The mangrove is an indicator plant for social and cultural values as much as it is for other pressures on the river.[28] It has been the field of geography which has engaged best with the shifting economic pressures of the human societies on the river, recognising the class, racial and gendered differences in human-environmental interactions, at the same time as highlighting the environmental changes.[29]

In the confines of the city, where space and nature of any sort have become increasingly limited, the circulation of ideas about nature have also been important in influencing how the Georges River is discussed. There are two streams of thought which have shaped scientific inquiry as much as they do the social sciences and popular media. One celebrates the survival of native, local species, and seeks to foster the appreciation of them and enhance the possibilities of their continued presence, whether by conservation or by reintroduction. Such an approach has characterised much of the rationale for creating National Parks in Australia, either at the time of their establishment or in hindsight – as has happened with the Royal National Park, set up in 1879 on the southern edge if the city and bounded in part by the Georges River. This approach which celebrates native species alone, has also often ignored the role of Aboriginal people in the cultural and material work of actively managing, cultivating and changing the native species on the river and its banks.

Most 'natural' landscapes in the city have for decades been deeply enclosed within residential areas, where 'exotic' species have been introduced from the earliest days of settlement. Such landscapes are regarded as compromised in this nativist view, requiring remediation or restoration to an imagined past 'native' state. In its protective approach to any native species, such a view has been slow to identify the damage which may be done by invasive native species.[30] Mangroves, as native plants which are both local and invasive, have been at the centre of long debates around just this question. Although their expansion in many areas reflects the damaging impact of urban intensification, the plants themselves may not always require protection if they are expanding into and eroding the habitat of other, more vulnerable species.[31]

The second broad approach is less judgmental than the nativist one about the origin of plants and animals. This approach is interested in and values the processes by which all non-human species interact and adapt to changing urban physical environments, without discriminating between 'good' natives and 'bad' exotics. From this viewpoint, even compromised city landscapes are worthy of intense study, and may also deserve protection as green space if they fulfil environmental and social goals – whether they are 'native' or not.

All these ideas have influenced the value placed on the natural landscapes within the city, including the Georges River. In 1961, local lobbying led to the designation of the remaining open space on the Georges River as a National Park.[32] Against intense local opposition, it was then stripped of this title in 1967, before being finally returned to its status in 1992.[33] As this brief but stormy history suggests, the meaning and role of National Parks has been contested. For Aboriginal people the story about 'national parks' has been even more complicated than conflicts over 'native' or 'compromised' environments. Tracy Banivanua-Mar has recently explained how, in the 1890s, Aboriginal land in northern Queensland was designated 'national park' to claim it for the white Australian nation, not only for the purposes of national defence but against claims by colonised Indigenous people from 'within'.[34]

On the Georges River, the widespread view among settlers has been that 'native' species were symbols of 'the nation' as a whole. The zoological icons of kangaroo and emu adorn the nation's coat of arms, while an even more pervasive 'floral nationalism' has celebrated wattles and waratahs as the emblems of the nation and state to evoke their imagined unique qualities.[35] This floral symbolism was widely available to working-class Australians, because the flowers were vivid, evocative and cheap. Native plants were increasingly cultivated in the houses and gardens of the developing suburbs, and the blossoms, although harder to domesticate, were readily visible in the Georges River environment where bush flowers were so abundant.

This current of nationalist ideas has flowed beneath the 'nativist' conception of the environment. It emerged strongly for the first time in the mid- and later nineteenth century, and can be seen also much later underlying the declaration of the Georges River National Parks in 1961. It also shaped the later emergence of a conservation ethic, which venerates local native species above all else.

In structure, *Rivers and Resilience* follows the shape of the lower, estuarine river, from where the fresh water flows into the brackish tidal water around Liverpool down to the Towra Point promontory which marks the entry of the river into Botany Bay. The chapters are organised chronologically, but each tackles a theme in the ongoing inquiry into how Aboriginal people have made lives for themselves in the city and on this river.

Each chapter tells its story by following the lives of key people as they grapple with the dilemmas which life on the river has demanded. Rather than regarding Aboriginal people as generalised and homogenous groups to be discussed only collectively, this book approaches the various communities which formed and re-formed along the river as networks of vivid and sometimes conflicting personalities. This writing is inspired by archival sources but also by Aboriginal autobiography, biography, and family stories which are widely used ways in which Aboriginal people have explained their pasts. We argue that such stories are a crucial part of making places meaningful. The stories Aboriginal people tell about their lives weave places into and through family histories, ensuring continuities of knowledge and attachment. The Tharawal Land Council explained the relationship between family stories and places in their 2005 campaign to save Aboriginal lands at Holsworthy: 'Each Aboriginal site has its place; every Aboriginal place has its story in the life of an Aboriginal family. Country is alive with stories.'[36]

The people in these chapters lived on and visited many places along the river – sometimes moving from one to the other and sometimes staying tenaciously in one space – but the river itself has continued to form a sustaining and ordering link between the people and the places. Its waters and its ecologies have been used differently and have changed as the impacts of settlement and urbanisation shifted over time. We will learn a great deal about our central questions by keeping in mind that the river is also an actor in these stories, even while we follow the complex lives of the Aboriginal people for whom it is home and who have been 'making locality' on it. In the end, we draw these threads together to ask: what is resilience and how have rivers contributed to it?

Many stories flow along the Georges River. Those in this book are only a few and we hope they will start the conversations about lots more. There are rich Aboriginal histories of all city rivers – especially this one – and now is a good time to start to tell those stories.

TWO

Rethinking the river: Pemulwuy and beyond

Pemulwuy is well known as a resistance hero, a man celebrated today by Aboriginal people all over Australia because his fearless challenges and audacious raids terrified the early settlers around Sydney.

It is almost a surprise to find that he was also a man from Salt Pan Creek on the Georges River. None of his challenges to settlers took place on the Georges River. Virtually all of the major conflicts he had were at sites on other waterways, like Sydney Cove and in Parramatta, or even on the Hawkesbury River further north and the Nepean to the west. Pemulwuy is much better known for his actions and his words at Parramatta than he is for any he took on his own country, Bediagal lands around Salt Pan Creek. Why?

The reason we know about Pemulwuy only on rivers which were not his own is the same reason that the lower Georges River has remained a blank area in the histories of early contact and settlement. This chapter will explore the major gaps in the early records of settlement to ask what these absences can tell us about the way the river shaped relations between Aboriginal people and settlers. It will look at how the river determined the patterns of settlement just like it had influenced Aboriginal people's economic and social life. In doing so, we argue we can draw even more from Pemulwuy's life and death than the story of resistance as a single strategy.

The river and its people: before the British

The Georges River was not simply a backdrop, but has been an active player in this story. We can find out a great deal about the river and its people, before the British arrived in 1788, by drawing on the later archaeology and at least some records from the period immediately after the landing of First Fleet.

This is a long river. It rises in the mountains to the south of Sydney, just inland from Coalcliff, as O'Hares Creek, before joining a smaller stream, the Georges, and tracing a great arc to the west. It then bends around to turn towards the east as it flows to the coast. Originally a river running fresh all the way to the distant ocean, this was changed dramatically when rising sea-levels drowned both the river bed and its valley floor many tens of metres deep in the Pleistocene age, over 10 000 years ago. The lower reaches of the river join with the fresh-water above Liverpool, then move downstream as a tidal salt estuary until, passing the diamond-shaped promontory of Towra Point which guards its mouth, the Georges flows with its smaller sister river, the Cooks, into Botany Bay.

Over the many centuries when the freshwater ran all the way to the sea, the river's flow had created the characteristic Sydney geography of richer, arable shale lands back from the river. As it carved a path through the high sandstone cliffs, it left sandy soils there and along much of the river bank. There were some small floodplains with rich alluvial soil but these were rare on this lower part of the main river because the steep, rocky escarpments make it impossible for floodplains to develop.

Many smaller rivers flow into the main Georges River: we know them now by names like Prospect Creek, Mill Creek and Salt Pan Creek, as well as the Woronora River. Yet they were all freshwater rivers, only becoming brackish and tidal as they neared their junction with the Georges. They rose as freshwater streams which nurtured very different vegetation and wildlife in their upper reaches than lower down. Their banks were often disrupted by other freshwater springs, like the one at the Cuttings on Salt Pan Creek. Even in the early twentieth century, this creek was clear and clean enough to catch or gather fish, mussels, prawns and oysters from, all of which sustained the Aboriginal residents. As Joe Anderson said in 1933: 'there is plenty fish in the river for us all'.[1] Its banks were clear too, with areas of sandy beach interspersed with some rocky sandstone outcrops and overhangs in the upper areas, a few mangroves and wide expanses of salt marsh, allowing an open vista down to the water. Closer again to the main river, the creek banks narrowed as its waters cut deeper into the high sandstone escarpments on either side as it flowed into the Georges.

When Joe Anderson spoke from the banks of Salt Pan Creek, the river had already been settled by the British and was facing a further increase in residential population. Cities are not usually thought to be places where Aboriginal communities had survived until the mid-twentieth century. But Sydney is a city of rivers whose rugged geography has shaped not only the urban topography but the eccentricities of its politics as well. There were good reasons that the site for such a richly activist and continuing influence on the colonial enterprise was a watercourse. Rivers, creeks and waterholes have been key sites of conflict between settlers and Aboriginal people in Australia because everyone needed water in an environment where rainfall was variable and often scarce. But because of their steep gullies and muddy banks, rivers have been places which colonial control could not secure. Neither troopers on horseback nor police on foot could be confident of following people far along the river banks. It was both the river's rich resources and also its unstable banks which had sustained the spaces for Joe Anderson's people to create a free community. Here they could escape the rigid constraints of the 'protection' system of the first half of the twentieth century and nurture a culture of economic independence and outspoken protest.

An 1802 map shows this process already in play even in the early period around Port Jackson. The geometric patchwork of cropped fields, housing and roadways has structured the landscape into a managed pattern, shown not only by the neat parallel ploughlines but by the gallows dotted across the open riverside plains, some with bodies still hanging from the crossbars. Only the irregular and unusable areas around the creeks and rivers interrupt the march of disciplined colonial order across the landscape. The rivers were an unreliable region, penetrating right into the heart of the colonisers' orderly fields, roads and fences. The rugged terrain of the river bank provided the space for a continuing Aboriginal presence. Perhaps even more important was that the river allowed for mobility and communication between the Aboriginal people living in those spaces all along it.

Yet if this estuary continued to be so important to its Aboriginal owners, we have surprisingly little recorded information about their understanding of it. We know little even of their names for the rivers and places along it. Pemuluwy and Joe Anderson shared the same home, on Salt Pan Creek, yet despite now knowing more about them, we have never learnt the Bediagal name of their little river. No record has been found yet in local Aboriginal memories or in settler writings. It must have had a Dharawal name too, because these neighbours all had an interest in this river, but we don't know those names

Drawn by French visitors to the new
colony in 1802, this sketch-map shows how
waterways shaped landuse, and the way river
banks remained out of the control of farmers
and fence-builders.

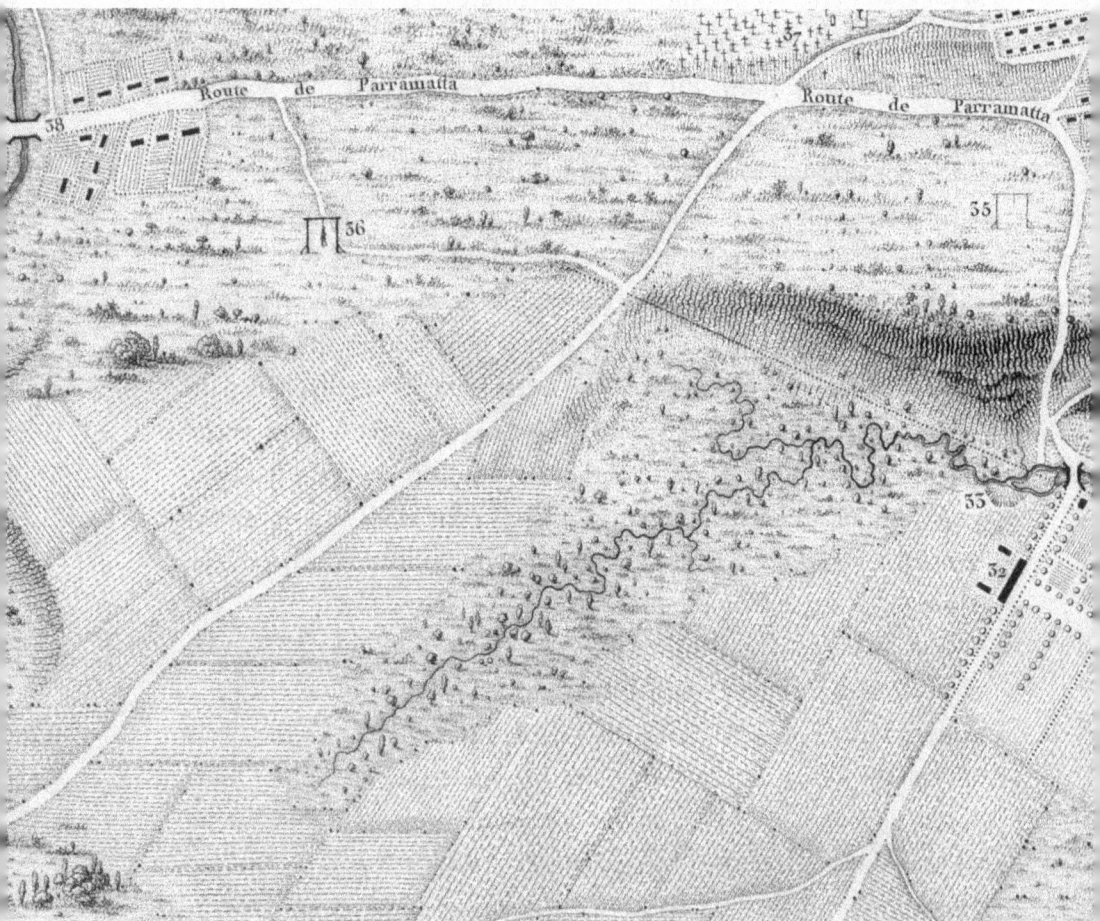

Jean Baptise Antoine Cloquet, after Charles Alexandre Lesueur, 'Plan de la Ville, Sydney
1802', in Francois Peron, *Voyage de Decouvertes aux Terres Australes*, 2nd edn, 1804:
Mitchell Library, State Library of NSW

either. So we are forced to talk about this rich and powerful place in the language of its invaders, who didn't even see it as a river but only a lowly creek.

That no local name survives for Salt Pan Creek is not because there were no Aboriginal owners remaining who had lived there before 1788. On the contrary, the rivers had been heavily populated before settlement, with the Dharug language spoken along the northern banks, from the coast in the east back into the western plains. On the southern bank the Dharawal language was used, uniting speakers who lived from Wollongong in the south up to the Georges River and perhaps beyond. To the west, on the upstream freshwater reaches of the river, were the peoples speaking the Gandangara language, whose land extended across the Nepean and further west into the Blue Mountains. Within each of these wider language communities there were smaller collectives (often called 'groups') formed through family networks and affiliations to more tightly defined areas. Within the extensive Dharawal language community, for example, the Gweagal group belonged to the eastern section of the southern bank of Botany Bay from Kurnell, while the Cobragal were associated with the stretch of the river around what became Liverpool. The Bediagal group of the Dharag-speakers, Pemulwuy's community, were closely associated with Salt Pan Creek and Bankstown.[2]

The land responsibilities of the Aboriginal people in this coastal area were not well understood by early European observers. As a consequence, the remaining documents show many variations regarding which language group was responsible for which precise area.[3] The generally understood Australian tendency of language speakers to be knowledgeable about the language and land responsibilities of their neighbours probably also held for this area. So it is likely that flexible and negotiable responsibilities were the rule for much of the time, particularly in resource-rich liminal areas like the rivers. The most reliable indicator of traditional affiliations remains the memories and practices of the Aboriginal families in the area who are most closely descended from the traditional owners. This book will follow the approach to language affiliation which is held by family researchers, such as the Anderson family among many others, which are based on extensive reading and discussion about the archival sources in the context of family memory and known current family practice.[4]

The Gweagal, Cobragal and Bediagal groups were all river people. Their societies have been described as 'canoe cultures'.[5] Because the British were focused on land tenure, they persistently categorised local people as being associated with either the coast, like the Gweagal, or with the 'woods', as they labelled the Cobragal. Yet all of them utilised the extensive network of Sydney's river system for transport and communication as well as for economic production and cultural life. They could draw their livelihood from the river waters as well as the land and from the banks which linked the two. The rivers offered them swift and safe means of transport around a land area which was riven with gullies, marshes, cliffs and hills. Canoes could be constructed rapidly by anyone, young or old, from everyday materials which were simple to replace. They allowed a rich experience of productive fishing with lines or spears, easy travel and ready communication across wide distances.

Aboriginal people also had many pathways through the bushland which seemed so impenetrable for settlers, and many of these paths allowed rapid movement across country. When considered with the waterborne movement from deep inland to the coast, it is meaningless to look for fixed boundaries between the 'coastal' and 'woodland' groups. The local economy drew on both land and water resources, including wallabies, kangaroos, possums and birds, along with fish, eels and many oysters. They also used plants from land and water, and the honey from the many flowers which grew prolifically along the sandstone.

The banks and escarpments overlooking the river were heavily used by many groups of people for making tools, camping and socialising. This is abundantly evident in the extensive middens of oyster shells all along both sides of the rivers, including Salt Pan Creek and Lime Kiln Bay, Oatley, Lugarno, Sans Souci and Liverpool on the northern side, Guragurang on the southern side, as well as numerous sites in the Holsworthy area and around Port Hacking.[6] From their campsites, people created artwork all along the caves and overhangs of the escarpments, like the beautiful stencil galleries at Sandy Point on the southern side and the carvings on the rocky points of Lime Kiln Bay, reflecting the complex social relationships of kinship, trade and conviviality. There too Aboriginal people retold the stories which made their landscape constantly alive with meaning. Few stories survive from the lower Georges River, but we catch a glimpse from an epic recorded in the 1890s, when Gandangara people from the Burragorang Valley explained how the massive struggles of their ancestors, Gurangatch and Mirragan, had flung up hills and gouged out valleys, making the waters flow along all the rivers from the Jenolan Caves to Parramatta.[7]

Another feature of the economy and social relations of the river communities was the gendered divisions of labour and technology. Early settlers noted that they more often saw Aboriginal women fishing from their small canoes, even outside the heads, while men usually fished from the rocks. Archaeology suggests that hooks were a technology which had been adopted widely along the Sydney coastal areas, and Grace Karskens shows that it was women using them; the men used spears. Although the British thought that men should have done the fishing, their records demonstrate that it was women who caught most fish and were more important in the political economy along the rivers and coast. This continued even after smallpox had devastated the Aboriginal population, probably killing more women than men. As the new colony struggled to produce enough to feed itself in the early 1790s, it was Aboriginal women's fishing which sustained both the white colonists and the surviving Aboriginal population.[8]

People, plants and animals had always interacted, and their relationships had changed over time. The invasion accelerated this process dramatically. We can see this happening most clearly in the relationship between salt marsh, mangrove, swamp wallaby and people. At the time of settlement, the mangroves lived on the edge of the water, their roots partially submerged, while the salt marshes spread out low wherever there was flat land behind the mangroves. The boundary between mangrove and saltmarsh is not stable or fixed. Instead it depended always the interaction of water, plants, animals and humans. The mangroves could always advance into the salt marsh habitat, except that the swamp wallaby, in one example of the pressures on the plants, fed on both young mangroves and on saltmarsh but preferred mangroves. So as long as there were plenty of swamp wallabies, the salt marsh would have some advantage over the mangroves. An increase in the human population hunting wallabies, however, would reduce the pressure on mangroves and consequently threaten the salt marsh.[9]

Overlooking
the river

The early accounts and drawings by British officers, settlers and the occasional French and Russian visitors allow us just a very partial reflection of the colony. They could only write from their expectations and experiences. Their encounters were shaped by the geography of the rivers they had arrived on – the biology, hydrology and geology they found – and how this met their immediate needs. So we do not have a bird's-eye view of the whole area, in which we would see all the actors across the harbour, the bay and the several rivers flowing into them. If we did, we would see the white convict men and women who could not write and leave records. And we would also see the many Aboriginal people who were watching but refusing to engage with the

British. Instead we see only the events which the literate British officers – who were all men – saw and then chose to record.

There has been a substantial amount of writing in which historians and novelists, white and black, have tried to understand the few short decades that mark the early years of settlement, from 1788 to around 1830.[10] They have had to use the same sources we have just described, and so their stories are shaped by both their creativity as well as the limits of the sources themselves. Fine historical research includes the non-fiction writing of Inga Clendinnen, Keith Vincent Smith and most recently the work of Grace Karskens, in which she looks at both sides of the interaction.[11] It is important to consider how the sources they were using have shaped the stories they could tell.

In most of this work, the tidal lower reach of the Georges River – from Liverpool all the way downstream to its mouth at Botany Bay – is eerily absent. This invisibility arises because the resources these historians have to draw upon give them few clues about what was happening on this long stretch of the Georges River.

The absence of the Georges River arose geographically because the pressure of settlement was not spread evenly over the land or river area of the colony. Instead, after a brief camp at Yarra Bay just inside the northern head of Botany Bay, Governor Arthur Phillip realised he needed deeper water to shelter the fleet and then the later vessels on which the colony would rely. So within days, all the first settlers moved to Port Jackson, and it was here that the first heavy impact occurred. But it was not followed by major impacts in nearby areas, such as the lower Parramatta River or the lower Georges River. The crops the settlers had tried to plant at Sydney Cove had failed, and the colony was desperate for food. So the settlers 'leap-frogged' over the poor soils and saline water of the lower Georges and lower Parramatta rivers to find some ground they could use for crops. This meant that the second heavy impact was in Parramatta and Rouse Hill, a long way upstream on the Parramatta River.

The Georges River only next felt the impact of settlement in the area around Liverpool, because settlers had moved south from Parramatta along Prospect Creek, and found the alluvial flats around what is now Liverpool and Fairfield. The settlers were not even sure the river they found was same river they had seen flowing far downstream into Botany Bay. Only in 1795 were Bass and Flinders able to sail all the way up that river to Liverpool, proving the connection. Even then, the long stretch of the tidal lower river, from Liverpool to the Bay, remained undeveloped. The few Europeans who did intrude there did little recording.

Those first few days when the British were at Yarra Bay, from 18 to 26 January, have left us few records about Botany Bay and its people, with only some quick exploration by boat far enough upstream past Towra Point to see the sandstone cliffs and the lower Woronora flowing into the Georges River. The one recorded incident was – revealingly – over nature and resources. Lieutenant William Bradley of the *Sirius* reported on 20 January: 'The natives were well pleas'd with our People until they began clearing the ground at which they were displeased and wanted them to be gone'.[12]

Overlooking
the river's people

Geography was one dimension of the limits of materials such as Bradley's account, but class and gender were also important. The initial settlement at Sydney Cove meant that the most intense scrutiny – and also the least prejudiced observations – took place around the shores of Port Jackson. In the early years, the people who were writing notes on their encounters and analysing their interactions with Aboriginal people were educated male officers who had been charged with establishing good relations with the Aborigines. The settlers' observations were limited, but were nevertheless of an extraordinary nature which was never to be repeated.

The conditions changed rapidly. Within a year, the Aboriginal population was decimated in the Port Jackson area by smallpox, leaving survivors scarred physically by pockmarks and psychologically by the horror of such massive mortality and the guilt of leaving so many dead loved ones unburied.[13] Aboriginal people had shown a careful refusal to interact with the settlers in the initial two years of the settlement, but for reasons not well understood even at the time this ended abruptly in 1790. Aboriginal people began to 'come in' to the settlement physically and economically, taking up residence in the streets and bartering their fish and game to the increasingly needy settlers. The officers and governor continued to observe and interact, leaving us the best glimpse of Aboriginal people in the area, but it is a sadly fragmented glimpse.

As Karskens has argued, the passage of time had undermined the early sympathies and communication, even in Sydney, where tempers frayed with familiarity and the rising impact of settler drugs like alcohol.[14] By the time the settlers had established their second intensive settlement at Parramatta, the white population was more diverse and the Aboriginal people were more trenchantly opposed to the clearing and exclusive land management of the new farms. Tension was high and feelings were mixed. Some settlers were sympathetic to Aboriginal people, finding them to be useful workers and informative guides. Others were deeply opposed to Aboriginal presence on their farms and contemptuous of Aboriginal people and their knowledge. So the observations recorded by settlers at Parramatta and Rouse Hill are of a very different nature to those of the early officers. Even the supportive settlers like Charles Throsby had little time for the intensive language learning of William Dawes or the close interactions of Watkin Tench. Before long, the most understanding of the officers had returned to England. The remaining officers and officials, such as David Collins, had lost patience as the Aboriginal people, whom they had never really understood, had become ever more hostile to the increasing settler dominance over land and resources. There are few records for the Parramatta people which are equivalent to the careful and relatively open-minded observations which the early officers made about the people of Port Jackson.

Yet even the records about the Parramatta people were more detailed than was documented by this time for those from the Georges River. There were virtually no settlers on the Georges River over the whole of the 1790s except in the small farming enclaves around Liverpool and to the immediate south of Parramatta. Botanists like Robert Brown and George Caley occasionally passed through and recorded some language and observations of practices or of economy, but they were more interested in plants. This was a great benefit to Aboriginal people remaining on the river because it gave them a decade or so of respite from the intensive interference which the Aboriginal people at Port Jackson, Parramatta and Liverpool had faced. However it restricted the source materials for later historians. It meant that the lower tidal Georges River had neither the thoughtful early attention of the officers nor the sympathetic later observations of a settler-employer like Throsby at Glenfield. Just as importantly to the overall settler conception of Aboriginal culture, it reinforced the early assumptions of the officer and settler observers that there was a great difference between the 'coastal' Aborigines and the inland or 'woods' people. For the settler observers the lands around Parramatta were indeed distant from Port Jackson and seemed to be an entirely different ecosystem.

The sharp distinction between 'coastal' and 'woods' people that solidified in the early settlers' imagination is another factor which has clouded our understanding, and there has been little motivation to go beyond it. But the view from the river opens up a different perspective. As we shall see, the ease with which Aboriginal people moved from east to west and back again along the Georges River – from Pemulwuy to the 1950s – raises many questions about whether such a sharp distinction could have existed between coastal and 'woods' groups before the British settlement began. After 1788 and the rapid onset and effects of smallpox and other diseases of the invaders, it is harder still to be confident about such a difference. Current linguistic analysis suggests a continuity of Dharug language from the western areas around Parramatta to the coast in the area between Port Jackson and Botany Bay. On the southern side of the Georges River, the Dharawal language was commonly spoken from the eastern coast to the far western areas around Liverpool.[15]

Perhaps the most valuable contribution to this coast/woods discussion comes from the recent analysis of the artwork and archaeology at Cubbitch Barta National Estate – the former military lands at Holsworthy. The rich and extensive artwork on the southern bank of the Georges River is so different from that to the north and in the rest of Sydney that it suggests a north/south cultural difference, with the demarcation line running along the river, rather than one running perpendicular to it and separating western woodlands from eastern salt-water people.[16] The means of rapid movement and communication along the rivers were so readily available that it seems as sensible to stress the links and collaborations as it does the differences.

A continuing
gap

Beyond the histories of early colonial interaction, there are some studies of Aboriginal language groups which have attempted a longer time-frame, but they cover areas that lie at some distance from the Georges River, rather than being along the river itself. This is the case, for example, with the Gandangara historical research of Jim Smith about the peoples to the west of the Georges River, or the Wadi Wadi research by Chris Illert and Allan Carriage for the people of the Illawarra region.[17] After its initial neglect by settlers, the Georges River faced a heavy impact from the later urban expansion of Sydney. This, ironically, continued to cause a gap in the recording of Aboriginal experiences, because historians who have been tracing language group histories have focused on people outside the most heavily affected area, rather than on those who might be inside it. These language group studies have also traced the histories of particular families through to the present. While each study is important in itself, they have focussed only on the descendants of those people who could be confirmed to be in the area at the time of the first British settlement. They have not analysed the interactions which may have occurred with other Aboriginal people beyond those from immediately adjacent groups, nor the way these local groups were affected by wider currents of political development. Local histories have taken a different approach by working within a fixed geographic boundary. Many have focused largely on settlers and more recent immigrants rather than Aboriginal histories. The strongest among them, such as the work of Sue Rosen at Bankstown and Christopher Keating at Liverpool, still struggle to find any Aboriginal history at all to write about for the long years after the early conflicts. More recent work, such as the forthcoming history of Fairfield by Stephen Gapps, will begin to address this absence of attention to Aboriginal people in the intervening century between first settlement and the present day.[18]

The exceptional case is Maria Nugent's *Botany Bay*, which explores the interactions between Aboriginal and non-Aboriginal history-making about the very small area of La Perouse. This area on Yarra Bay, just inside the northern head of Botany Bay, was where Phillip's First Fleet had landed initially, followed closely by the La Perouse's ship. Eventually the place had become the site of widely publicised Aboriginal settlement.[19] This site has acquired intense symbolic significance for both black and white people. Nugent's study is, however, largely limited to the specific site of La Perouse and to the period after 1880. So while *Botany Bay* is extremely helpful in understanding the currents of thought circulating among Aboriginal people and white Australians – about Aborigines, La Perouse (the place and the man) and 'first settlement' – it gives us little detail about the people and events on the rest of Botany Bay, and the Georges River which empties into it.

Finally there have been recent collections of the life stories of the Aboriginal people in some of the communities in Sydney which are about the people in relation to the places they or their parents left when they came to live in the city. Many are by Aboriginal authors like Ruby Langford Ginibi whose autobiography and other stories discuss the importance of community life in south west Sydney.[20] Gillian Cowlishaw has focused on western Sydney in a contemporary study which is too far west to encompass the Georges River people, as also is the work of Jim Kohen and Jack Brooks.[21] In each of these, however, there is little sense of how the people who came from Bourke or Wellington to live in the post-war housing developments in western Sydney might have developed a relationship to the land on which they were living. Nor has there been any investigation of how these incoming Aboriginal people might have related to those who had lived there in the decades before, let alone in the centuries prior to British settlement.

Rediscovering Pemulwuy:
setting the scene

So if we know little about the lower Georges River, what can we draw from the early settlers' accounts to frame the retelling of Pemulwuy's story?

Port Jackson long remained the focus of the interactions between Governor Phillip and the Aboriginal people with whom he was able to negotiate, even when they had been brought in from more distant areas. Though the devastating impact of smallpox swept through the dense waterside groups within a year of the British landing and its effects in mortality were dramatic in the immediate vicinity of the settlement, little is known about areas even a few miles away from Port Jackson. The psychological and other impacts were undoubtedly far-reaching.[22] Whatever the impact of the terrible disease, there were survivors on whom, ironically, the settlers came to depend for food.[23]

These often vivid and careful descriptions from the early officers reveal glimpses into what was happening at Sydney Cove, but little about how the new settlement was being viewed by Aboriginal people outside Sydney Cove. There is enough, however, to realise that much of Aboriginal Sydney was carefully watching the goings on at the tiny settlement from a safer distance, including from Botany Bay. Bennelong, for example, the most famous of the local people who interacted with the invaders, had negotiated with Phillip in 1790 to build him a house on the point below Government House – now known as Bennelong's Point and the site of the Opera House. Proud of the house as an indication of his status among the British, Bennelong reported to Phillip some months later that the Botany Bay people had created a whole new song about it which they had sung in a large gathering he attended at the Bay. As Bennelong explained it, the song's stanzas had commented not only on the house but on 'the governor and the white men at Sydney' demonstrating that all the people and goings on at the new settlement were observed closely enough to provide fodder for creative and public comment within the local community.[24] Communication and comment of this sort must have continued over many decades – and news of the Sydney Cove events would have passed rapidly between communities camped all along the river up to Liverpool.

Until 1795, the long deepwater stretches of the Georges River and the sandstone escarpments had remained secure in the hands of their traditional owners. The promise of the Liverpool Plains for European agriculture was limited – the river was still tidal up to this point and only a short distance downsteam the alluvial flats disappeared, the river bank narrowed and the sandstone cliffs crowded in. The wood of the river had some attraction. A few timber-getters began to enter the turpentine forests of what became Punchbowl and Mortdale, while others harvested the mangroves on the lower river banks near Botany Bay to make ash for soap. But there was little to entice farmers, which accounted for the slow penetration of the British along this length of the lower river.

This view of the way the river shaped settler actions allows us to understand why Pemulwuy was most visible in his confrontations with settlers in the places where they were causing the most intense disruption – the Parramatta River and Prospect Creek – and not in his own country further south. The sites of communication and conflict were those in which the British were most concentrated, and Aboriginal people from the less heavily impacted areas were noticed and recorded most when they moved into the zones in which most British were living, observing and recording their presence. Pemulwuy was moving towards the points of most powerful British pressure, rather than waiting for the British to come close to his own country.

Governor John Hunter's map of the British colony in 1798 shows both the focus of the early agricultural land grants and the way in which the whole area was seen as being defined by its rivers.[25] The close proximity of the Georges River tributaries, like Prospect Creek, with the Parramatta River explains the way Pemulwuy and others associated with him could move so widely and rapidly across the landscape in ways which the settlers found mystifying.

The tactics of resistance

Pemulwuy first came to the notice of Governor Phillip during December 1790, when he was blamed for the death of Phillip's gamekeeper, John McIntyre. McIntyre was widely resented by Aboriginal people, and officer Watkin Tench suspected that he had earlier killed and injured some of them. In response, however, Phillip launched two punitive expeditions aimed in particular at Pemulwuy. These were spectacularly unsuccessful, due by all accounts to skilful distraction by the Aboriginal guides and contacts, as well as the caution of participating officers like Tench, who was unhappy about the consequences to which such retribution might lead. In his account of the expeditions, he detailed their attempts to surprise the local people and noted repeatedly how swiftly they moved by canoe and on foot, outwitting their pursuers.[26]

Pemulwuy was prominent but elusive in the raids which occurred with increasing frequency after that, and which demonstrated a development in the tactics being used by the Bediagal and their neighbours. These raids were more often aimed at sabotaging the crops, stealing corn and scattering stock than they were at injuring people. So they were effective in disrupting farming but potentially led to alienation of settler sympathy.

David Collins, Deputy Judge Advocate reported in 1798 that both settlers and natives believed that Pemulwuy 'was ... at the head of every party that attacked the maize grounds'. His most famous confrontation was in 1797. In March, farmers close to Parramatta had become frustrated with the increasingly effective raids on their crops, supplies and clothing. Rising tensions had led to a conflict in which a white man and woman had died and Aboriginal people were blamed. A group of farmers pursued the Aboriginal people through the bush until sunrise, eventually finding a camp of 100 people – only to have

Pemulwuy, or 'Pimbloy' as his observers spelt it, in an etching which is understood to show him at or near his home on Salt Pan Creek.

Samuel John Neele, 'Pimbloy: Native of New Holland in a Canoe of that Country', in James Grant, *Narrative of a Voyage of Discovery Performed in HM Vessel Lady Nelson 1803–1804*, 1804: Mitchell Library, State Library of NSW

them all escape, leaving only abandoned corn and musket shot. They were 'fatigued', Collins reported, and so entered the nearby township of Parramatta. But Pemulwuy, rather than fleeing, came into Parramatta after them with many fellow warriors to confront the settlers. Pemulwuy, whom Collins described as 'a riotous and troublesome savage', challenged the armed settlers: 'they intended, if possible, to seize upon Pemulwuy; who, in a great rage, threatened to spear the first man that dared to approach him, and actually did throw a spear at one of the soldiers'.[27]

The settlers opened fire on Pemulwuy, wounding him severely, while five other people with him were killed. He was taken to hospital, under arrest, his body riddled with musket shot, yet he not only survived but then escaped – with leg irons still on. He reappeared in May, just two months later, healed, assertive and back in his own country near the junction of the Georges River with Botany Bay. This movement of Pemulwuy raises questions about the helpfulness of the distinction between 'woods' and 'coastal' people. There were unquestionably very local differences in style, ornamentation and habits. But where the east-west routes along the rivers were used with such frequency between the 'coastal' Botany Bay area and the 'woods' areas like Parramatta, the important issues may be the underlying similarities between all the peoples of the Sydney basin, rather than the elements of local distinctiveness.

Instead of fleeing westward, away from the settlement altogether, Pemulwuy had used the river to travel from the west to east, into the area of the lower Georges River which although closer to Sydney Cove was ironically under least impact from the settlers, until he was ready to re-emerge. Pemulwuy was said to have confidently approached a member of the settler party at Botany Bay, which was being led by Governor Phillip's successor John Hunter himself, inquiing about whether the governor continued to be angry with him and 'seemed pleased at being told that he was not'.[28]

This meeting seemed to have laid the groundwork for a more civil relationship. Less conflict occurred for a year or so, but before long, settler activities had begun to penetrate more actively into the Holsworthy area of the Georges River, east from Liverpool, on what had been the previously safe Georges River. As attempts were made to establish farming there, Pemulwuy was again involved in an increasing number of raids on settlers. Tensions escalated until the military were sent to Georges River area by Hunter's successor, Governor Philip King, on 22 November 1801, in a recognition that guerrilla warfare was occurring and causing major difficulties for farmers and their crops. King ordered that: 'This detachment is to prevent the natives from firing the wheat ... They are to fire on any native or natives they see'.[29]

With Aboriginal tactics so effective, King made it illegal for whites to 'harbour' Aboriginal people near farms: an edict aimed to undermine any white sympathy with Pemulwuy and his fellow Bidiegal. It was also effective in splitting Aboriginal supporters away from the rebels, as the governor feared that runaway Irish convicts had joined forces with Pemulwuy and the Bediagal to assist in further attacks on settlers. King outlawed them all, declaring martial law and offering rewards for their capture due to the 'outrageous acts' which were being perpetrated. His draconian strategy of exclusion of Aboriginal people from the settlement may have been effective in disrupting Aboriginal alliances, with some people seeking exemption by claiming that they had been forced by Pemulwuy to take up arms.[30]

Eventually, it was the British tactics which won. The *Sydney Gazette* reported on 24 June 1804 that Pemulwuy had been killed by Aboriginal people, though historians have favoured the account that it was settlers who had shot him, then cut off his head to send to England.[31]

Pemulwuy's legacy

These intense conflicts of 1801 and 1802 can be seen very differently, however, as was suggested in the letters which explorer and naturalist George Caley wrote during his time in Sydney to Sir Joseph Banks. Caley was opposed to King's declaration, and argued that it was white settlers, with their violent behaviour and lack of respect for Aboriginal people, who started many of the disputes. He commented on the declaration of martial law in a letter of 25 August 1801: 'I have every reason to believe the whites have been the greatest aggressors upon the whole'.[32]

Caley's interpretation points to divisions between the settlers in their interactions with Aboriginal people, shaped by their self-interest and the ways it led them to interact with Aboriginal owners. His work in searching for the plants and animals, although it was as self-serving as the settler farmers', was greatly assisted by developing active communication with Aboriginal people. Yet there were many others in the settler community whose interest lay in removing any Aboriginal claim on their land or criticism of their management. Where settlers did not employ or interact with Aboriginal people, they had little communication, making them easy prey for unfounded scare-mongering. It was these settlers who had supported King in his 'war' on the Bediagal. Caley, on the other hand, found himself accused of being partisan with the Aboriginal insurgents. He was attacked particularly savagely by the Reverend Samuel Marsden, who insisted that 'there never would be any good done until there was a clear riddance of the natives'.[33]

Although Pemulwuy was depicted as the leading figure in the resistance, it may be that we have more details about him only because Watkin Tench, Arthur Phillip and later Philip King and others were seeking to identify leaders among the local peoples with whom they could negotiate, or blame. Although King generally portrayed Pemulwuy as an implacable and heartless enemy, he also recognised his stature, describing him as 'an active and daring leader'.[34]

The challenge to the settlers was far wider than just one man. The catalyst for clashes was invariably the intensification of settler interventions in any area. The conflicts around Parramatta did decline after Pemulwuy's death, but this also reflected the changing circumstances of the area, in which close farming and heavy settler presence had finally been effective in marginalising Aboriginal people. On the Georges River, on and even further to the east, and on the lower river around Salt Pan, conflicts escalated as the pressure from settlers there continued. Timber getters were penetrating the area and settlers were trying out small-scale farms even without formal tenure or permission.

By April 1805, hostilities on the lower Georges River had resumed. There were only rumours about who was leading it, perhaps Musquito, or Pemulwuy's son Tedbury, but the same tactics as Pemulwuy had used were re-applied, aimed at undermining the viability of settler commercial enterprises by burning green corn, removing all portable goods and scattering or destroying stock.[35] This challenge to settler intrusion reached a peak when the first formal land grants were made around the upper Salt Pan Creek in 1809. Four grants had been made, each on the alluvial flats and these were the focus of the attacks.

This time, however, the river peoples' tactics worked. Unlike at Parramatta, where the weight of settler numbers had ensured their dominance, the odds at Salt Pan Creek went the other way. Two of the landholders, Bond and Meredith, appealed to the acting governor. Bond stated that he had been 'driven off by the Natives, with a providential escape for his life'. Meredith had been wounded as he assisted Bond, and both wanted land elsewhere.[36] The attacks ensured that settlers were more cautious about residing on their properties, even if they did retain their grants. White occupation of the area actually fell until the 1830s, when further alienation of land finally took place in the area. Even where grants were held, the owners often ignored the grant conditions, failing to develop the land in any agricultural sense and leaving it unoccupied.

Yet again it was the river and its landscape which had shaped both the resistance and the settlers' mood. The poorer, sandy soils, the narrow river banks and the forbiddingly steep sandstone escarpments towards the main river had all deterred initial settlement for farming. The richest forests, the turpentines, which appealed to timber-cutters in the area were well away from the river on the higher shale soils.[37] Not only did the environment of the lower river discourage settlers, it offered safer spaces to which the Bediagal and their neighbours could retreat to assess the impact of their strategies on the upper, alluvial river areas.

Pemulwuy's story has been retold over many years, celebrating his daring and courage in challenging the invading settlers. Yet there was a range of other ways of interacting with the British. Pemulwuy himself tried out different approaches – alternating confrontation and negotiation – in attempting to create a workable outcome. Eric Willmot, an Indigenous writer, has drawn a fictional but carefully researched portrait of the dramatic life and death of Pemulwuy, in which he suggests that Pemulwuy even chose the timing of his death. Willmot proposes that Pemulwuy recognised that he would live on as a powerful symbol of resistance even after the settlers had shot him down.[38] If Willmot is right, Pemulwuy was looking beyond his own death to see how the people of the river could shape their future. Pemulwuy's real challenge would then be to look at this broader range of strategies, to see a context for his personal sacrifice, but also to see the directions for the continuing histories of Aboriginal people on the Georges River.

THREE

Holding on to country: Goggey's river 1830–1890

The river and its landscapes may have allowed a more successful Aboriginal resistance in the 1810s on the lower Georges River, but there was no respite in the pressures on the river upstream. The population of the settlement was increasing and so the demand to clear and farm the alluvial and clay soils higher up the river was increasing. Liverpool was declared a centre of settlement in 1810 and more blocks were granted and measured out. Settler intrusion was escalating too, even further upstream beyond Minto to the freshwater stretches around Appin and what was to become Campbelltown. As settlers moved to the west and south from here, they intruded more often and more violently on the land of Gandangara people of the mountains and of the southern Dharawal and Wadi Wadi from Jervis Bay. They in turn began to react with anger and frustration at settler abuses.[1]

Through this, Dharawal people around those areas already settled were trying to negotiate new ways to work with the settlers. Kogi was one such person. A charismatic figure among the Dharawal groups around Liverpool and further south on the river, he had been noticed by observers like Francis Barallier and George Caley when, as a young man, he was in conflicts over relationships within his own society as well as with the settlers.[2] Kogi was one of the Dharawal party who met with a newly arrived Governor Lachlan Macquarie when he first toured the Cow Pastures in 1810.[3]

Having spent some time with Gandangara people to the west, Kogi had a varied relationship with them: in conflict with them as often as in alliance. But he was also developing close relationships with some of the settlers who had begun to employ Aboriginal people as shepherds, and in particular with the farmer Charles Throsby at Glenfield.[4] Although the upper Georges River beyond Liverpool was a frontier of the settlement over these years, the settlers there included some men like John Warby and Hamilton Hume who, like Caley some years before, were primarily explorers and naturalists and who sought out the Dharawal and associated with them extensively. So there were at least some areas of mutual interest in sustaining peaceful and collaborative relationships.

When drought struck in winter in 1814, many Gandangara people apparently moved eastwards towards the rivers, as they would always have done. But this was interpreted as threatening by those settlers eager for excuses to act against local Aboriginal people.[5] Rumours circulated of Aboriginal plans to fire all the crops and attack the more isolated settlers, which put pressure on Macquarie to mobilise not only military protection for settlers but pre-emptive strikes against all Aboriginal people. Macquarie agreed, but carefully specified that attacks were not to be launched against the local Dharawal. Nevertheless, Kogi and other Dharawal were targetted by aggressive settlers, happy to have an excuse to act against any Aboriginal people. Kogi moved his family onto Throsby's property Glenfield for protection, as did other Dharawal. Throsby was outspoken in his criticism of the motives of the other settlers, whom he accused of fomenting the violence and then escalating it with hysteria and baseless accusations.

The Gandangara moved back to the mountains in spring, but during the severe drought of 1816 they again moved eastwards towards the coastal rivers. Settlers once more demanded the governor act pre-emptively to protect them. This time, Macquarie was less restrained, allocating soldiers rather than authorising settlers to take up arms, and ordering knowledgeable locals like John Warby to act as guides in company with any friendly Dharawal. And once more, Kogi and others moved to the homes of protective settlers like Throsby, expecting to be safe. They were relaxed enough for Kogi to spend a day fishing on the Georges River with John Wentworth, the son of the settlement's surgeon D'Arcy Wentworth.[6]

As the military party began targetting Dharawal people, however, such refuges no longer seemed safe enough. Kogi moved his family further eastwards along the river towards Botany to avoid the soldiers altogether. This movement along the river from west to east to avoid conflict was the same tactic Pemulwuy had used after his arrest and imprisonment in 1797. Warby argued with the military commander as the party broadened its attack to include the Dharawal as well as Gandangara, and he obstructed the soldiers when they tried to follow Kogi to Botany. When the army simply turned back to the attack on the Gandangara, Warby refused to assist any further, leaving with the remaining Dharawal guides. Undeterred, the soldiers continued south along the river, eventually finding a convict workman who was willing to lead them through the night to surprise a camp of Gandangara families near Appin. The soldiers shot the people down as they fled in disarray. Fourteen people died, including a number of women and children, while others fell to their deaths over nearby cliffs as they tried to escape, their bodies unrecovered and uncounted.

Kogi, 'King'
of the Georges River

The Appin Massacre, as these killings came to be known, was often regarded as the final blow to both the Dharawal and the Gandangara of the upper Georges River. The deaths had certainly horrified the surviving local Aboriginal people who kept well out of the way of settlers for some time afterwards. The memory and the accounts of these killings have lived on continuing to disturb and anger Aboriginal people in the area in the later twentieth century. Judy Chester and other Aboriginal women growing up around Liverpool in the 1960s (whose story comes in chapter 8) have explained that learning then about how the colonial governor had organised the Appin hunt and murders had driven them to become active in land and civil rights protests in the coming years.

Yet these 1820s killings did not signal the end of either the Gandangara or the Dharawal people in the area. Instead, many Aboriginal people continued to live there, and they kept coming to the governor's events – like the annual feast and blanket issues at Parramatta and other areas – for decades afterwards. Aboriginal people were themselves also conducting ceremonies. In 1824, the French visitor Dumont D'Urville reported that Bungaree had hosted a 'great gathering' of tribes near Sydney Cove to which D'Urville had been invited. He witnessed the Aboriginal people from Liverpool (including Kogi) and Windsor attending, as well as many others from as far afield as Emu Plains, the Hunter River (Newcastle) and the Five Islands at Wollongong.[7]

Along the river introduced diseases continued to ravage Aboriginal people – even after the initial smallpox epidemic of 1789, which was repeated in the 1830s. There were as well other epidemics of unfamiliar bacterial and viral illness like measles, and other conditions like pneumonia which attacked people already weakened by worsening poverty, alcohol abuse and declining nutrition.[8] Yet there were numbers of people who survived across the area and, as leaders like Kogi came home, the community regrouped as best it could.[9]

This process of building a new life in the spaces in between settlement has been little understood. In this early period we can find only traces and hints of Aboriginal life, scattered through the records like broken shells in a midden. They can only suggest the rich tensions, the laughter, the plans and the stories which might have accompanied the gathering and eating of the oysters and mussels whose remains were left behind.

We know only a little more about Kogi, who had returned from the Botany area to take up an active role among the western Dharawal community. He had responded to Macquarie's call later in 1816 for Aboriginal people to lay down their arms in return for food, education and secure title to land in the Liverpool area. While there are no records of what formal arrangements Kogi came to, he retained Macquarie's favour, and his status was recognised when he received a 'King Plate' from the governor, in which he was identified as 'King of the Georges River'.[10] He was recorded again at the annual feast at Parramatta in 1826 as the head of his tribe.[11] He may have been recorded again, aged about 60, in the Return of Aboriginal Natives in 1834, but he then disappears. (It is unclear because the British kept spelling his name differently, including as 'Gogy', 'Goguey', 'Koggie', 'Cowgye'.) He was however survived by his wives, Nantz and Mary, and their children, and in the same 1834 list his son Jackey appears. After that, it was Jackey alone who was recorded: in 1837, aged 27, and then in the subsequent censuses in 1838, 1842 and finally 1843, when he was 33 years old.[12]

Goggey's claim on
Williams Creek

Such official documents make no mention of where Kogi and his family lived, and the assumption has been that they were itinerants around the town. But just because we lose the trail in the settler records does not mean that the Dharawal people were not still living on the river. Whether or not the agreement in 1816 had involved a formal transfer of land is not clear. The legislative mechanism of reserving Crown Land to be exclusively 'for the use of Aborigines' was not established until 1850, leaving land grants as the only vehicle to transfer land formally to Aboriginal people before that. While there are a few records of grants made to Aboriginal people in the area – like those to Colebe and Maria, the children of Yarramundi, in the 1830s – there are no records of land being granted or otherwise secured for Kogi and others in 1816.[13] Yet the understanding that land would be offered in return for peaceful relations was widespread, and the rumours that there was Aboriginal freehold land along the Georges River persisted into the late twentieth century. Where then did the Dharawal of the Liverpool and Holsworthy area live after 1816? Was Kogi settled on land of his own?

The answer lies in a furious petition written in 1857 by Kogi's grandson, Jonathon Goggey. He had been living with other Aboriginal people on a block of 100 acres (40 hectares) at the junction of the Harris and Williams Creeks, just upstream from where they join the Georges River at Holsworthy. This area is now known as Voyager Point, and had originally been granted to Captain JT Williams. It had however been left vacant and undeveloped, like much of the land granted in this period on the Georges River.[14] The grantee on the other side of Williams Creek, Captain Thomas Rowley, had set up a shipbuilding business there which was active into the 1840s. He also collaborated with a neighbour on a water mill to produce flour.[15]

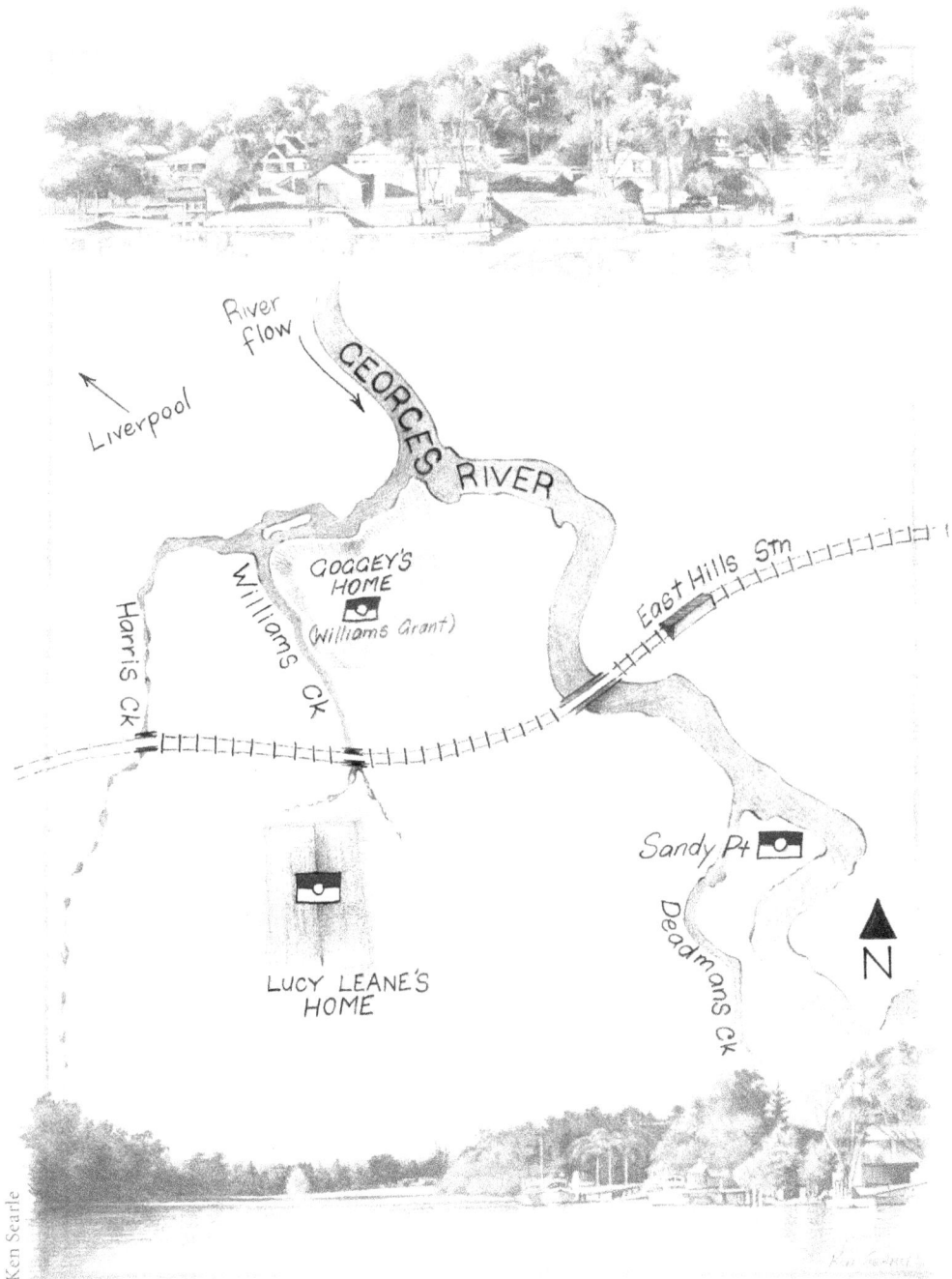

Williams and Harris Creeks, where
Goggey's family and later Lucy Leane
lived in the nineteenth century.

River Flow

Liverpool

GEORGES RIVER

GOGGEY'S HOME
(Williams Grant)

Harris Ck

Williams Ck

East Hills Stn

Sandy Pt

Deadmans Ck

LUCY LEANE'S HOME

N

Ken Searle

Thomas Rowley's son John was sympathetic to Aboriginal people, and he recorded the Appin people's language and culture, before moving away from the area. Thomas' grandson, another John Rowley and the focus of Goggey's petition, held different views.[16] He remained on the Holsworthy block and planned to expand his businesses and land holdings there – regardless of Goggey's presence.

In his petition, Jonathon Goggey explained that his father Jack had also been living on the Williams block for over 21 years, from before 1836. This was not a backwater: Thomas Rowley's shipbuilding enterprise, and water mill formed some of the earliest industrial sites in the colony. Along with the stone quarry just downstream, there would have been a substantial movement of labourers and goods through the area.[17] However the Williams block, where Goggey lived, was low-lying land, including some wetlands with mangroves and salt marsh, so it had not been suitable for either extensive farming or large-scale residences. It had therefore been able to provide a refuge for the Aboriginal families in an otherwise busy area. Now, Jonathon wrote to the governor to protest that, despite their long unchallenged residence, a great injustice was being done. Their neighbour John Rowley, the grandson of Thomas Rowley,[18] had begun trying to expand across Williams Creek and wanted to turn the Goggey family off the land they regarded as their own. This demand for recognition of long tenure must have been a commonly expressed Aboriginal concern, but it was rarely recorded. Jonathon Goggey's 1857 petition, however, has survived:

The Petition of Jonathan Goggey, an Aboriginal, of the Colony praying for redress, reporting his ejectment from certain lands –

Humbly Sheweth

That Petitioner's father resided at Holdsworthy [sic] near Liverpool, on a Plot of Land, Known as Captain William's

Grant, for upwards of twenty one years.

That a Person in the name of John Rowley had turned him off the Said land without showing just claim.

Petitioner therefore a Supplicant at the Hands of your Excellency, requireth that divine prerogation to be executed, which alone [might?] stoppeth the Other and the Petitioner will in duty Bound

Ever pray

Jonathan Goggey

George's Hall

Near Liverpool

PS it may be as well to state that the land in question is subject to no personal claim, having been originally granted to Captain Williams.[19]

Goggey's appeal met confusion in the government because there was in fact no coherent policy about Aboriginal people and land in 1857. But this was not because the issue had been ignored: ten years before the British Colonial Office had forced the New South Wales government to investigate the conditions of Aboriginal people in the colony. At this time, graziers of sheep and particularly cattle had been aggressively attacking Aboriginal people on the land they wanted to use to pasture stock. News of the battles and massacres during the 1830s and 1840s across south-eastern Australia had reached England where, having recently legislated against the slave trade, the vocal humanitarian faction of the government had turned its attention to colonised indigenous peoples.[20]

The New South Wales government had reluctantly conceded to British insistence and agreed in 1850 to set aside forty reservations of Crown land for the use of Aborigines, located on the advice of local Crown lands commissioners. These reserves were to be one square mile in area (640 acres, or about 260 hectares), with at least one in every Crown land division. Some of the Crown land commission-ers and the surveyor general had begun discussions with Aboriginal people to determine what land they might accept. Although this proc-ess occurred less often in settled districts like Holsworthy, it was likely to have been well known among Aboriginal people across the colony.[21]

Few of the 1850 reservations had been of real interest to Aborigi-nal people. Most did not wish to be confined to small plots as either farm or refuge, despite coming under continuing frontier pressure to move away from the grazing and agricultural properties on their tra-ditional lands. But the discovery of gold in 1851 dramatically changed the land and labour situation across the state. Workers all over New South Wales and the newly created colony of Victoria downed tools and left their jobs to head for the diggings. This meant that all avail-able workers were needed to fill the jobs that had been left vacant. Suddenly many Aboriginal people, previously subject to attack and exclusion, found themselves from 1851 being cajoled to come back to work on the settlers' properties.

Soon, however, a new pressure emerged in the coastal agricultural areas. As men flooded into the goldfields from all the Australian col-onies and from overseas, the demands for food escalated, and so too did the demand for farming land to produce it. Previously unfarmed land adjacent to existing farms became highly desirable and neigh-bours began expanding onto it wherever possible. At the same time, more farming land was clawed out of what had been reserved land. For Aboriginal people in agricultural areas like Holsworthy, blocks which had previously been of no interest to surrounding farmers (and avail-able for Aboriginal camping) suddenly became appealing as farmers scrambled to feed the population on the goldfields. Just a few years later, Aboriginal people from the south coast who were coming under similar pressure began making demands on the colonial government for new reservations over land. Before long this occurred in other areas even closer to the Georges River, like the Burragorang Valley.[22]

In this context, in 1858 the surveyor general's office replied sympathetically to Jonathan Goggey's plea for support against the encroaching Rowley – but it offered little practical help. Although its officers had been unable to acquire any further information, the surveyor general seemed to accept that Goggey was justified in demonstrating ownership by long residence. Since the land was no longer Crown land, but rather a land grant for which a title deed had been issued to Captain Williams, there appeared to be little the government could do to help Goggey. They could take the step of appealing on his behalf to the Supreme Court to demand that 'Mr Rowley show a better title than the 21 years possession which Goggey alleges and can possibly prove'– but that was unlikely to happen.[23]

There are sadly no further records which explain what happened to this land as a result of Goggey's demand, although parish maps over the following decades show that the land was neither sold nor subdivided. Did Goggey win in his battle with John Rowley? Certainly the belief persisted amongst the broader population of Holsworthy that this was in some way officially authorised Aboriginal land, although it was assumed that it was a formal reservation for the use of Aborigines.[24] (We return to this story in Chapter 7, because events of 1949 finally allow the riddle over whether Goggey won his 1857 battle to be solved.)

Women and colonisation: relationships and the river

Holsworthy was a second point of impact of the colonisers on the Aboriginal people of the Georges River. The first point of impact had been Botany Bay, into which the Georges River flows on its way to the sea. This was where the British first arrived in 1788 and to which they kept on returning to fish, hunt and gather timber and reeds. Right at the junction of the Georges River and Botany Bay, a diamond-shaped promontory juts far out into the Bay from the southern bank, guarding the river mouth. At its northern corner lies Towra Point and its western corner is Pelican Point, while the eastern corner enfolds within it the rich shallow mud flats and fishing grounds of Weeney Bay. This is the site of the next story about Aboriginal people holding on to country.

So far, this chapter seems to have been a story about men. Women appear very seldom in histories of early invasion and settlement. Instead we find evidence from the early years to be largely about Aboriginal men as leaders of an armed struggle, like Pemulwuy and Tedbury, or as family leaders like Kogi and his son and grandson, all asserting their status and rights to land on their own country. However, women as well as men had survived the violence and the sickness of the first years of the colony. There has been important recent recognition of the active role of Aboriginal women in the early interactions of the settlement. The writing of Ann McGrath, Inga Clendinnen and Grace Karskens have each shown that at the time of the British invasion, both Aboriginal and British social conventions discriminated against women, even though they did so in different ways.[25]

The lack of information about Aboriginal women as actors in the history of colonisation arises from the biases of both settlers and Aboriginals – which tend to emphasise men as leaders and spokespeople. Yet as we discussed in chapter 2, from the very beginning of the settlement women were observed to be the main fishers among the Aboriginal people of the rivers. A telling suggestion of their active role in the economy of both local Aboriginal and early settler societies are the breast plates inscribed for Cora Gooseberry, from the area to the south of Port Jackson. They are engraved with images of fish, one alive and swimming but the other image of two dead fish, dangling on a carrying line, ready for cooking or for sale.[26]

When it comes to the impact of colonisation on women, we must remember that invasion and dispossession were not just conducted between men over land, water and resources. Brutalities occurred sexually as well, and as the earliest British authorities admitted, both convicts and officers sometimes raped and sexually abused Aboriginal women. Yet interactions between Europeans and Aboriginals were not always confrontational either. There were also some sexual and personal relationships which seem consensual, affectionate and enduring. Accounts of such relationships were few, and were often distorted in their transmission back to England, where the published works tended to be little more than demeaning caricatures. And we have only fragments of evidence for the early parts of the story, which probably began in the 1840s but achieved greater visibility in the 1870s. Tracing the continuing presence of Aboriginal people on the Georges River opens up glimpses of each of these kinds of relationships. This is a story about women who, more quietly but just as tenaciously, sustained culture and teaching so that their children were able to continue their heritage and culture. It is also a story – to be told many times in this book – about interactions between Aboriginal people and the newcomers, building families and at the same time, holding on to country.

Mahroot and Weeney Bay in the 1840s

Mahroot is one of the few members of the Sydney fishing communities whose knowledge and speech were recorded at all. His responses indicate clearly that many Aboriginal women were present in the fishing communities along the river. He gave evidence before the colony's Select Committee on the Condition of the Aborigines in September 1845, describing his busy life on the waters of the Cooks River and Botany Bay, as he made a living from fishing and selling his fish to whites in the township. His home was near another creek named after a mill, but this time on the northern shore of Botany Bay. Mahroot's home on this Mill Creek was just one of the many ranged along the shore from the Cooks River mouth, in an area which later in the century became known collectively as 'the Botany camp'. This area was initially not only a rich site for fishing but was surrounded by grasslands in which game such as wallaby were abundant, and wetlands with prolific birdlife.[27]

Mahroot was one of the adventurous Aboriginal people who had left Australia for periods of time as a crew member on whaling vessels.[28] His nickname 'Boatswain' seems to have been derived from his role on these voyages, overseeing deck crew and cargo loading. Throughout his travelling life, Mahroot always returned to his own place and was buried close by, in 1850, on a site which continued to be used for Aboriginal burials until at least 1868, near the Sir Joseph Banks Hotel at Broadmeadow.[29] Mahroot was not the only Aboriginal person who was surviving well in the new environment: James Tegg was working successfully as stockman and overseer in 1841 for Charles Throsby at the upper end of the river.[31]

Yet such stories of effective cultural negotiation were not of interest to Mahroot's interrogators in the Select Committee. In a common obsession for the settlers, they wanted to know whether he would try to force other Aboriginal parents to send their children to school and if Aboriginal communities would accept mixed-race children. Mahroot, between digressions to answer their questions, described his community of around 50 people, of whom he said there were only four – three women and himself – who spoke the language of the group from the area where he was born, at the mouth of the Cooks River. (Significantly, none of his questioners at the Select Committee asked for the names of these three women.)

The other people in the community, Mahroot explained, were people who had grown up in the area near the Bay and who had then left it to live upstream on the Georges River, towards Liverpool, but had returned once again. Mahroot was married to a woman from Liverpool and he implied that the three women were also married, some to Aboriginal men from Liverpool or elsewhere. Others, like the women among the wider Aboriginal community in which they lived, were married to white men. Some of these men welcomed a distance from the main settlement: they were perhaps escaped convicts or naval deserters like the man met by one 1860s traveller who had 'found a resting place among the shell-getters of Weenie Bay', losing his identity as 'Tom' and becoming 'Damper' for the rest of his life.[31]

Mahroot explained that the Aboriginal men and women who were involved with the British did so with an underlying suspicion. They sold fish and sometimes possum and other game to the white settlers, for example, but did not trust them with either their children or their sick. They retrieved any vulnerable kin from white control in schools or 'poor houses', however benign these situations might appear to have been. This was hardly surprising given the attempts – and often the success – of settlers abducting Aboriginal children from the early days of the settlement, either to train them as interpreters or 'civilise' them as examples of a 'superior' culture.[32] The extended Botany community came to be known for its fishing, on which the settlers depended for the first few years of the colony and so settler fishermen were drawn to the Aboriginal networks around the Bay, forming families and building up a community of fisherfolk which drew on both cultures.

The Malones: passing on knowledge of country

One of the three women who spoke Mahroot's local language began living with, or was married to, a white man called Malone. She was able to pass on to their child, John, some knowledge of her language and her country, and John Malone became a notable figure in the area. He was thought to be about 30 or 40 years old in 1858 and, if so, born between 1828 and 1838.[33] Yet none of the women in these extended fishing communities have been named in written records we have examined. We only know they were there and that they had 'half caste' children, indicating their ongoing relationships with white men. John Malone was written about by later settlers as 'the last of his tribe' – and yet he had a daughter Elizabeth, and a son Harry. Although Harry lived for some time in Liverpool, he was survived by his widow and daughters – John's grand-daughters – who had returned to Kogarah Bay by 1883. Yet this story of largely female descent was not noticed by white observers.[34]

John assisted a German doctor Karl Scherzer in 1858, who was searching for the grave of a senior Aboriginal man, Tow-weiry, who had died about 1846 and had been remembered as Tom Ugly. (This Tom Ugly has a bridge across the wide lower Georges River named after him although his Aboriginal origin is not widely known.) In 1858, however, Karl Scherzer was well aware that the Aboriginal community would be able to tell him about Tow-weiry, and he recruited John Malone to show him around. John used his own boat, described by Scherzer as 'safe and well-built', to carry the searchers around to the land between the junctions of the Cooks and the Georges Rivers. Here he showed them rich evidence of extensive and lengthy human residence, with the remains of many cooking fires, oyster-shell middens and camps in all directions, before returning to his home at Kogarah Bay.[35]

John Malone continued to live in this area, and in the mid-1870s he recorded with ethnographer A Mackenzie the vocabulary he remembered from his mother. This was later published in 1878 – although still without recording this woman's name.[36] Malone's wife was at least better recognised: Mackenzie recorded her as a Shoalhaven woman, Lizzie, who explained her knowledge of Wadi Wadi, her people's language, and of Dharawal, the language she described as being used from Wollongong to the north, across the Georges River and on to Port Jackson. (Her implication is that John Malone's language was Dharawal.)

Mackenzie's report named the European contributors with titles like 'Mr' or 'Rev' and provided their given and family names. For John and Lizzie Malone though, Mackenzie used only 'Malone' with '(half castes)' noted after it. The use of the surname alone and of the singular form to indicate a couple are examples of the linguistic distinctions often made in records of all sorts in the colonial period, and are clues to Aboriginal identity even though often ambiguous and confusing.[37]

Here the maps and archival records suggest other clues.[38] One of the sites at which Aboriginal people were living in the 1840s was around Weeney Bay, the shallow, rich fish and shellfish area enfolded within the Towra Point promontory. In 1831, James Malone made an attempt to regularise his ongoing residence on the southern side of Weeney Bay by claiming a 30-acre block (12 hectares). A neighbouring white settler, John Connell, took exception and in March 1831 began a lengthy correspondence with the Colonial Secretary's Department, insisting he had been granted precisely the block on which Malone lived – but without apparently producing enough proof to convince the officials of the Surveyor General's Department. They advertised the land as owned by James Malone in September of the same year. Connell persisted, and in the absence of any documentation from Malone (suggesting he may have been illiterate), Connell succeeded in having the grant notified officially in his name for the first time in October 1831.[39]

Yet there continued to be doubts and, it seems, Malone and his family continued to reside on the block. In a parish map of 'Southerland' drawn apparently after 1831, the block appears with only the name Malone and '/30' inscribed on it. But there is no impinging or adjacent landholding to that of Malone. It stands alone on Weeney Bay.[40]

In 1861, the entrepreneur Thomas Holt bought up huge swathes of land along the southern shore of the river, stretching down in many cases to Port Hacking. On another map, drawn soon after, the large word 'Malone' continued to dominate the space of the block – reflecting a continued belief in the Lands Department that Malone, or the

John Malone, probably from about the time he helped A Mackenzie compile a Dharawal 'vocabulary', c 1875.

DECC, photo 2004.526.118

Malone family, had a claim on the land. One further undated map shows the continuance of the Malone name in large letters in the block, despite Connell's name still appearing in the smaller annotation about the grant. Only in 1884 does Malone's name disappear from the official maps.[41]

So the Malone family seem to have managed to keep some hold on the Weeney Bay land for at least 30 years – from the time Connell first tried to contest their tenure in 1831 until Holt arrived in 1861 – and then beyond for close to 50 years, until 1884, when the Lands Department finally accepted John Connell as the owner. Over that time, John Malone had grown up learning from his mother the language and the country of Towra Point and the surrounding Georges River. But this was not all he had learnt: he was noting the way her language had been changing to engage with the new working and social relationships with whites – from the intimate family relationships between his Irish father and Aboriginal mother to the master-servant relations into which the settlers were insisting Aboriginal people must fit. In the mid-1870s John Malone could confidently discuss with Mackenzie the vocabulary in his mother's language for the environment and for the game on which his family had lived, like kuruera (possum), kundyeri (duck) and manma wulimai (he has caught some snapper). But her language was also expressing change with the sentences for new interactions, like 'What do you want mistress?' and 'Our father here will pray for us'.[42]

William Rowley:
life at the river's mouth

The Malones were not the only Aboriginal family living on the Towra promontory. William Rowley was born there around 1851, on its western corner at Pelican Point, and grew up there with his family – also learning about the river from his mother.[43] (He appears to have been no relation to the John Rowley whose family had caused so much distress to Jonathon Goggey further upstream near Holsworthy.) As an adult, William Rowley fished across the whole of the mouth of the river, as well as collecting shells on the mudflats of Weeney Bay. This river mouth area was dotted with small communities, like those at Ellesmere at Kogarah Bay and at Kyle Bay, the next inlet to the west, each community built on the relationships between Aboriginal people, particularly Aboriginal women, and white fishermen

The residents of these fishing communities lived on their catches and sold their excess fish to the surrounding settlers. Often impoverished and looked down upon by more affluent neighbours as the settlement consolidated, they contributed to sustaining relationships among the Aboriginal people along the length of the river.[44] William Rowley for example travelled often by canoe and rowboat between La Perouse and Weeney Bay. At La Perouse, where a substantial Aboriginal community interacted regularly with local whites, Rowley sold his catch of fish, shells and octopus skeletons (used to make jewellery moulds) and made, in his own recollection, 'a fair living'.[45] He petitioned the newly formed Aborigines Protection Board (APB), as a member of the La Perouse community, for boats for fishing in 1883. But he continued to live at Weeney Bay, close to where he was born.[46] The 1891 census listed William Rowley as the householder of the only dwelling there, in which he lived with an extended family of four men and one woman.[47]

Like John Malone, William Rowley's knowledge of the local environment and resources was valuable to white interests in the area. In 1893, he was acknowledged by the manager of the large Holt Company estate in the area as the caretaker of all of the Holt oyster racks in Weeney Bay, and empowered to stop unauthorised people, including white settlers, from taking resources from any of the surrounding Holt lands.[48] Rowley, apart from earning extra cash, may have used this role as a way of keeping an eye on his own country and protecting

The entrance of the Georges River into
Botany Bay, and nearby Port Hacking,
where many Aboriginal people lived and
worked in the late nineteenth century.

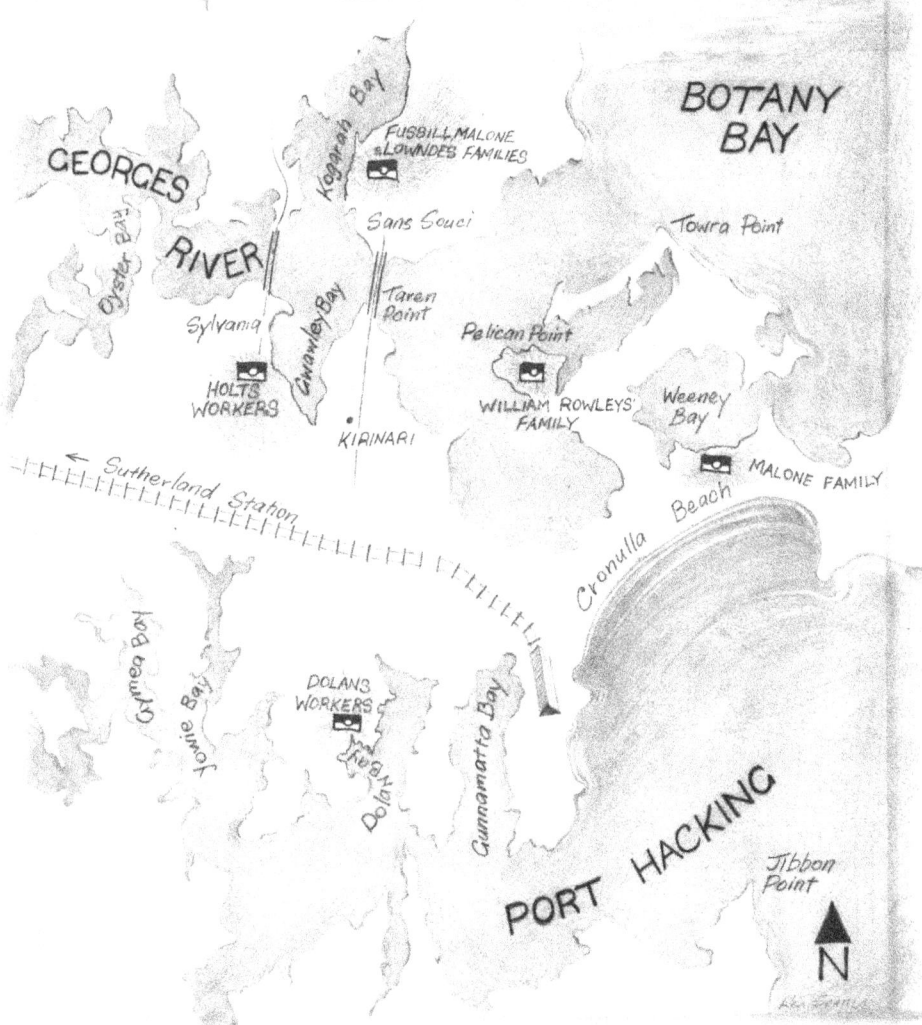

Ken Searle

GEORGES

Oyster Bay

RIVER

Kogarah Bay

FUSSILL, MALONE
& LOWNDES FAMILIES

BOTANY
BAY

Sans Souci

Towra Point

Sylvania

Gwawley Bay

Taren
Point

Pelican Point

Weeney
Bay

HOLTS
WORKERS

WILLIAM ROWLEYS'
FAMILY

MALONE FAMILY

KIRINARI

← Sutherland Station

Cronulla Beach

Gunnamatta Bay

Gymea Bay

Yowie Bay

DOLANS
WORKERS

Burraneer Bay

PORT HACKING

Jibbon
Point

N

it from being overexploited. In the 1910s, Rowley and his wife moved upriver to settle at Salt Pan Creek where they participated in the vibrant community life which supported Joe Anderson's demand for recognition in 1933.[49]

John Malone died in the 1880s, but his grandchildren, Mary (13) and Eliza (7) were living just across the river mouth at the Ellesmere camp on Kogarah Bay.[50] They were seeking what many Aboriginal families had begun to demand in these years: access to the newly established public education system. Other Kogarah Bay Aboriginal parents and guardians such as Teresa Fussell, J and W Fussell (a labourer) and Anna Lowndes also signed the successful 1883 petition to the government. The Malone family remained at Ellesmere over the next two decades at least.[51] But they continued to be alert to the country around them – although this irritated the schoolteacher, who complained that these children wandered off at play hour 'looking for five corners and gathering bush flowers'.[52] The continuing influence of Aboriginal women in this mixed community, both in their fishing and in their fostering of their children's awareness of country, can be seen in this community's history – even though their names were so often unrecorded.

Lucy Leane's demand for recognition in the 1890s

If women are shadowy figures in the written history of the Malones and the Towra Point communities, they step onto centre stage with the story of Lucy Leane, who lived upstream on Williams Creek, not far from Jonathon Goggey's home at Voyager Point.

Jonathon Goggey in 1857, in the face of pressure from a white neighbour, was defending land on which his family had lived for three generations. John Malone and the women in the fishing families at the mouth of the river were holding on to their country through the 1870s by engaging in an economy in which they had both traditional and present-day market experience, even though they were facing opposition and discrimination from local whites. Lucy Leane was holding on to country in a different way again. Having established herself as a respected and well-connected local citizen, in 1893 she demanded recognition specifically as Aboriginal, and as an Aboriginal woman linked with a broader Aboriginal movement to assert rights to land and an economic future. To understand why Lucy made her stand, it is necessary to see her actions in the context of events across the rest of the state.

Many things had altered in the 36 years between Goggey's protest and Lucy's demand. The area around Holsworthy had become more closely settled and had attracted a diverse population. The parish maps for the 1890s are dotted with landowner names like Passanisi, Haerse and Belotto – suggesting the Italian, German, Russian, Polish and French immigrants who had been arriving for some decades. Initially brought to establish wine-growing in the area, many settled into independent farming around Holsworthy, stimulating vineyard planting on surrounding properties.[53]

Similar shifts towards intensive food horticulture meant that the pressure on land which Jonathon Goggey had felt had been just the beginning of a wave of settler expansion across the whole of the eastern half of the state. One by one, community by community, Aboriginal people in the most affected areas had started to petition the government for secure tenure over small parts of their traditional lands. In 1859, just two years after Jonathon Goggey's protest, the Goulburn Valley people began to petition for land, in a long campaign which led in part to the achievement of family farming blocks on the Murray River at Cumeragunja.[54] Then the Yuin people on the mid-south coast of New South Wales began calling for land in the 1860s,[55] followed in the early 1870s by Gandangara people in the Burragorang Valley just to the west of Sydney,[56] and by Aboriginal people around the gold-fields areas of Braidwood and Yass.[57] Late in the 1870s, demands began to emerge from the north coast of the state, as agriculture, dairying and sugar cane farming increased in the fertile river valleys.[58]

Some of their petitions or deputations echo the ideas behind the small government reserves set aside in 1850, but most were presented in the language of 'free selection' – a white working-class settlers campaign in the 1870s which aimed at secure freehold. Aboriginal petitioners sometimes met with local authorities like police and local members or parliament, or forwarded petitions to the state government. At other times they took direct action – occupying and beginning to farm the land over which they wanted secure tenure.

There were consistent elements to all the Aboriginal petitioners' demands which were expressed in words or writing: they all wanted land in perpetuity, as an inalienable freehold tenure. Their goals included gaining land from which they could earn a living in the new economy, sometimes drawing on traditional subsistence harvesting as well as from cash incomes. Some petitions and deputations included, for example, a desire to live close to fishing grounds or to hunt on the land granted, while others asked for land to farm. A key element of each demand was for security over land of importance to them. They might express it as Jack Bawn of Braidwood did in 1872 when he led the deputation of his people to the local police to demand land: 'We think the blacks are entitled to live on their own country'. Or they might explain it by using a Christian analogy, as William Cooper from Cumeragunja did in 1887 when he asked for enough land for a selection and 'for a small portion of this vast territory which is ours by Divine Right'.[59] But for all of them, the central point was that they did not want land just anywhere – they wanted land which meant something to them for cultural as well as economic values.

The government had reacted to all these early claims with confusion, sometimes granting a reservation of Crown Land on the model of 1850, but at other times simply explaining that there was no policy to deal with the request. In the face of this confusion, many of these claimants turned their appeals towards local bodies. The most successful of these was in 1876, when the Aboriginal people in the Burragorang Valley recruited the local priest, Father Dillon, to support them. This led to a local subscription which raised enough money to purchase a 70-acre (28-hectare) farm on the junction of the Cox's and Wollondilly Rivers which continued to support a substantial community of Aboriginal people well into the 1920s. Some people were able to purchase land outright, while others gained permissive occupancies.[60]

Although these many demands were not formally consolidated into a movement, there can be no doubt that Georges River Aboriginal people were well aware of them. The first claimants in the 1860s were from the south coast of the state – close to the communities from which John Malone's wife came. The next were from the nearby Burragorang Valley, from which there was regular movement into the Georges River; and then from Yass and Cumeragunja, both south-western regions from which there were people moving into the urban area. Police reports in the early 1880s confirmed Mahroot's 1845 statement that people from the west, including the Burragorang Valley and the south-western areas like Brungle continued to move along the Georges River all the way to Botany Bay.[61] The Aborigines Protection Board was only set up in 1883 – still without a clear land policy but led by a 'chief protector' who hoped that land allocations could be used both to foster self-sufficiency and to entice Aborigines to cease their visits to the city and move back to 'their own districts' in rural areas.[62] A key element in the first protector's report in 1883 was to document the large and growing number of Aboriginal claims for land and for other means for economic independence, usually boats, building materials and seeds.[63]

In its early years the APB merely reacted to each demand made upon it, rather than formulating and implementing its own policy. It still responded to calls from both whites and Aboriginal people to use land to further community goals. In some areas, local white communities began to call on the Board to set up reservations aimed at confining Aborigines or at securing their labour in conveniently nearby locations – despite their removal from newly subdivided properties. Most reserves established from the 1870s to the early 1890s, however, were the result of Aboriginal requests. The Board's response looked both backwards and forwards: acting on the model of the 1850 reserves, it created reserves instead of inalienable freehold, but explained that the land was being handed over permanently. The Board was less interested in the old model of rations and blankets, and preferred instead to provide tools and materials for future independence. As word spread among Aboriginal communities that the new Protection Board was responding positively, further petitions and deputations for land were undertaken. They were mostly successful until the full impact of a severe economic depression was felt in the early years of the 1890s. It was in this early flush of the Board's largesse, in 1883, that the group of men at La Perouse, including William Rowley, applied successfully for boats, fishing tackle and building materials.[64]

Lucy Leane entered this process late in her life, in 1893 when she was already 53 years old. She still lived close to where she had been born as Lucy Burn, in Holsworthy around 1840, but her life was very different from the caricatures of Aboriginal women which have survived. Lucy had grown up to marry an Englishman, William Leane, and had purchased two blocks of land with him on the eastern side of Williams Creek – just upstream of Jonathon Goggey's family home. There she had successfully reared their 13 children.[65] They developed a flourishing farm of 82 acres (33 hectares), with a 10-acre orchard and, like their Italian neighbours, a successful vineyard. They also owned milking cows, horses, carts and farming implements. This is likely to be the farm at Holsworthy noted by the APB in 1892.[66] By 1893 they were sending their younger children to school and had already raised their older children to go off to lives of independent work and marriage. Several of their children married in Liverpool and some continued to live there.[67] Lucy had developed good relations with the dignitaries of the settler community there, and was held in particularly high regard by the mayor of Liverpool, who had known her for over thirty years. In 1893 Lucy decided to write to the Protection Board, penning her own petition which she had the school teacher witness, to seek the allocation of a boat to use in selling her farm produce along the river.

Lucy could conceivably have 'passed' into the settler community at this stage of her life, whatever her visible ancestry, as she had established herself very much on its terms. She had no need to advertise her aboriginality nor to assert her connections to country and to the wider Aboriginal community. Yet she chose to stand proudly on just these grounds:

> Your Petitioner … is the only surviving Native Woman of the Georges River and Liverpool District, residing here ever since her birth, Fifty Three years ago, as the undersigned witnesses can vouch for, and attest.
>
> Being a bona fide Original Native of Australia & of this District, your Petitioner requests of you the supply of a boat as granted by Government in all such cases, for the purpose of carrying on trade on the Georges River.

The witnesses who supported her petition included the mayor, numerous aldermen, the local bank manager, the school teacher and other leading gentlemen who added comments like 'This is a most deserving woman'.[68]

The Protection Board responded that they intended their allocations to be made on the basis of need, not of the right of Aboriginal people to claim such recognition. Lucy was probably aware of the paternalistic intention of the Board, so it is all the more interesting that she chose such an assertive tone and recruited the support of such an array of local authorities. It is significant also that she explained her purpose to be one of using the boat to trade along the river, expanding still further her independence and demonstrating her established position in the local economy. For all Lucy Leane's success in establishing herself in the eyes of the settlers, the river continued to be central to trade and culture as it always had been. While Lucy may have been disappointed at the Protection Board's refusal to acknowledge her claim, she and her family continued to farm the land, though she died just two years later.[69] They may also have appeared in the fictional work of local author Robert 'Falder' (Kaleski) who lived close by and wrote of local Aboriginal people. The Leanes kept their blocks in the family name until at least 1925, no doubt continuing to assert the continuation of local Aboriginal heritage into the new century.[70]

There were many people along the river trying to hold on to patches of their land in the mid- to late nineteenth century. As long as they were successful, only a few of them came to the notice of white people who recorded their stories. Mostly they appeared in the written record only when they became embroiled in a conflict as they tried to formalise or protect their continued occupation. Even so, these three situations each involved a different type of hold over land in the official sense: the Goggey family at Voyager Point was squatting on private but undeveloped land; the Malones and others at Towra Point were living on some unalienated Crown land as well as lands which may have been permissive occupancy, or were in dispute. The Leanes at Holsworthy were living on farming land of which Lucy was an owner. Together they indicate the varied ways in which Aboriginal men and women might be successful in securing a foothold along the river despite the pressures of settlement. Each of these communities would have remained isolated, however, if there had not been active communication between them. Such communication and movement was another major strategy which Aboriginal people adopted to build new lives for themselves under colonisation.

FOUR

Travelling Guragurang: Biddy's river 1850–1890

Holding on to particular pieces of their land was what Jonathon Goggey, the Malone women and Lucy Leane were all trying in their different ways to do. But there was another strategy to build new lives in the challenging conditions of invasion and settlement, one which was widely practised.

This strategy was travelling. It was a way of managing land and kinship relationships which had been a key part of pre-invasion cultures right across Australia. Travelling was among other things a means of land management, harvesting and sustaining relationships between people and country. After the invasion, travel continued to allow Aboriginal people to keep in contact with many parts of their own country, as well as with the people who remained from their language networks.

This strategy of travelling was often denigrated and caricatured by settlers – who called it 'going walkabout' and said Aboriginal people were 'failing' to become 'civilised' because they were not 'settled' on one block of land. Yet when we can trace whole lives, we can see that Georges River people were sustaining contact with their country and kin even at the same time as they travelled widely outside traditional language areas, were taking part in new settler economic and cultural activities, and were building even wider networks. Mahroot, introduced in the previous chapter, was an adventurous traveller who undertook whaling journeys as well as being a fisherman at Botany Bay. Another key person who travelled east and west along his river was William Rowley. He was born at Pelican Point at the mouth of the river, and at different times in his life lived close to his birth place at Weeney Bay, then at La Perouse (1883), back at Weeney Bay in 1891, then at Salt Pan Creek from the 1920s and finally Roseby Park where he died in 1941.[1]

The people we focus on in this chapter travelled even further. Jimmy Lowndes and Biddy Giles were each well-known figures in the area. They came from different places and travelled for diverse reasons, but they each called the Georges River home, and each of them returned to it. Rather than focusing on well-defined patches of land to defend and build on, they instead spent much of their lives moving around. Their travels were sometimes on long-established routes, like Biddy's journeys between the Georges River and the Five Islands. Other movements, like Jimmy Lowndes' travels for work, were far outside traditional pathways. This generated a two-way interaction: his journeys seem to have drawn Aboriginal people from the new areas which Jimmy visited, into ongoing contacts with his own country and people back on the Georges River. A common feature of all their travels was the ability to have free access to all their country on the river, even as changes were occurring in the way settlers were using the area. Each of the people we focus on had open and available places to live. They had the freedom to move across country, by land or water, between communities and camps. They encountered few fences (or at least passed through them with ease), and accessed and knew of of sites of cultural significance. All of these conditions enabled them to continue to draw on both the traditional and the settler economies and cultures as they used travelling as a way to survive.

The people who travelled by choice, like Jimmy and Biddy, were not the only ones moving around. Long before the Protection system was set up, there were vulnerable people who were facing enforced moves. Children had from the earliest days of the settlement been seized or enticed into settler control. Initially Governor Phillip had wanted to learn local language and culture, and negotiate with local people through the young hostages. Before long, the settlers argued that their motives were to educate or 'civilise' children.[2] Some of these institutions were located along the Georges River, such as the Orphan School at Orphan School Creek, north of Liverpool, to which a number of young boys from the old Black-town Aboriginal school were sent from 1828 to 1832 under the Reverend Cartwright.[3] Other children were moved from rural areas. This home was later merged with children's homes, like those developed by George Edward Ardill, a philanthropist and influential early member of the Aborigines Protection Board from 1883.[4] Later still, Aboriginal children were drawn into the wider practices of child labour and 'bonding' which were occurring also with white working-class or orphaned children – unofficial, often exploitative and commonly accepted until public outcry developed against child labour much later in the nineteenth century. Children may at times have welcomed the role of cultural explorer, but when they found themselves trapped in coercive 'schools' and blocked from returning to their families, the attractions wore off and the children, like their parents, came to see these as punitive incarcerations.[5]

Jimmy
Lowndes

Jimmy Lowndes was born sometime in the 1830s around Camden, and in his adult life he travelled long distances following new work in the settlers economy. Yet he sustained links both to country and kin, returning to the Georges River later where he came to be recognised as highly knowledgeable on Dharug language and culture in his last years.

Jimmy Lowndes' distinctive surname, perhaps acquired from a white father, was used frequently, distinguishing him from the many other men whom the setters called 'Jimmy'. His visibility in the records is perhaps the reason we know more about him than about other men who may have been travelling in the same way. The first mention of Jimmy Lowndes is in William Macarthur's correspondence, in which he discussed the number of mixed-race children born on his father's sheep grazing Camden estate during the 1820s, from relationships between local Dharawal women and the estate's staff.[6] Macarthur expounded on the topic which obsessed the British: how did local Aboriginal people accept such children or did they kill them instead? Mahroot's questioners in 1845 had repeatedly raised this issue and, like them, William Macarthur referred to it at length. In the midst of this, Macarthur mentioned that one child, Jimmy Lowndes, had been protected by Budbury, a senior Dharawal man, who had hidden the child to save him from danger.

Macarthur may have been very wrong about Aboriginal attitudes to the young Jimmy, because he grew up safely to adulthood within the community where he spoke his own Dharug language and became familiar with the neighbouring Dharawal and Gandangara people.[7] At the same time, he developed skills in the pastoral industry, moving on to handle much larger stock than the Macarthurs' sheep. Lowndes became a highly regarded horseman and an acclaimed bullock driver

– the major form of heavy transport, especially for the fleeces which were the new colony's main export.

As the industry expanded westwards, Lowndes moved up to the Castlereagh River, where his stockmanship was honed. Here he may have worked on the properties of Thomas Holt, the Sydney wool merchant and financier who in the 1850s had invested heavily in sheep runs in both north-western New South Wales and Queensland. In 1861, Holt sold some of his inland runs to purchase an extensive property which ran from Botany Bay to Port Hacking, filling in all the 'vacant' areas on the map with the Holt name. This encroached on the land of the Malone family and the scattered blocks of settlers John Connell and Gregory Blaxland.

Jimmy returns to the river

Holt found, however, that he was not able to use the land as intensively as he had hoped. Successive attempts at establishing pastoral enterprises with sheep and then cattle each failed and ultimately he turned to oyster farming, with canals dug initially around Gwawley Bay on Port Hacking, to timber-getting and coal-mining. Each of these land uses caused even less impact than grazing could have done on the potential for Aboriginal people to move across the extensive lands under Holt ownership.[8] So while Holt's purchase altered the land-holding map dramatically, his businesses made surprisingly little impact on the ground. But they did markedly change the way the Aboriginal community was built up and organised living and working arrangements.

Jimmy Lowndes came back to the Georges River to work on these big Holt properties. So far we don't know anything further about his relationships with the Gamilaraay and Wiradjuri people who may have been living on the Castlereagh River. Aboriginal people on the

Georges River often told white commentators of their connections with the people of the southern and south-western districts like the Shoalhaven or Brungle, but even by the later nineteenth century there were still few connections into the north-west of the state. However in the 1920s, at a time when general movement from the north-west into Sydney was still thought to be rare, there were members of at least two north-western families – the Groves and the Williams – living at Salt Pan Creek.[9] There is at least a possibility that this movement had been opened by relationships built up in the most active period of grazing expansion, when Jimmy Lowndes was working on the Castlereagh. Once Jimmy had returned to the Georges River, his renown as a horseman and bullock handler grew and became another identifying characteristic which was invariably remarked on by white commentators.[10]

During the 1860s, when Jimmy was working on the Holt properties, he lived in the Aboriginal labour camp, near what is now Sylvania, and developed extensive contacts with both Aboriginal and non-Aboriginal residents of the river. He married Betsey, an Aboriginal woman from Liverpool, who brought her children with her – including her daughter Emma, who later married George Timbery the fisherman from La Perouse.[11] By the 1880s, Jimmy may have been living across the waters at the camp at Ellesmere on Kogarah Bay, a community of workers in the fishing industry that included Aboriginal people. He certainly visited as an elderly man at least once in 1887, as APB expenditure records show 'Joey and Jimmy Lownes [sic] received clothing, hat, shirt and trousers' at the camp.[12] Over the same time, Lowndes also moved across the peninsula between Kogarah itself and Sans Souci, the eastern beach facing Botany Bay. In 1883 members of his family (their name spelt 'Loundes') were involved in the petition to gain a public school for all the children of the fishing community. James Loundes, perhaps a grandson of Jimmy, aged 12 and his mother Anna were listed as living at Ellesmere and planning to send James to the school if it could be started.[13]

During this time, white residents often saw the aging Jimmy Lowndes on either side of the peninsula. His extraordinary athletic skill, his talents with the lasso, his overall horsemanship and his long employment with Holt were often discussed. One day in the mid-1880s a set of photographs was taken at a camp somewhere in the vicinity – perhaps in the western side at Kogarah Bay or the eastern shore at Sans Souci or even at Sylvania, the old Holt camp across the water. Jimmy Lowndes is there, as tall, severe and stalwart as he is remembered, towering over the other Aboriginal people present.[14]

Jimmy Lowndes towered in other ways. Although he excelled in the Anglo-Australian pastoral industry, it was as a man of traditional knowledge that he made his final mark. As a Dharug man who had grown up around Camden where Gandangara and Dharawal people regularly met with Dharug speakers, Jimmy Lowndes was in a unique position to discuss the language and culture of all his people. He was found in the 1890s by those two prolific recorders, Mary Everitt and RH Mathews, and he worked with them in their compilations of vocabulary and customs, particularly offering insights into the comparative relationships between the three groups of people. Mathews, who seldom acknowledged his informants, mentioned Jimmy Lowndes specifically:

> The Dharrook dialect, very closely resembling the
> Gundungurra, was spoken at Campbelltown, Liverpool,
> Camden, Penrith and possibly as far east as Sydney, where
> it merged into Thurrawal. A very old Dharrook blackfellow,
> named 'Jimmy Lownds' only recently deceased, informed us
> that the Gundungurra and Dharrook natives could converse
> together with but little difficulty.[15]

Rare as it is, this mention points to the key role Lowndes was able to play as he looked back over his journeys in the months before his death in 1900.

Biddy Giles:
tracing a life

Biddy is a pivotal figure in relating the Dharawal people of the early nineteenth century with those who came afterwards, in the 1920s. The initially careful observations about Aborigines written by officers dwindled through the early nineteenth century, and even those by settlers became less frequent after 1830. So there were few documents at all about Aborigines until the establishment of the Aborigines Protection Board in 1883 led to official records which occasionally named individuals. In trying to fill that gap, the key questions for historians and for families have been about Biddy's kin: to whom was she related and who were her children? These questions simply cannot be decided on the basis of the European documentation, which is too fragmentary and inconsistent to allow firm conclusions. The families most directly concerned will hold in their family memory the strongest resources to solve such puzzles. In Biddy's story, we will be focusing not on what remains unclear about her family but instead on the information we do have about where she went and what she did. Her story shows some of the key ways that the Aboriginal community, living close to the heart of the British settlement, was at the same time rebuilding itself and emerging from the tragedies of the early colonial conflict. This process is resilience: the creation of a viable social network for the mid-nineteenth century by drawing on earlier, traditional values and strategies.

There are a number of things we know for certain about Biddy. She was a Dharawal-speaking woman who moved actively across the whole of Dharawal country, which ran from the Georges River in the north to the Five Islands near Wollongong in the south. But her travels were shaped by her relationships as well as her country. She was born around 1820 within the Gweagal group, whose part of Dharawal country was on the southern side of the Georges River and Botany

Bay – towards what became known as Kurnell. Biddy's daughter Ellen explained it this way in the 1920s when she said that her mother was 'from the north' of Dharawal country and her father was 'from the south'.[16] Mary Everitt, an ethnographer who knew Biddy Giles, said that Biddy spoke 'the pure Botany Bay Thurrawal', suggesting her close connections with that northern country.[17]

Mary Everitt also knew Emma Timbery, the stepdaughter of Jimmy Lowndes and by then a senior woman from La Perouse. As a woman only a little younger than Biddy, who had lived most of her life among Biddy's circle of friends, Emma must have known a great deal about Biddy's personal story.[18] Emma explained to Mary Everitt that Biddy's Dharawal name was Bi-yar-rung, and that, as a teenager, Biddy had been married unhappily to an elderly, well-known man from the Georges River called Cooman or King Kooma.[19] After a short time, Biddy had left Cooman to marry Paddy Burragalang (also known as Paddy Davis), moving to his country in the Five Islands in the southern areas of Dharawal country. Biddy and Paddy had two daughters, the younger being Ellen, whose son was Joe Anderson of Salt Pan Creek. Joe knew that his grandfather was named Burragalang, and it was from this name that he took his title of King Burraga in 1933.[20]

This family and Aboriginal community information is consistent with some of the scattered settler memories and early government records. An aging settler's memoirs, recorded in 1905, recalled a meeting at Kurnell in the 1830s with a teenaged Aboriginal girl called Biddy, then about 13 years old, who told him about her uncle's memory of witnessing Cook's landing there.[21] The census of Aboriginal people who were receiving blankets or rations in the early years of the nineteenth century, which recorded some people's names and estimated ages, show that a woman who was known as both Biddy and Byarraw, and aged 20, was living in the Five Islands area and collecting blankets at Wollongong in 1840. She remained there for 20 years and had two children: Rosie, born perhaps in the 1840s and Ellen, born in 1855.[22] By the early 1860s – about the time of Paddy's death – Biddy returned to live on the Georges River. There she began a long relationship with an Englishman, Billy Giles, whose name she took and kept for the rest of her life. Around this time Biddy told a number of different settlers about her first marriage, as a teenager, to King Kooma.[23] Emma Timbery thought that after Billy's death in the mid-1870s, Biddy had moved along the river to the Holt property at Sylvania where her brother Joey was living. She is thought to have again moved with him across the river mouth to Kogarah Bay, where she died early in the 1890s.[24]

There have been a number of attempts by historians to trace Biddy's familial relationships but disagreements among them persist. Recently Jim Kohen, Chris Illert and Keith Vincent Smith have each examined the few archival records from colonial authorities and the reminiscences of white and Aboriginal people, while Jim Smith has touched on Biddy's life in references to her daughter Ellen's time in the Kangaroo Valley in the 1890s.[25] Kohen alone suggests that Biddy was also known as Betsy and had another entirely separate set of family connections. But they all agree with Biddy's family that she was a Dharawal-speaker. There is debate about whether she was born in the northern area on the Georges River as most believe, or whether she and her brother Joe originally came from around the Five Islands.[26] There is also some confusion about the names and sequence of Biddy's husbands, with Emma Timbery describing Biddy as having a fourth husband in the last years of her life at the Holt property.[27]

There also remain puzzling questions about why Biddy did not mention her long relationship to Paddy when she talked with the many settler adventurers for whom she acted as a guide from the 1860s onwards. She chose rather to stress her earlier and brief relationship to someone more unequivocally linked to the Georges River locality,

Biddy's river: showing the
places to which she introduced
travellers in the *1860s*.

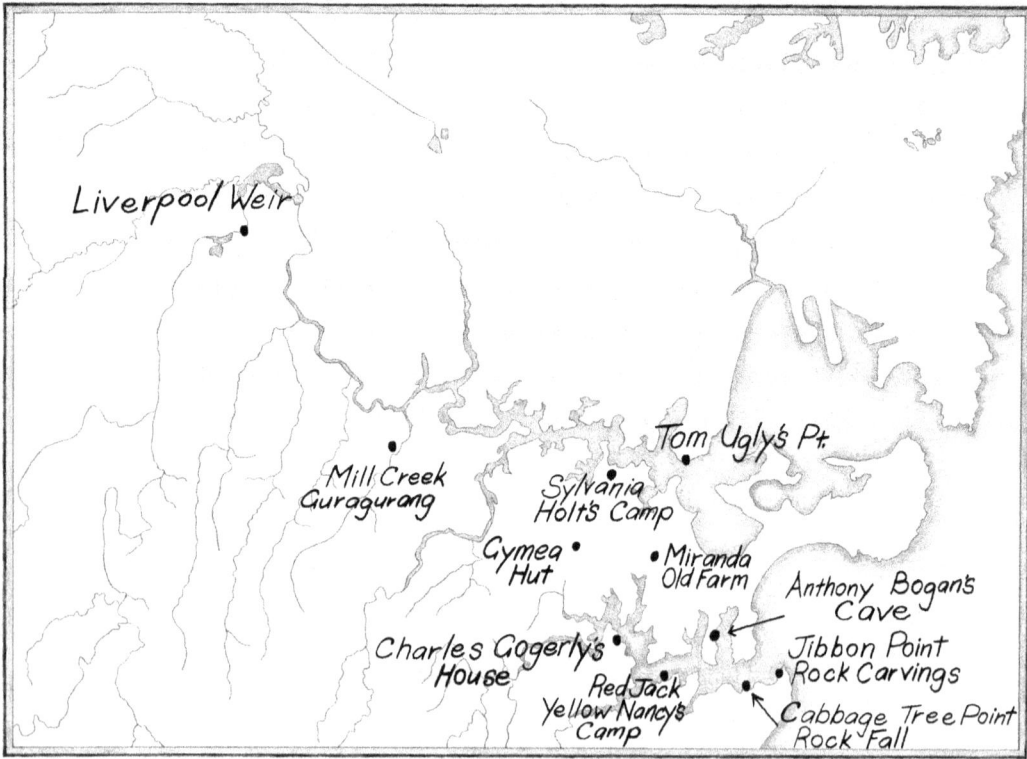

Liverpool Weir

Mill Creek
Guragurang

Tom Ugly's Pt.

Sylvania
Holt's Camp

Cymea
Hut

Miranda
Old Farm

Anthony Bogan's
Cave

Charles Gogerly's
House

Jibbon Point
Rock Carvings

Red Jack
Yellow Nancy's
Camp

Cabbage Tree Point
Rock Fall

perhaps to strengthen her own authority to speak about the place as an Aboriginal woman in terms that European people would understand. Yet there is no difference of opinion that Ellen was her daughter. Ellen was born in 1855 or 1857, late in Biddy's relationship with Paddy and she was raised mostly with Paddy's family in the southern districts – when she wasn't visiting her mother after Paddy's death around 1860.[28]

The Aboriginal families involved will be in the best position to sift through these complexities. It is important to recognise that many of these problems stem from the characteristic failure of documents written by British or white Australians to name the Aboriginal women they wrote about. This means that far fewer women than men can be identified with any certainty, and so genealogical confusions are compounded. We have already discussed the repeated failure to name the women involved in the fishing communities at the mouth of the Georges River, like Johnny Malone's mother, although there were some exceptions – like his wife, Lizzie Malone, who also became a key informant for ethnographers Mary Everitt and RH Mathews. As Illert has pointed out, it was most likely to be the few female ethnographers who recorded the names of these women who told them so much language and cultural knowledge.[29] Everitt's diaries recorded her correspondence or conversations with 'Bessie Sims, Granny Giles, Emma Timbery, Lizzy Malone, Clara Phillips ("Gungee"), Kate Saunders, Jimmy Lowndes and Robert Racklin'. Yet when RH Mathews did the final editing of their article in 1901, which was based largely on Everitt's work, he removed all of the names of the female informants. This erasure of the names of Aboriginal women continued to be common throughout documentation of Aboriginal presence.[30] It is not surprising that there remain confusions in the usual records of the life stories of women, but for Biddy we have another type of source altogether.

Mill Creek
in the 1860s

After Biddy married Billy Giles in the 1860s, they lived on the western bank of Mill Creek, close to its junction with the Georges River, in a farmhouse built earlier by Dr Alexander Cuthill.[31] By the middle years of the decade, Billy and Biddy had become well known for offering hospitality and local knowledge to white travellers and adventurers on what was then the undeveloped southern side of the river. It is through the reminiscences of those travellers, written many years afterwards, that a rare window is opened on to a world of interaction between white and black in Sydney's river borderlands. However imperfectly, they show how Aboriginal people lived on and moved frequently across their country, by river and by land. They mixed with an extraordinarily varied network of Europeans who were living outside the conventional social boundaries of the small colonial world of Sydney.

We have a glimpse here also of Biddy's astute management of a new sort of interaction with settlers. As transport increased through this area to the south coast, and as roads penetrated through to the new large properties like Holt's, there were some men who came venturing across the Georges River as recreational hunters and fishers. These men liked to see themselves as adventurers in 'wild' country which, nevertheless, was not too far for comfort from the centre of the settlement.

As we have seen, some Aboriginal people closely connected to this river country had continued to live on it. The patches on the map marked 'vacant' on both sides of the river created few obstacles to their travels. Where fences had been erected, they were not at this stage intended to keep out either travellers or people who might be potential workers. Both fenced and unfenced land marked 'vacant' had often been transferred into private hands, having been granted very early or sold on. But like so many properties on the infertile lower river, they had not been developed. This had been the case with the Williams block, on which Jonathon Goggey was living, and with many others which had never been farmed or built on because it was sandstone escarpment country or low-lying and swampy. This middle section of the river was notorious for landholders who failed to develop their land and simply left it lying abandoned for decades.[32]

Often there were advantages to this type of land not being 'public'. It meant it was not regulated or inspected. The economy of the settlers was already a mixed economy, in which formal cash incomes like wages were widely supplemented by 'informal' activities like hunting or fishing on the surrounding undeveloped private land. Another way to use this 'vacant' land was to encroach on it even more permanently to raise chickens or graze stock, not to mention the illegal gaming and other illicit activities. Some of these economic activities, like hunting game, may have been learnt from Aboriginal people who continued to camp on these areas and to carry on their own subsistence uses of land and river, as well as ceremonial and social uses. Such an unregulated space allowed interactions between Aboriginal and non-Aboriginal people in the unpoliced and undisciplined bush country on the edge of the city.

The movement along the river and the use of waterfront camps on the northern side of the river and Botany Bay by Aboriginal people throughout later nineteenth century was a continuation of life before the British invasion. The Aboriginal fishing people living in the camp at Kogarah Bay were not alone: there were camps all along the river in sheltered inlets like Kyle Bay, and from the Cooks River mouth all the way around the northern shore of Botany Bay. La Perouse was the most remote of these camps from the Port Jackson settlement, but in the mid-nineteenth century it was just one of an arc of camps and living places. These camps were concentrated round the creeks flowing into Botany Bay near the mouth of the Cooks River like Shea's

Creek, Bunnerong Creek and the other Mill Creek, on which Mahroot had been living in 1832.[33]

The southern bank of the river was even less alienated or developed than the northern side and so the impact of white settlers was far less. Much of the land had not even been granted before Thomas Holt purchased his large runs in 1861, and even when he did buy in the area we have seen in Jimmy Lowndes' story how little of it was fenced or closed in any way to Aboriginal movement. At the farm on Guragurang/Mill Creek, Biddy and Billy were living with an extended family, including two Aboriginal children.[34] The practicalities of their lives reflected both their backgrounds: they ate settler produce like goat's milk from their flock, made dampers and ate the abundant quinces growing in the orchard. Yet Biddy maintained her preference for wild honey and oysters, local fish, game and fruits. She offered guests goanna and black bream rather than the increasingly common rabbits. Biddy cooked in a traditional style, encasing goanna in clay, for example, baking it in the campfire and breaking open the clay at the end to reveal a succulent meal.[35]

Travelling with
Biddy Giles

A cluster of settler memoirs by three different authors describe a number of trips with Biddy in 1866, 1867 and 1868 in which she guided shooting or fishing parties. Each of them detail her confident movement across the country on the southern bank of the Georges River from Liverpool far across to the eastern coast and Port Hacking. SBJ Robinson wrote in 1911 of his visit to meet with a 'distinguished native lady – one "Biddy" Giles'. He explained how Biddy and her husband Billy:

acted as guides, philosophers and friends to a party of us who, in 1866 … came down the Georges River from the Liverpool dam in the Giles' boat, camped where Sylvania now is, and crossing over the peninsula, went fishing in Port Hacking in a whaleboat belonging to Mr Simpson who had taken up a selection on the south side.[36]

Billy was an enthusiastic partner in these encounters with travellers, and he clearly relished many Aboriginal aspects of his life with Biddy. He regaled visitors with stories about Aboriginal traditions, habits and other Aboriginal people. He seemed particularly to enjoy the way the common pursuit of hunting allowed him to move between English and Aboriginal worlds.[37] This was a well-developed sport among colonial men, in India and other colonies, in which they married the aristocratic form of hunting in England with the local traditions. They created an exotic image of the 'white hunter', with native bearers and beaters to carry gear and flush out the game. It was a practice which both demonstrated white colonising men's supposed superiority and claimed dominance over native people and environments.

Despite this very masculine setting, Billy was also recorded as being warmly supportive of Biddy in each of the travellers' accounts. And it was always Biddy who remained the focus of Robinson's stories. Her fishing prowess was one central feature of his account, and his respect for her skill is obvious: 'And such fishing! It seems to me now that no matter what hour of the day it was, or what was the state of the tide or what kind was the weather, "Biddy" could put us "on" to the fish.' Robinson also wrote glowingly about Biddy's food: 'I remember how Biddy cooked an iguana and how well its flesh tasted!' He was even more fascinated by her control of her hunting dogs:

Biddy's nondescript and nearly wholly starved and most variegated pack astonished me. She worked them by hand without a word. At her bidding they would form an extended

line at the top of a gully and beat downward to the guns
without a whimper until a wallaby was sighted and started.
Then the whole pack gave chase and down the gully they
came![38]

Over the next few years, more groups of white adventurers sought out
Biddy and Billy, travelling along the river from east or west to meet
them. One, calling himself 'Woolla Nora,' wrote to the newspaper in
1907 about one of his visits to the Giles family around 1867, in which
he travelled with three other men and three women on what was evi-
dently a journey he had made many times before. Rowing across from
Kogarah Bay, the party landed at Little Moon Bay and walked up to
the top of the steep ridge running north-south above the creek. They
looked down on 'the masses of white blossom which adorned the
blood red trees on the adjacent hills' which 'gave the impression they
were covered with snow'.[39] Then they trekked down to the bank of
Mill Creek, opposite Biddy and Billy's home and 'coo-ee'd' across the
creek. Biddy appeared with a boat lined with stringy bark and, 'after
according us a friendly greeting', came across to ferry them back to
her home. 'Woolla Nora' then described how Biddy, Billy and other
Aboriginal people shared a plentiful meal with the visitors, a mixture
of local food and the produce of the small farm and its orchard. Some
of the party then went hunting, under Biddy's direction, while others
remained and listened to Billy's tall tales. 'Woolla Nora' must have
kept in touch with Biddy and Billy, as he lamented their deaths, writing nostalgically of the passing of some of his white friends as well as
the Aboriginal hostess and her family.

Another traveller from the 1860s, also writing in 1907, signed
himself 'One of the Old Sort'. He was a friend of Woolla Nora and
had shared some travels with him, but in this series he wrote about
the time he had spent with Biddy and Billy on a trip from Sydney to
the Shoalhaven. When he reached the southern bank of the Georges

River, which he crossed from Kogarah Bay, he met up with and stayed some days with Biddy and Billy, who may have been living at this more easterly point at this time.[40] The party was guided around by Biddy in particular as she showed them hunting and fishing places. She took the writer for a number of long journeys but more especially pointed sites out as they went along the river and across the peninsula between Kurnell and Port Hacking.

'One of the Old Sort' was less sentimental than 'Woolla Nora' and more inclined to caricature those he encountered, but he was nevertheless impressed by Biddy's extensive knowledge of the country. He not only recounted her fishing, hunting and cooking expertise, but recorded her wide knowledge of the botany and zoology of the country she took them through. At the Bottle Forest, for example, Biddy gave the travellers the Dharawal and more recent English names for the trees and shrubs they were passing. At the same time she described earlier shooting trips that she had guided through the area in search of animals and birds such as kangaroos, wallabies and paddymelons, various pigeons and lyrebirds.[41] He noted that she gave frequent explanations about past events and retold what he understood to be traditional stories for the country. Biddy was introducing him to a peopled landscape which needed both recent human history and age-old stories to be understood.

One of the stories which the writer mentioned in some detail was Biddy's account of the purpose of stone engravings on Jibbon Point – a broad sandstone platform set back from the actual cliff face on the southern side of Port Hacking – which she said had been explained to her by her family, including her first husband Kooma. These included a huge image of a whale, other large fish and 'a splendid specimen of the form of a wallaby', which Biddy said had been carved to commemorate outstanding events like successful hunts or whale strandings.[42]

Another site she took them to was a large rock fall, probably on George Simpson's property, just west of Jibbon Beach and within present-day Bundeena.[43] This rock fall had been the result of the collapse of a huge sandstone overhang dislodged, Biddy explained, in a lightning strike. As it fell, the rock had crushed more than 100 Aboriginal people who had been camping in the cave beneath. The travellers, at Biddy's instruction, looked into the crevice within the rock and saw white material inside which they took to be a great many skeletal remains. Biddy dated this event by referring to the grandfather of her first husband, King Kooma, which given the practice of oral transmission, located the event before Biddy's own lifetime.[44] It may, however, have been evidence of another type of catastrophe: the devastating smallpox epidemics which had swept the colony in 1789 and again in 1830. They had been so terrible that, as in other such traumatic events, the survivors had not had strength or will to bury the many dead with proper ceremony.[45] 'One of the Old Sort' did not, unfortunately, offer enough information to consider further how Biddy was telling her story.

The rock fall and its cause were the subject of another episode in the travellers' journey with Biddy, and this demonstrated the extraordinary network of Aboriginal and non-Aboriginal people which her travels had allowed her to nurture. At many points in this series of articles, 'One of the Old Sort' wrote about other Aboriginal people whom Biddy and Billy introduced them to, many of them with stories about places and people, although very few were named. There was far more detail about the non-Aboriginal people encountered, who were more often named although not necessarily with their legal names. They included naval deserters like Damper and escaped convicts like Anthony Bogan, and there were eccentric recluses like Charles Gogerly, an ex-convict and controversial journalist, transported initially for minor theft but later imprisoned over conflicts about his publications.[46] Gogerly retired from public life in 1853, living in a four-room house on the point named after him on remote Port Hacking, refusing to associate with town society, keeping an extensive library behind glass-doored bookshelves and training dolphins and gropers to eat from his hand.

'One of the Old Sort' had initially scoffed at Biddy and Billy's stories about Gogerly, but an Irishman he called 'Pat' from his own party had met him also, so they travelled overland with Biddy's guidance and met Gogerly themselves. Gogerly proved to be just as eccentric as the Giles' stories had suggested, and just as good at taming wildlife, demonstrating his skilful handling of a large blue groper on the shore near his home and feeding numerous wallabies and magpies. His sarcastic greeting to 'Pat', which 'One of the Old Sort' put down to an anti-Irish sentiment, speaks just as strongly about the racialised sexism which operated in this river society: his first salute, on recognising Pat, was 'Hullo, what kind of a bushman do you call yourself, bringing a black gin to pick the way – or perhaps she's your wife!'[47]

Yet despite this denigration of both the Irishman and Aboriginal women, Gogerly was deferential with Biddy, often debating with her but apparently always including her in his discussions about places and stories. Their conversation about the rock fall at Simpson's was particularly interesting: while Biddy held to her account of a lightning strike, Gogerly argued – although without producing any evidence apparently – that it had been campfires which weakened the overhang. His implication may have reflected a wider and convenient settler sentiment: that the Aboriginal people had themselves caused the disasters which had befallen them. Just as important was 'One of the Old Sort's observation that Gogerly consistently turned to Biddy for authorisation of the truth of any of his statements: 'When in doubt of any assertion Gogerly invariably appealed to Biddy, and the same response was always at hand, "My word that's true Mr Gogerly."'[48]

Robinson had observed a similar characteristic in Billy Giles' interactions with his wife: Billy constantly sought Biddy's approval and endorsement for his claims and tales. It suggested a need on the part of both these white men to seek an Aboriginal confirmation for their stories, a recognition which was in some contradiction to their other interactions. It reflects a desire – described by Maria Nugent in later narratives about landmarks around La Perouse – in which Aboriginal people were accorded a limited role in settler stories but largely to bring an authenticity to the locations where settlers claimed the events of their plot had happened.[49]

We can locate the places to which Biddy took these travellers and where she confidently introduced them to creation lore, historical stories and environmental information about trees and animals. The map of these places shows her to have been knowledgeable not only about the river and land around Guragurang or Mill Creek, but across the whole expanse eastwards of the land between the Georges River and Port Hacking, encompassing what would have been Gweagal country up to Kurnell and probably that of the immediately neighbouring groups. Biddy explained often that she knew about this country because she had been taught about it when she was young by her own and Kooma's families.

This whole expanse of the river was country in which Biddy clearly felt comfortable and to which she belonged. Yet her explanations to these travellers move beyond merely demonstrating her own knowledge of place. They suggest Biddy's shrewd awareness of the need of the white visitors to have 'authenticity' for the accounts she was giving them. This may explain also her decisions to speak to them only about her early relationship with Kooma and not her longest relationship living with Paddy Burragalang near Wollongong. The marriage to Kooma linked her not only to a man unequivocally tied to that very country, but also with someone styled as a 'king' – a symbol of authority which whites understood. This would have reinforced Biddy's demands that they recognise her legitimacy as well as satisfying their tourists' desire for an 'authentic' experience.

Travelling communities,
communities of travellers

The network of reclusive whites to whom Biddy introduced the travellers were not the only people on the river. All these travellers mentioned that there were other Aboriginal people there as well in the 1860s, but they named very few. An example was the description by 'One of the Old Sort' about a shooting party at Jibbon Point made up of himself, his fellow travellers, Billy Giles and Charles Gogerly while 'a number of blacks were engaged to "wall-bung" (to beat the bush)'. Just a few were named, suggesting the Aboriginal networks Biddy was maintaining in her travelling. One was Yellow Nancy, a woman who was, her name suggested, of mixed descent and who lived with a white man called Red Jack on the shores of Port Hacking. Another was Bundong, a guest at Biddy's table and clearly an old friend of hers, who shared stories with her, Billy and their travelling visitors about places and personalities along the Georges River and Port Hacking.[50] Bundong knew the river well: he continued to live around the mouth of the river and fish its waters into the 1880s. He was listed by the Sands Directory as a resident local fishermen, along with George Timbery, the senior Aboriginal resident of the area associated with Yarra Point and later La Perouse.[51]

There were also larger Aboriginal camps all along the river, despite the 1860s travellers only writing about those in which Aboriginal people were living with white people like Biddy, Yellow Nancy and the mixed fishing communities around the mouth of the river. The travelling which Biddy and others were doing was possible because the land was so open and their passage was unobstructed, and because they had learnt about their country from their people. The outcome of their travelling was the sustained connection between river people, not only those noticed by whites, but the small scattered communities like those at Kyle Bay and the fishing communities on the shores of Botany Bay.

The southern side of the river faced what seemed like a major change after 1861, when Thomas Holt acquired his huge property. Yet the attempts at pastoral and other enterprises had little success there, and there were few developments on the land other than the consolidation of Aboriginal work camps near Sylvania and, to the south, at the Dolan's property near Burraneer Bay.[52] These brought more Aboriginal people in to the area, or brought home those like Jimmy Lowndes who had been working elsewhere. Furthermore, the shift to oysters on the Holt properties had consolidated the presence of Aboriginal people living in the area, as it had done for William Rowley when he was recognised as the overseer and manager of the Holt oyster beds in Weeney Bay.[53] Biddy's travelling drew all these people, pastoral workers, fishers and oyster workers, into the network of Aboriginal society along the river.

In the 1880s, after Billy's death, Biddy moved up to the work camp on Holt's property at Sylvania where her brother Joey and Jimmy Lowndes were then living.[54] From there, each of them moved at various times to the places around the mouth of the river, often at the Kogarah Bay camp but sometimes over on the eastern side of the promontory at Sans Souci beach on the shores of Botany Bay itself.[55] A number of the older Aboriginal people like Biddy had become well known to whites in the area by this time. Around 1885 a Carlton photographer, J Robinson (perhaps the traveller who was later to write in 1911 about his treks with Biddy in the 1860s) took a series of photographs of them either at Kogarah Bay or at Sylvania, giving us our only glimpse of Biddy herself, along with her brother Joey and Jimmy Lowndes.[56]

These photographs reflect the diversity of origins of the people in the riverside camps. The brash young man in the police uniform, known to whites as Jimmy Brown, was thought to have come from Western Australia, while the fourth man, the older Joe Brown, who may have been a brother from the same distant location, was reported

Biddy Giles in later life, with others
who lived on the Holt Sutherland
Estate in the 1880s: (l-r) Jimmy
Brown, Jimmy Lowndes, Biddy
Giles (front) Joey, (Biddy's brother)
and Joe Brown.

'King' Albert, wearing a breast plate indicating his standing as a senior man for the Georges River. These plates were given by graziers or police to senior Aboriginal people in the hope they would assist with negotiation. Although ambiguous symbols, the plates do indicate the high standing of the person for whom they were made.

Local Studies Collection, Rockdale Library and Information Service

to be little known but widely respected.[57] When this photograph was published in 1904, it was presented with nostalgia about disappearing natives, as were stories about 'King Albert' and Aggic, two elderly personalities also associated with the Kogarah Bay camp in the 1880s.[58]

Yet at the same time there were younger and more assertive members of the community. The Aboriginal families at Ellesmere at Kogarah Bay had joined the 1883 attempt to have a public school sited close to their camp, while in the 1880s, Bundong, William Rowley and others continued to be recognised as members of the local fishing industry.[59]

From the 1860s the shores of both the Georges River and Botany Bay were scenes of recent or current Aboriginal activity, as Scherzer had pointed out in his 1858 diary entry about travelling with Johnny Malone looking for graves. This reflected both continuing populations along the river, but also the movement which Mahroot had described in 1845 as being both north–south, between the Five Islands and the Georges River, and east–west, from Liverpool and beyond to Botany Bay and back. The north–south movement was extensively demonstrated in Biddy's life as well as that of her brother Joey. It was well recognised that many of the longer-term residents of the camps around the north shore of Botany Bay, down to and including the large settlement on the headland at La Perouse were, like the Timbery family, related to communities from the south around Wollongong and the Five Islands.

There were many living among the Botany encampments who had moved around the Bay itself. The important story of William Rowley was told in chapter 3. He had been born at Pelican Point near Towra Point, fished the Bay, and lived at La Perouse before moving back up river to the Holt property and then to Salt Pan Creek. The movement to the south-west, which linked Sydney with not only the Shoalhaven but the areas to the west over the ranges, was also well established. By the 1890s, the Protection Board was trying to force people from

Brungle and Kangaroo Valley out of Sydney and to 'return [them] to their usual abode'.[60]

The east–west movement was less well known but nevertheless sustained. Jimmy Lowndes was one who moved from the west of the Georges River at Camden to Sylvania and Kogarah Bay, while Mahroot's wife, another unnamed woman, had come from the west at Liverpool to live with him on the northern shore of Botany Bay. Emma Timbery herself had been born at Liverpool and so had moved from that town right to the coast at La Perouse when she married George Timbery. The populations just outside the metropolitan area were substantial, particularly on the Hawkesbury and Nepean rivers. The number of Aboriginal people recorded by the police in the census in 1882 is known to be an underestimate. Authorities often discounted people of mixed descent, so such figures can only be regarded as an indication of the comparative size of any community, not of its absolute numbers. Those figures show the Aboriginal population of 17 at Liverpool to be about the same as that at Camden, but significantly less than the 37 in the Burragorang Valley, where an independent farm was being run by Aboriginal farmers on land at the junction of the Cox's and Wollondilly rivers. There was an even larger community, indicated by the census figure of 75 recorded as living around Windsor.[61]

It was from these areas that longer journeys continued backwards and forwards to the coast. An important example was Jean Timbery of La Perouse, the daughter of Emma and George Timbery. Jean had married a Gandangara man, Henry John Simms, in the 1880s and moved with him to his country in the Southern Highlands.[62] The unhappy marriage collapsed and when Jean died during the birth of her third child in 1890, her mother Emma walked up the river valley to bring her grandchildren, and another young child from the Simms family, back to La Perouse. Their long and difficult journey back, largely on foot, left a rich legacy of stories in the memories

William Rowley (front, fourth
from r) with his wife and child, and
a group of Aboriginal people from
La Perouse in the 1890s.

of the families involved. It further consolidated the networks which stretched, like those of Jimmy Lowndes, far beyond what had been traditional boundaries prior to the British settlement. By the 1880s, there were a number of people in the Georges River communities and in camps in the Sydney town centre, as we have already seen, who had travelled from other areas, largely from south-west and south coastal areas like Brungle and the Kangaroo Valley. Others had come from further afield like Western Australia and the Castlereagh River in inland New South Wales, to live on the Georges River.

Biddy's life and travels from 1860 into the 1890s allow us an insight into the way resilience was taking place. Her travels, along with others, had built the networks between all the different small communities, consolidating the sense that the river people were connected right along its length. She was a central figure too in explaining and introducing Aboriginal culture and people to inquiring settlers, shaping her stories in ways which she could see they wanted, but building on her own confident knowledge of the river and its history. With her skill in finding and using the resources of the river and the landscape, and in her dignity and charisma in relating to the many white settlers she encountered, Biddy made a powerful impact on white awareness of continuing Aboriginal presence on the river.

FIVE

River of flowers: Ellen's river 1910–1930

Biddy Giles' daughter Ellen was another woman whose travels were shaped by new personal relationships as well as her kin and country. She travelled further than her mother: from her childhood at the Five Islands near Wollongong to the the Georges River as a young woman and then on to Cumeragunja on the Murray River where she married into the community. From there, as a young mother, she moved backwards and forwards between the Shoalhaven River and Kangaroo Valley, and finally returned with her family to the Georges River to play a key role in the free community at Salt Pan Creek. This community was later to become a beacon for the many people forced into travelling by the events of the 1920s and 1930s. But all that was in the future.

The Protection Board and
local Aboriginal camps

As Ellen was growing up, she moved between only two places: her father's southern Dharawal country around Wollongong, and her mother's and her other relations' home on the Georges River. By the late 1870s, when Ellen was coming often to Sydney, Biddy had moved to the Sylvania and Kogarah Bay communities, closer to the mouth of the Georges River near Botany Bay. The steady movement between north and south by Shoalhaven and southern Dharawal Aboriginal families drew many of them to the camps scattered along the northern shore of Botany Bay, as well as the most remote of them – at La Perouse on the northern headland. So it was to these camps that Ellen often made her way, where she could not only be close to her mother and uncle Joey but could be in close touch with people she knew well from the south coast.

About the same time, the state government established its new bureaucracy, the Aborigines Protection Board, although only a lone protector, George Thornton, was appointed at first. He was charged with inquiring into current conditions but in fact he had already been instructed to reduce the numbers of Aboriginal people in the city. He and his superiors assumed that Aborigines in the city must all have come from somewhere else – their 'own district' – because by definition they could not belong in the city. His first report in 1882 confirmed the frequent and regular Aboriginal movement backwards and forwards between Wollongong in the south and the western Burragorang Valley into the camp sites on the Georges River itself and to those all around Botany Bay and out to the more isolated La Perouse at its northern head.[1] This continued mobility was exactly what had troubled the government, and what it had appointed Protector Thornton to end. The main focus of Thornton's attention was the inner-city area, and the Aboriginal camp at Circular Quay was rapidly shut down and its residents forcibly moved away. But soon he began to exert pressure on the camps around the northern shore of Botany Bay. Some were on a government reserve which the state could merely revoke to force people to move on.

At the same time, Thornton was persuaded that the La Perouse settlement itself was far enough away from the city to offer little threat. He saw potential for self-sufficiency among the fishermen in the community, calling it 'settled' and the people 'intelligent' and 'willing to work'. Without losing his momentum about clearing the rest of the camps, he began to offer recognition for the continuity of La Perouse by granting applications for boats, fishing tackle and building materials, as he did for other communities outside Sydney. This was just the type of recognition Lucy Leane was to call for in 1893 – only to be denied because Thornton and later the full Aborigines Protection Board did not grant such applications to any other metropolitan Aboriginal community besides La Perouse. They concentrated all the rest of their grants on more distant and rural areas. Maria Nugent has pointed out that this was a turning-point in the history of La Perouse:

> In the closing years of the 1870s … the camp of Aboriginal
> people at La Perouse was probably little different from the
> other Aboriginal camps in the vicinity of Sydney … However
> during the 1880s this camp on Botany Bay's north head
> underwent considerable change in ways that distinguished
> it from others … The first effect was that this little piece
> of Botany Bay came to be seen as the camp residents' 'own
> district', and the second was that they were forever within the
> government's orbit'.[2]

And in these ways, it came to be very different from the other camps along the Georges River. While La Perouse, Nugent argues, became 'enmeshed in the colonial government's practice of segregating

Aborigines', the other Aboriginal camps on Botany Bay simply melted out of sight, as Aboriginal people looked for refuge upstream in the quieter, less developed areas along the length of the river. Aboriginal people who had previously made a living from fishing or shell-gathering at the mouths of the Georges or Cooks Rivers moved further back into these rivers, away from Botany Bay and away from the risk of falling into the APB's hands. And on the rivers themselves, the smaller camps disappeared too, as people moved from camps like Kyle Bay and the Dolan's work camp into larger ones like Kogarah Bay, either for support among their own people, for access to schooling or because of pressure from neighbouring whites and police who wanted more readily controlled groups. So the effect was that Aboriginal people moved, but mostly they moved locally rather than travelling any great distance away. Some, like William Rowley, moved first from Weeney Bay to La Perouse in 1883 but by 1891 he was back living in Weeney Bay and some years later had moved even further to the west to Salt Pan Creek.

As Thornton moved against most of the inner metropolitan Aboriginal camps, he received an offer from Daniel Matthews to take the residents of these camps, and anyone else who could be persuaded to go, down to the Murray River mission of Maloga which he had established some years before. This was an attractive offer for Thornton, despite the fact that the APB was increasingly hostile to private, church-operated missions. Nevertheless, in 1881 Thornton and the Board were still happy to work with missionaries as long as the state remained in control. In this instance, it was convenient to all – except of course for the Aborigines being forced to move.

Maloga and Cumeragunja
on the Murray

Ellen, aged in her mid-20s, was living on the northern Botany Bay camps in 1881 when she became entangled in this move. It was to shape the rest of her life. With Matthews and the group of people he had rounded up she travelled by train to the Murray River, where she found Maloga was more familiar than she might have expected.[3] There had been many contacts in the past across the southern highlands between the south coast and the Murray River communities, and Ellen found they shared much in common. She soon formed a bond with the articulate Goulburn River man Hugh Anderson, who was living at Maloga and had become a close associate and supporter of Matthews and of Thomas James, a Mauritian school teacher who had married a Yorta Yorta woman.[4] James had been living at Maloga for many years and his committed teaching had fostered a high rate of literacy and general education in the population there.[5]

Ellen and Hugh were married in 1882 and began raising their children on Maloga over the next few years. However, the Board intervened later in the 1880s, incorporating the buildings and residents of the Maloga mission onto the adjacent Cumeragunja reserve, which was established with Matthew's support in 1883. The Protection Board took over the two other church institutions at Warangesda and Brewarrina, and out of the three it created civil institutions called 'stations', each under the control of a Protection Board manager.

As missionaries, Matthews and his wife Janet were now marginalised, and while some Aboriginal people supported the Board, Hughie Anderson was one of those who did not. His letter protesting the government approach to managing the community was published in the *Riverine Herald* in 1889. His passionate defence of Daniel and Janet Matthews is important not only to indicate his position in this particular conflict but because it showed his view that missionary activity should be engaged with outspoken assertiveness about the value of Aboriginal identity and culture. Hugh Anderson did not believe in a subservient Christianity, but instead one which fostered defiance:

> When we lived at Maloga we were better cared for ... Mrs Matthews did her best for the sick but it is not so here on this station ... We have been treated very badly ... there is no nourishing food for the sick, only bread, meat, tea and dirty black sugar. All hands have stopped working at the station, for we cannot work any longer on a place where we are not treated right![6]

Hugh Anderson's letter is a good example of the links between a Christian ethic of care and an active stance of egalitarian protest, something he shared with Thomas James and which was characteristic of the Cumeragunja community. Anderson was quite openly championing a strike: he argued that the Cumeragunja population was justified in downing tools and refusing to work under Protection Board management. This link between Christianity and assertive, practical egalitarianism was to continue to be an important one for the Anderson family.

Building networks and the return to Salt Pan Creek

Ellen had travelled to Maloga under duress in 1881 and after the APB's takeover she and Hughie had felt unhappy in staying at Cumeragunja. Yet their destinations after this were of their own choice and they moved in a circuit which traced links between kinfolk as well as suggesting their plans for the future. They went to live for some time in the Kangaroo Valley, near Barrengarry, where a reserve of 370 acres (150 hectares) had been established beside the Kangaroo River in 1890.

Hugh took a leading role in drawing together the small community. The reserve had been established over poor land, however, with only patches suitable for cultivation, and this compounded the community's problems.[7] Eventually the Andersons returned to Cumeragunja, but they travelled frequently with their children to the Shoalhaven where Ellen had relations, sometimes (unsuccessfully) seeking Protection Board passes to do it.[8] Ellen said later that she had been in Minnamurra in 1896 when her brother-in-law Mickey Johnson had been honoured as 'King of the Illawarra' at the Wollongong Show.[9]

Throughout all their travels, the family maintained their involvement with the Christian network including Thomas James and other Cumeragunja community members. When Ellen, Hugh and their family returned to Sydney, probably in the 1910s, they were living around Botany.[10] There they encountered the Aborigines Inland Mission (AIM). This was a Protestant organisation established in 1905 to evangelise among Aboriginal people at La Perouse and later at St Clair on the Hunter River. It was a different body from the Maloga missionaries, but was still one with which the Anderson's could sympathise. Not long after arriving in Sydney, the Andersons moved up-river to live on the land they eventually purchased on lower Salt Pan Creek where it flowed into the Georges River. They were happy to encourage the AIM missionaries to come to visit them there, and so the mission journal *Our Aim* often contained snippets of news from this little community. Before long, William Rowley and his wife also moved up to Salt Pan Creek, buying a block of land beside Ellen and Hughie.

Now middle-aged people of great experience, between them Ellen and Hugh Anderson and William Rowley and his wife held a formidable body of traditional and contemporary knowledge. There were the traditional stories and language from the Wollongong of Ellen's childhood, from the Goulburn Valley years of Hugh's youth, and the Cumeragunja time that he and Ellen had shared, along with the stories they had learnt in the Kangaroo Valley. For William, and no doubt his wife, there was lifetime of living and working on Botany Bay, with close relationships with the people of La Perouse and Kogarah Bay.[11] They brought their stories and knowledge with them to Salt Pan Creek, consolidating what Ellen had learnt from Biddy's time on the southern side of the whole river and William Rowley's own knowledge of his country at the mouth of the river on Botany Bay. They could in many ways embody 'tradition' on the river in the early twentieth century. Yet they were also deeply engaged with the contemporary economy, most successfully in William Rowley's case in his fishing and oyster management, but also in Ellen's strategies for making a viable living from the cash economy.

But traditional knowledge was only one part of their lives: Christianity formed another, although related, part. Ellen and Hugh in particular kept in close contact with the elements of Christian missions which had fostered militancy and activism. In this the AIM was in close accord with the traditions of Thomas James and Daniel Matthews. So it was to be both the traditional and the contemporary connections which were important in the next episode of their lives.

Salt Pan Creek
in the early 1900s

When Ellen and Hughie Anderson settled down at Salt Pan Creek, they purchased a block of land on the eastern shore just a few metres from a large midden which spilled glistening shells across the sandy beach, demonstrating centuries of Aboriginal fishing and feasting.[12] Their block was only a mile or two downstream from Mill Creek, where Ellen's mother Biddy had lived. Yet the social and natural environment had changed from Biddy's day, often dramatically, on both the northern and southern sides of the river. On the northern side, the suburbs which surrounded Ellen's camp at Salt Pan Creek were Herne

Salt Pan Creek showing Biddy Giles' home on Guragurang/Mill Creek, and Ellen and Hugh Anderson's home on the Salt Pan Creek blocks. Mickey's Point is understood to have been named for an early Aboriginal fisherman, and Doctor's Bush was another area where Aboriginal people camped.

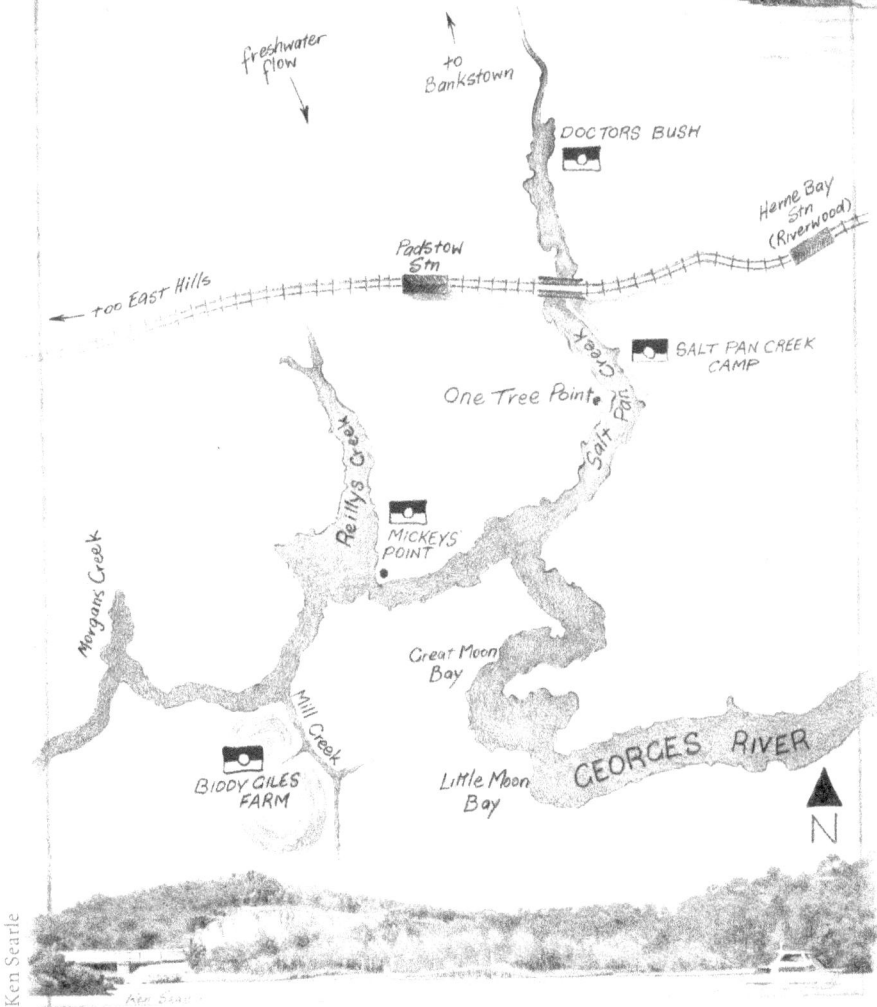

freshwater flow

to Bankstown

DOCTORS BUSH

Herne Bay Stn (Riverwood)

Padstow Stn

too East Hills

SALT PAN CREEK CAMP

One Tree Point

Salt Pan Creek

Reillys Creek

MICKEYS POINT

Morgans Creek

Great Moon Bay

Mill Creek

GEORGES RIVER

BIDDY GILES FARM

Little Moon Bay

N

Ken Searle

Bay, Peakhurst and Mortdale. They were not so remote from the city as the areas across which Biddy had travelled on the southern side of the river. Nor were they so empty. So why did this family – and the many who joined them – decide on Salt Pan Creek as their home?

One reson may be that, despite the growing city, many bushy points and bends had survived. Since the 1880s, these had been preserved as parklands around 'pleasure grounds' like Parkesvale opposite Picnic Point. These were a mixture of theme park, dance hall and recreation area which became enormously popular over the period until World War I. They had been set up on the many patches of private but undeveloped sandstone lands along the river. People travelled by train, bus, steamship or dray out to the Georges River at the weekends for picnics, boating, dancing and drinking.[13] The clue to the Georges River's attraction was only partly its scenic beauty and fishing productivity. It was just as relevant that at that time only legitimate 'travellers' could purchase alcohol on Sundays, and to be a traveller you had to be beyond a certain limit from the city. The Georges River fell just beyond that limit, so the pubs at the pleasure grounds were as busy as their dance floors.

Despite the increase in local tourists coming into and through the area, these sandstone escarpments were still regarded as useless for farming or even for backyard gardens. Although towns away the river, like Bankstown, had increased their population, there was still in the 1920s a low density of permanent residents in the suburbs close to the river. So there continued to be areas into which Aboriginal people could move at low or no cost and with open space around the residential areas. Such characteristics were attractive to some working-class white Australians too, because it meant the river was just beyond the constraints of established society. They were certainly a very different and more urbanised group than had been those scattered eccentrics of Biddy's acquaintance so long ago. Although white residents on the eastern bank of Salt Pan Creek were like those in Bankstown – mostly

Catholic and working class – they were more likely to be poorer than those in the towns and to have less regular work. They were far more likely to be in factory or labouring jobs than those on the western side, who worked on the farms of Padstow. By the 1890s, brickworks and other industries had grown up around Mortdale which brought the railway line out in 1897. This made Mortdale the furthest point away from the city at which workers could live and yet still commute to inner-city jobs. The shifts for dock work, for example, came out in the early edition of the papers: if your name was there, you just had time to jump on a train at Mortdale and get to the wharves by the time the whistle blew for the start of the shift.[14] This waterside workforce included all types, from committed activists and communists to men who didn't want too much attention from the police. Mortdale and Peakhurst were good places for all of them: these suburbs was just far enough away from a close police scrutiny to make it a good place for outspoken views, hard drinking and some shady dealings.[15]

So Ellen's new home was still just at the edge of respectable society. She and Hugh were established there before 1911, and in the 1920s they purchased a block on the eastern side of the creek, low down near the junction with the Georges River and opposite One Tree Point.[16] Their land was at the end of Ogilvy Street in Peakhurst, where it curves in what is now called Charm Place towards a steep gully down to the creek – from which Hugh made a living by fishing.[17] William Rowley from Weeney Bay bought the block next-door, which he may have purchased from someone associated with the Kogarah Bay Aboriginal camp.[18] As Eric Dickinson – then a young boy often visiting his aunt on the western side of the Creek – remembered, Salt Pan Creek was a clear, unpolluted stream in 1913 with open, accessible banks not yet choked with mangroves.[19] Dickinson always wrote about his visits there as an 'an adventure' because of the Aborigines living there, suggesting that he was both nervous of them and fascinated by them too.[20]

This part of the river was an area which remained thick bush and where the little community's few neighbours were people like themselves who, although not Aboriginal, were making a precarious living from selling locally grown produce or fish. The resources of the area were another of the reasons this was such a valuable spot. The Andersons, Rowleys and others drew much of their livelihood from fishing, hunting and gathering in the large areas of sandstone and bushland. Hughie and William Rowley made a cash income from fish and probably prawns and oysters, and as well as what they sold, they were able to feed their families from the produce of the river. The kids in the camp were part of this economic process. Jacko Campbell arrived as a ten-year-old in 1926 and he recalls catching prawns in hessian bags in Salt Pan Creek with the other boys from the camp, using stringy bark torches as they waded through the water. The boys could sell them for ninepence a quart, or just catch themselves a feed! In the parts of Salt Pan that were really boggy, they'd catch eels and as Jacko recalled, 'We'd go up when we wanted a feed of anything, fish and all that! But it was a terrible place for sharks there, in the murky water!' The land too continued to be an important source of food, with not only the native swamp wallabies being hunted but the now abundant rabbits making up an important part of the family diet.[21]

Gathering wildflowers, gaining knowledge

Ellen and Hugh would have stood out most from their white neighbours for two reasons: one was their continuing association with the church, and the other was the way Ellen and her family were able to make a cash income from wildflowers. The wildflowers that grew along the Georges River were riotously abundant in spring. George Peake, an elderly white resident writing in 1981, described his memories of childhood on the sandstone escarpments near Salt Pan: 'wildflowers grew in profusion, waratahs, boronia, bells and flowers of every colour, as well as Christmas Bush in every gully'.[22]

These extraordinary flowers were no accident: they grew in the bush there because of the iron and minerals in the sandstone on the escarpments. The flowers were an enriching element of the ecology and central to much of the traditional Aboriginal symbolism of the river. The commercial potential of the flowers only emerged, however, with the growing urban white populations of late nineteenth century and their rising nationalism which drew on 'native' environmental icons to express an emergent 'native' Australianist identity. In a way that Biddy Giles, for example, never had open to her, the flowers and gumtips offered a source of income to early twentieth century Aboriginal residents at Salt Pan Creek. They could use their knowledge about where to find the best flowers, and then gather and sell them door to door or at the local and city markets, as way to supplement their income in the informal economy.

Ellen was renowned for her local selling of armfuls of flowers and gumtips, and her sons would later take gumtips into the city markets.[23] Her granddaughter, Ellen James (née Williams) has many warm memories of trips into the bush with her grandmother to find the flowers before trailing along after her as she walked the streets to sell them. Her recollections also cast some light on the differences between the approaches this Aboriginal community brought to the flowers, compared to those of the white neighbours who purchased them for their decorative style. On these trips into the bush, Ellen Anderson taught her young granddaughter not just about which plants would sell to the white market, but much more about the medicinal and food value of both the plants they were gathering and those which were not necessarily of interest to white buyers. Ellen taught her about the landscape too: about how to follow the tracks criss-crossing the sandstone to find the best plants flowering in each season.[24] The wildflower trade flourished because of the white fashion for nationalism and decorative taste, but it was built on the continuing foundations of a very different set of values, those of an indigenous harvesting culture which saw the landscape as productive and fruitful, not just as picturesque.

The growing
Salt Pan community

Ellen and Hugh Anderson's home became the focus of a growing community of Aboriginal people. They had built three weatherboard cottages and some sheds, one large enough to be used as a church, by the mid-1920s. Other visitors were camped in tents, spread out across a 3-acre area.[25] While some of their white neighbours may have lived in more conventional houses, others lived in far more precarious circumstances. Across Salt Pan at One Tree Point impoverished white families, some with heavy and abusive drinkers in them, were living in makeshift dwellings and camps throughout the 1920s and 1930s.[26] The Anderson's continuing involvement in the AIM network is shown in the regular notes about their family in *Our Aim,* and in the wonderful photographs taken by AIM members at Salt Pan around 1925 and conserved in their photo album.[27] They give a glimpse of the way the little community was building up in those years. There are striking photographs of Ellen and Hugh Anderson, as well groups of the Anderson's growing numbers of adult children and their families, which linked these families with those even further across the state.

Ellen and Hugh's youngest daughter Dolly, for example, had married Tom Williams who had come from the Castlereagh River near Coonamble – a north-western link which may have built on past connections through people like Jimmy Lowndes. Tom Williams had served in World War I, an experience very common among the working-class men living along the Georges River. Many veterans came

*Hugh and Ellen Anderson (on left)
and some of the growing Salt Pan
Creek community in the 1920s.*

Identified by Ellen James, née Williams: AIM Collection PXA 773/Box 1 #78, Mitchell
Library, State Library NSW

Tom Williams senior, with his son
Tom at Salt Pan Creek, c 1923.

Shayne Williams' family collection

back from the war stressed and injured, and poured their energies into constructing a network of memorials and gathering places, like the RSLs, throughout these suburbs. Tom Williams had an intense desire for independence and while he wanted to live close to Dolly's family, he was in regular work and he bought a house not far away, near the newly cleared land where Herne Bay station was going to be built – the last stop before the rail line crossed over Salt Pan Creek. This was where his children were born, young Tom in 1922 and Ellen in 1923, and where the family stayed until the Depression wiped out the work of many of the men in the Aboriginal community.

Tom was forced to sell their land and, for a couple of years, take his family to live on the block where his mother-in-law, Ellen Anderson lived. He eventually found work again and moved a few blocks further east. Ellen remembers hearing her father say many times that he would not live on a Protection Board mission under any circumstances. He told his family he would rather take them to live in a bag hut than go on to a mission with a manager standing over them! Yet the Salt Pan families continued to be regular visitors up and down the river to the Protection Board settlement at La Perouse. There are photographs of the Williams and MacKenzie children in front of the high corrugated walls at La Perouse around 1928, with Tom junior in school uniform. Another shows William Rowley and his wife at La Perouse during the interwar period.[28]

The Salt Pan Creek community and its neighbours

The Salt Pan Aboriginal families also had a lot to do with their neighbours across the suburbs of Peakhurst, Herne Bay and Mortdale. Except during the worst of the Depression, Tom Williams and many of the other men were in steady employment and lived with their families scattered through the suburbs, not just in the recognisable setting at Ogilvy Street. Tom socialised with his war mates and was an active member of the local RSL, becoming widely known among white returnees.[29] The children went to the local school, Peakhurst Public, and both Ellen James and Jacko Campbell remembered the long treks which they made in the late 1920s along Belmore Road and then cross-country to the school, in company with Ellen's brother Tommy Williams, Bob (Sago), Charlie and Sally MacKenzie and Evelyn Rowley, the younger children trailing along after the older ones. The most moving of the AIM photographs is the one of some of these school children, with the very young Ellen and Tom Williams in the front row.

This photograph shows the great diversity in background and interaction already occurring there, with fair-colouring just as frequent as darker skin among the group. The wide open spaces of Salt Pan Creek are clearly visible behind them, which supports the memories of Ellen, Jacko and others who talk about the sandy beaches and broad flat sandstone rocks on the shore, which they remember climbing over and perching on.[30] The photograph shows the river just as they remember it, and the contrast is striking with the river in later years, when mangroves were to expand dramatically to take over all the banks.

Despite this level of economic, social and educational interaction, the relationships between Aboriginal and non-Aboriginal people in the area were not simple. There were conflicts, and it was these tensions which were the more public, because they were reflected in the media coverage of demands on Hurstville Council to move the families on in 1926. Reports of fighting were recalled between camp residents as well as fights with white neighbours – and not only the rowdy drunken ones from One Tree Point.[31] The Aboriginal families in the area were often living under the intense stresses of poverty and Protection Board harassment and in a time when it was illegal for Aborigines to drink

Children on the banks of Salt Pan Creek in the mid-1920s. Ellen and Tom Williams jnr are the very young children in the front row.

Third class at Peakhurst Public
School, c 1930. Ellen Williams
is in front row, second from left;
Evelyn Rowley is in middle row,
second from right.

Identified by Ellen James, née Williams: Brian Shaw, St George Regional Museum

alcohol. Methylated spirits was the only intoxicant freely available and there are records and memories of its abuse by some of the camp members.[32]

But there were many warm relationships too. Members of the white community in the area remember going to school with the Aboriginal children from the Anderson family and others like the MacKenzies, the Williams and the Barkers. Young Tom Williams was dux of the primary school. He is remembered by the Webb family, who owned the general store from 1927 to 1935, as the boy who could remember two pages of shopping orders.[33] The Webb children remember being taught to throw boomerangs and blow gum leaves by the Anderson brothers when they stopped at the family store.[34] The MacKinnons were another well-remembered Aboriginal family, with Mrs MacKinnon selling haberdashery from door to door.[35] When the store-owner LC Webb died in a car accident in 1933, the Aborigines from Salt Pan were the first to arrive at his funeral. They had walked overland on the bush tracks which were common knowledge among Aboriginal people in the area, to reach the cemetery at Woronora. Their 'lovely wreaths, sprays of native flowers and beautifully handwritten note were greatly appreciated by the Webb family'.[36]

Some former residents remember long, close childhood friendships, with hours spent in the bush, on the banks and in the waters of the creek. Ellen remembers seeing her brother Tom Junior, with his white and his black mates, Ern Blewett and the MacKenzie boys playing frequently throughout their childhoods down at the creek or on billycarts on the one sealed road in the area which, luckily, was on a steep hill.

Once school was over, the boys were off down to the creek or along the bank into the bush, making spears from the pliant swamp oak to hurl mud balls at each other or more distant targets, fishing or hunting rabbits.[37] Ellen watched from a distance, seldom permitted to join this boys' adventure except for the odd times when Ern was sick or couldn't come along, and then Tom allowed her to be his partner for the games along the bank.

Ellen has memories of her own adventures on the creek, although they were more often with Aboriginal relations than with white friends: getting oysters from the rocks and fish from the river, as well as armfuls of gum tips and Christmas bells from the bush all around. As told in chapter 4, she used to go with her grandmother Ellen or her father Tom to gather the profusion of bush flowers to bundle up and sell in the streets for some extra money. The Christmas bush and gum tips were everywhere, painting the bush red in spring and summer, but there were also just a few special places for Christmas bells – and Ellen's Nana knew them.

Merging economies: mangroves, wildflowers and the tourist trade

Mangrove wood had become a key part of a new cash industry, again building on traditional knowledge to create a way to interact with the new economy. This has been described as if it were a craft based on tradition but adapted to a new market which was practised only by the men of La Perouse. This major Aboriginal settlement had become a well-known site for tourists to visit so they could meet Aboriginal people, who in turn could make some cash by selling them souvenirs. But the acquisition of the wood for the manufacture of the boomerangs involved Aboriginal communities right up the estuary, to Salt Pan Creek and far beyond.

Making boomerangs and other curios depended on local and traditional materials, and mangrove wood was important for two reasons. One was the shape of the curved mangrove branches and roots: the most prized were the 'elbows' or 'knees' which could be readily carved into the boomerang shape. The other was the characteristic qualities of this wood which was adapted to regular inundation with the tide. Joe Timbery, a senior La Perouse Aboriginal man interviewed in 1963, described the advantages of using mangrove wood because it didn't warp and, after being carefully treated, gave the best finish:

> we always left the natural colour of the wood. If the wood
> didn't have a good colour or grain, we used to shape it up
> roughly and then bury it in wet ground for a few months. That
> made it blue-black and tough, and it polished up well.[38]

Then, to attract the eye of the tourists, the Aboriginal carvers would use hot wire to burn in contemporary popular images, using poker work skills taught to them by south coast Aboriginal visitors. They chose particularly the furry native animals which were so popular with white Australians at the time – echoing the passion for wattle, waratahs, wildflowers and gumtips which allowed Ellen Anderson and her family to make a living.

From the late nineteenth century, the Georges River up to Liverpool had been the source of this mangrove wood.[39] But the trade in mangrove wood between these Aboriginal river people and the coastal La Perouse settlement escalated with the gradual filling in of the swamplands around Kurnell, reducing the mangrove wood which could be supplied from nearby La Perouse. Eventually people on the coast were forced to use three-ply wood – although they were unhappy with the quality of the boomerangs it allowed them to make when compared with the more traditional mangrove.[40]

Ellen James remembers that her father, Tom Williams senior would go along the river from Salt Pan Creek in the family's small boat, searching for elbows of wood which would have just the right shape for boomerangs which he'd then carve for 'pocket money' to help the family along. Ern Blewett remembers watching as a boy while Tom carved the boomerangs and then burnt delicate ornamental patterns into the wood with a hot poker. Tom's knowledge of the bush in the area, learned when he came to the river after he married, was eagerly sought by the younger men from La Perouse. Ellen remembered they would often row up the river to Salt Pan to find Tom so he could show them the best places to get the wood they carved for the tourists at La Perouse.[41] So the river, and their use of rowboats to navigate it, were essential elements in the processes of boomerang production.

This was a common situation for Aboriginal people in the mid-twentieth century. Whether working for wages and attending the RSL like Tom Williams or owning land freehold and selling gumtips for cash like Ellen Anderson, they were active in the market economy and they interacted with the growing non-Aboriginal society in the area. Yet at the same time, as Tom did whether he was carving boomerangs or fiercely defending his independence, or as Ellen did when she took her granddaughter out to find bush medicine plants along the river shore, these Aboriginal people were drawing on a heritage of traditional values and skills to weave a life for themselves which contained all these varied and sometimes conflicting elements.

Such mixtures of economies – the adaptive uses of traditional cultural knowledge to create viable livelihoods in the city – were just some of the ways in which these Aboriginal people were creating resilient communities. And it was the spaces of the river which enabled them: the woods and the flowers remained accessible because the rugged or sandy or swampy or tidal conditions of the river had deterred development.

Another example of how people went searching for ways to make these connections between tradition and modern city life can be seen in Ellen's interaction with the author Charles William Peck. Ellen's vivid knowledge of traditional stories, learnt from her own parents, and no doubt from talking over many years with the great variety of people who she had met in her travels, are known because she recounted some of them to Peck. He had been born at Woonona on the New South Wales south coast in 1875, and then raised in nearby Thirroul. As was to become clear only many years later, Peck had also been at the Wollongong Show in 1896 and witnessed the coronation of Ellen's brother-in-law, Mickey Johnson, as 'King of Illawarra'. Ellen had been there on a visit from Cumeragunja, to see her sister Rosie and the rest of her family. For Peck it had been a moving event which had nurtured his continuing interest in Aboriginal traditional knowledge.

After serving in Palestine during the Great War and teaching secondary schools on his return, Peck had eventually opened a business selling tyres in Bondi.[42] Following his interest, he had over the years collected Aboriginal stories and published some in the Sydney newspapers and then in his book *Aboriginal Legends* in 1925. He was drawing largely on stories he had been told by Aboriginal people in the Burragorang Valley and the Illawarra – many of which were of course well known to Ellen when she read them in their published form. Peck was obsessed with stories about the waratah, spending much of his energy in a fruitless conflict within the floral nationalist movement, trying to oppose the overwhelming symbolic prevalence of the wattle by claiming a more important heritage and significance for the waratah.[43]

But Ellen was less interested in the waratah stories than in his many other stories. After his early publications she searched him out and introduced herself to him in his Bondi tyre shop. Peck described the meeting in florid language in the early sections of his expanded 1933 edition of *Aboriginal Legends*. He began visiting Ellen at Salt Pan Creek and drew actively on Ellen's knowledge for many of the stories he published in his later volume of Aboriginal legends – although he only acknowledged her in the second of the publications.

What is clear from comparing Peck's writing with Ellen James' memories of her grandmother, is the difference between the romantic nationalism expressed by Peck and Ellen Anderson's approach to the land as a rich resource for food, stories and medicines as well as enjoyment. It was this deeper understanding of country which Ellen had taught her young granddaughter. Peck, however, was not interested in the uses of plants as foods or as medicines, nor indeed in the places they were found and how they related to the other species around them. They found no place in any of his published stories. Yet it was all of these ways to understand the country which Ellen was able to teach to teach her grand-daughter.

Some commentators have felt that Peck's account of an Aboriginal 'princess' visiting him in his shop was far-fetched.[44] Once Ellen's way of life in Salt Pan Creek in the 1920s is considered, however, the possibility that she would have seen the book, known its contents and found her way by train, bus and tram to Bondi, where she then approached him to talk about it, is a logical and plausible story. (It is far more believable than some of Peck's melodramatic language in recounting speeches he attributed to her.) In all the mundane day-to-day existence of Bondi trams and tyre shops, Ellen was following up leads to people who had some knowledge of her past and culture. She was well able to negotiate an active role in further recognition of the importance of traditional stories. This was another important strategy for resilience. What she taught her grandchildren like Tom and Ellen was this same mixture of ways to survive in the very contemporary world they faced while also drawing on knowledge from within the traditional culture of which she was heir.

SIX

A free community: King Burraga's river 1920–1940

The community that Ellen Anderson and her family were so much a part of creating at Salt Pan Creek was not the only camp along the length of the river. We know at this time there were Aboriginal people living in small protected creeks and rivers like Prospect Creek and Cabramatta Creek all the way downstream to Kogarah Bay. Salt Pan Creek had been no different in the 1910s. Soon it became something else.

The pressures on Aborigines in the 1920s

By 1926 there were 30 people living in the Salt Pan Creek community. Their growing numbers were no accident. This was a time of intense turmoil among Aboriginal people. The Aborigines Protection Board had finally settled on a policy and gained legislation, after years of making ad hoc decisions in response to pressure from either

Aboriginal people or local white settlers. Board members believed that issuing rations to Aborigines during the severe depression of the 1890s had sapped their independence. Perhaps more importantly, Board members were alarmed by the growing number of mixed-descent people who identified themselves as Aboriginal and who were growing up within Aboriginal communities.

The Board decided it needed to be aggressive in dispersing the Aboriginal population to 'solve' the problem. With its new laws in 1909 it secured most of the powers it proposed to enact its 'solution'. It had already begun to end the widespread independent Aboriginal farming on reserved lands to break any sense of family economic connection there. Its first intervention was at Cumeragunja, Hugh Anderson's home, where equipment was seized in 1906 and people began to be expelled soon after. Then with the new legislation the Board began to act more widely to move people on, to cut them off its ration lists and to turn those judged not to be 'aboriginal enough' off reserves. Those who protested, like the south coast families who argued the point with Board managers and the Cumeragunja people who took up legal cases against the APB, found that they needed to escape Board control as far as possible.[1]

The Salt Pan camps were an important resource for these Aboriginal people because they were not on reserved land and had little surveillance from the authorities. By 1915, and after much campaigning, the Protection Board had gained the final element in its plan: the power to remove children from their families. This increased the numbers of people fleeing the Board, either to take their children out of harm's way or to escape punishment for resisting the managers or inspectors as they tried to remove children. Further intervention in independent farming dispossessed more, and by 1924 the farming families like the Shepherds and others had been forced off their farms on reserve land in the Burragorang Valley and on the Hawkesbury after bitter struggles with both the Board and the Catholic Church, which believed it had a claim on part of the Hawkesbury farm.[2] The Sherrit and Shepherd families from the Burragorang Valley and others from the Hawkesbury River moved to the La Perouse settlement.[3] Many others, however, chose Salt Pan Creek on the lower Georges River rather than the tightly monitored La Perouse reserve.

The Salt Pan Creek camp was not the only safe place in this district. It seems that there were Aboriginal families scattered right across this area, both in workers' cottages and in camps in the sandstone areas of bush like Wolli Creek and others in a corridor which ran from Kingsgrove and Wolli Creek down onto the river at Riverwood and then both east to Padstow and west along the river itself towards Lugarno and Oatley.[4] The communities in all of the camps seem to have been swelled, ironically, by the movements generated by the dispersal campaign. But Salt Pan was the place which attracted the most militant of the refugees. Their camps were spread around the Anderson and Rowley blocks and the growing numbers of people shaped a clearing in the bush above the gully – clearly visible in the first aerial photographs of the area taken soon after.

Maintaining connections

Ellen and Hugh Anderson had extensive family ties themselves, and these links brought people to camp near them. Hugh's Cumeragunja connections brought people like the Pattens and others from the south-west, like the Glass family, while Ellen's south coast connections continued to draw people from there. Their children extended those links further still. As Ellen's children had grown to adulthood some had married and, like Dolly, had brought their new partners to Salt Pan Creek. Ellen and Hugh's unmarried sons continued to live with them on the Salt Pan Creek block, and none was better known

Salt Pan Creek from the air in 1930.
The Anderson and Rowley blocks are clearly
identifiable on lower eastern bank.

Map 3427, I56–5, Sydney, 1930 © Commonwealth of Australia, Geoscience Australia

than Joe, the eldest and most outgoing. Jacko Campbell in particular was grateful for Joe's assertiveness. When he arrived at Salt Pan as a ten-year-old, Jacko recalls Joe had sat him down and said:

> 'Well I'm the boss here. Anything you want to do, anything goes wrong at that school, see me!'... and oh yeah, he used to go up and talk. He'd put it into them. He didn't mess around![5]

Others among the Anderson children had moved to live with their partners' families, like Ellen and Hugh's son Jack, who had moved to Hill 60 and become part of another family network with connections to both the north and far south coast.

We can see some of these connections in photographs taken around 1926 or 1927. Charles Peck was still visiting Ellen and her family at that time, both at Salt Pan Creek and also at Hill 60, and on one trip he brought along photographer John Price. Price's nephew Jack was an actor in the new movie industry who had become a friend of Ellen's son Jacky, who had also began to take roles in locally produced films. John Price took some extraordinary photographs of the family group.[6] A sharp-eyed and astute woman, Ellen looks out unsmiling but directly at the camera, while Hughie and sons Joe and Jacky look more relaxed and jovial.[7] Jacky's wife was from the north coast Walker family and her sister, also seen in the photographs, had married into the Duren family of the south coast.

The Andersons still kept closely involved with the Aborigines Inland Mission and were mentioned enthusiastically in *Our Aim* as holding church services on their land and encouraging one of their sons to take up a proseletysing role for the organisation. In fact the AIM claimed him as a missionary.[8] Yet as Ellen and Hughie's story shows, the Anderson family had an ambiguous relationship with the missionaries. When Hughie had lived at Maloga in the 1880s he had supported Daniel Matthews because of his egalitarian ethos rather than for his welfare or missionary work. The Andersons continued

Jack Price, a family friend, Ellen Anderson
(left) and a family group, probably at Hill
60 near Wollongong, c 1928. With her

... are Hugh Anderson (r), Lena Anderson (née Walker) holding an infant Ernie Duren, and Annie Duren (née Walker) behind.

this approach with the AIM in Sydney. Rather than this affiliation with missionaries leading to a submissive attitude, the Andersons regarded Christian networks as a means to link up the Aboriginal people in many parts of the state who were protesting about the increasingly oppressive Protection Board regime.

The other group the Anderson's were linked to through Ellen's interest were the Australian nationalists like Peck. They not only saw waratahs and wattles as emblems of the new Australia, but organisations like the Australian Natives Association and others were at this time attracted by the idea of 'traditional' Aboriginal people as romanticised symbols of what was distinctive about Australia. In the work of emerging Australian poets and artists, Aboriginal flourishes were beginning to appear. The souvenir-makers at La Perouse were one source of 'authentic' Aboriginal articles, but the Anderson family through Ellen, as well as her son Jack in films, were just as accessible for the nationalist networks which were taking shape.

Finding a political voice

An emerging Aboriginal political organisation was also forming in the early 1920s which drew on both the AIM structure and the nationalist movement as ways to form political networks. This was the Australian Aboriginal Progressive Association, led by spokesman Fred Maynard, a waterside worker originally from Singleton. His family had suffered under the Board's revocation of reserves there but had remained around the Newcastle area. Maynard had left to work first as a drover and then as a waterside worker, living in Woolloomooloo in inner-city Sydney from 1907. He shared executive roles with his fellow countrymen Sid Ridgeway and Lionel Lacey who were both also from the central north coast of New South Wales.

Maynard, Ridgeway and Lacey were actively campaigning by the early 1920s, influenced not only by local conditions and by their union experiences but also by the militancy of coloured and African-American seamen whom Maynard knew as a waterside worker. They were in formal contact with the Garveyite Universal Negro Improvement Association in the United States and wove the Garveyite doctrines of liberty and cultural assertion (both traditional and contemporary) into the Australian Aboriginal Progressive Association platform.[9]

One strong ally of men like Ridgeway and Lacey in Newcastle was JJ Moloney, the influential editor of the newspaper *Voice of the North*. By 1920 Maloney was visiting the Aboriginal settlement at Karuah near Newcastle and had strong ties with many Aboriginal people in the region around this Hunter River city.[10] When the AAPA launched their public political activities in Sydney in 1925, they were less obvious than in Newcastle, but they also had the strong support of a maverick AIM member, Elizabeth McKenzie Hatton.

The history of this movement has so far been analysed in terms of the public leadership, foregrounding the personal and familial relationships particularly of Fred Maynard.[11] Important though Maynard and his fellow north coast countrymen were, there is a need also to understand better the city Aboriginal support which buoyed the movement from its earliest days. These urban networks drew on the rural links already well-established in the Sydney communities to circulate news of the new movement and to alert the AAPA spokespeople to the conflicts occurring in rural areas outside their own north coast networks.

The early AAPA activities drew the attention of Elizabeth McKenzie Hatton, a middle-aged woman living independently from her husband and raising a child. She had moved to Sydney from Melbourne in 1924 with the goal of supporting the AIM to set up a home for girls absconding from the hated Protection Board's indentured apprenticeships. The Aboriginal activists supported her in this, as did the AIM, and so McKenzie Hatton set up the girls' refuge in Homebush – just a few suburbs away from the Salt Pan Creek camp. The Andersons must have known about this project and followed the active AIM role in its planning and establishment. However, the missionary organisation soon withdrew its support. As the AIM saw it, McKenzie Hatton's close links with Aboriginal people had turned the home from a centre of church activity, for 'the evangelisation of the aboriginal races of Australia', into 'an Aboriginal Institute' and 'the present headquarters of an "Aboriginal Progressive Association" for both men and women, having for its object the social betterment of the people'.[12]

The AAPA's wide links with Aboriginal people across Sydney were reflected in its first public meeting which was held in Surry Hills in April 1925. This meeting heralded the public debut of the organisation with Maynard, Ridgeway and others as office bearers and McKenzie Hatton, the only non-Aboriginal member, as organising secretary.[13] The most interesting aspect however was that it was attended by the extraordinary number of over 200 local Aboriginal people.[14] Who were these people and where had they come from?

Such a large attendance must have drawn on networks of people scattered over the city but already connected in some way. The most effective connections – including those along the river – had been developed by AIM's activities.

The AAPA's influences and agenda

One insight into these wide connection are the memories of Jacko Campbell. Jacko arrived at Salt Pan Creek in 1926, escaping from the Burnt Bridge Aboriginal station at Kempsey after his mother had defied the Protection Board's Inspector Donaldson when he demanded she hand over her children. She had threatened the 'kids collector' with a shotgun, leaving the family no choice but to flee.[15] So Jacko was a witness to the unfolding of the activism of the camp, and his memories are alive with accounts of the debates and arguments around the campfire at night 'whenever there was anything to be done about the Aborigines Protection Board', and particularly how they wanted to push Jack Lang's government to stop the revocation of reserve lands.[16]

He insisted that this 1920s movement had a connection to religious organisations, and said that they used newspapers, like a Christian one he remembered as the 'War Cry', to spread their message about the need to challenge Protection Board control. This use of Christian networks to circulate news about campaigns for political justice is very similar to the approach which Hughie Anderson and Thomas James had both used in the long disputes at Cumeragunja in the 1880s to resist Protection Board encroachment on Aboriginal residents' independence and later, in the 1900s, on their family farming blocks.

Jacko's memories suggest the ways the early political movement was built on networks established initially by missionaries. But Aboriginal people had used those networks towards very different goals than those of AIM. Rather than being influenced by the missionaries into compliance with government policy, these Aboriginal participants were using the missionary network as a leaping off point for a social justice campaign.

It had other important influences as well. At the same time as McKenzie Hatton came out of the AIM structure to support the AAPA, Salt Pan Creek was being visited by Charlie Leon, initially from Taree but by the 1920s a widely travelled working man. Leon had joined the Communist Party while working on the docks in Tasmania and, like Fred Maynard, was strongly influenced by the radical left-wing politics which were circulating in the waterside industries.[17] So the political ideologies which were shaping the Aboriginal movement and the communities were mixed but the structures of communication which the AIM had set up were valuable for circulating all these ideas, not just those endorsed by the missionaries.

The other role of the city Aboriginal communities was to make the links between rural disputes and the north coast-focused leadership of the fledgling AAPA. By 1925 there had been many long-running rural disputes as the pressure on Aboriginal people increased. One underway since 1918 was the bitter conflict in Batemans Bay on the south coast in which local council and the citizens' Progress Association had been trying to remove the established Aboriginal settlement on the edge of town to make way for urban expansion. The council had tried a number of strategies but when the Aboriginal community continued to refuse to move, and the Protection Board offered no effective solution, the local Parents' and Citizens' Association voted to segregate the school on racial lines – a power which any white parent had held under Education Department regulations since 1902. One of the grandparents of the 20 excluded Aboriginal children, Jane Duren, led the protests locally, and in a formal letter to King George V in June 1926 protested about the hypocrisy of the Australian claim to 'fair play' when a system of education – declaring itself to be both compulsory and public – could still exclude all children of Aboriginal members of the public.[18]

The Sydney and north coast-oriented AAPA had had no contact with this or other south coast campaigns in April 1925, but quite suddenly during 1926 the connection was made. By November 1926 Jane Duren was speaking on the AAPA platform.[19] A photo of the Anderson family at Hill 60 shows how these connections were made. Ellen Anderson's son Jack was married to Lena Walker, and Lena's sister was married into the Duren family, one branch of which was living around Wollongong while others were at Bateman's Bay. Ernie Duren, the son of Jack Anderson's sister-in-law, is a baby in these photographs and years later he identified the people and their relationships. These family links generated frequent contact and the rapid flow of news, particularly among families with a history of outspoken protest like the Andersons.

Such networks offered their practical support for the building protest movement and meant that an elderly rural grandmother like Jane Duren was by October 1927 accompanying Maynard and five other members of the AAPA to a public debate in Sydney with senior church figures in the Australian Board of Missions like the Reverend JS Needham. The church bodies were then advocating a 'native state' within the Northern Territory which, while understood as a philanthropic proposal by the churchmen, would have necessitated the removal of Aboriginal people from places like Sydney to the remote interior of the continent. Duren, like Maynard and the other Aboriginal representatives, rejected the proposal, insisting that they wanted secure land in their own country as their primary demand.[20] This was an important example of a key difference in policy between the missionary establishment and the Aboriginal movement, which led not to compromise but to a bitter open conflict.

'They could talk on politics!'

Despite the increasing organisation and militancy, the pressures of the times were forcing more and more Aboriginal people into travelling, and the Salt Pan Creek community remained both a focus and popular way-station. Young Ted Thomas had arrived at Salt Pan around 1924, having walked up from Wallaga Lake 'with a spear and me swag on me back' – as he recalled in 1980. He was around 16 when he moved in to stay there with Joe Anderson in his small camp on the block owned by Ellen and Hughie, and he used to go to Brighton-Le-Sands with Joe and some of his brothers when they went to busk there with a gum leaf band. Young Ted used to go round with a hat for them and collect the money from their audiences. Ted remembered 'They were great blokes on politics too!' There were others from the south coast too, men like Paddy Pitman and Jimmy Lukum who had a good reason to avoid any interference by the Protection Board after their defiance earned them a 'walking ticket' from the Protection Board's stations. As Ted recalled, 'That's the time when they got hunted off Roseby Park for shit-stirring with the manager!'[21]

Jacko Campbell, whose memories of the Salt Pan camp allow such valuable insight into its complex history, came by water from Kempsey in 1926 and was about 10 when he arrived. Following the incident with the shotgun, his family had fled in Jacko's father's fishing boat and come down the coast, first to Putty Beach and then into Botany Bay and to the Georges River, where Jacko's sister was already living. Jacko remembered a number of families living in the Salt Pan Creek community. His family lived for a while next to Joe Anderson's camp. Ellen Anderson and her family had a nice house, Jacko remembered, as did old Bill Rowley, but others lived in little mia-mias and bag huts. After a while the Campbells moved a little bit away to rent a house from an Italian market gardener. Jacko also remembered Joe Anderson and his brothers busking, gathering gum tips to sell around Hurstville, Penshurst or Mortdale, or selling blackberries, gooseberries and wildflowers.

At the camp there were the north coast Kelly family from Foster and Charlie Leon from Taree. Charlie was by this time leading a travelling vaudeville troupe, but he pulled up at Salt Pan Creek camp when he was in Sydney. From the south-west there was the Glass family from Cowra, and from the Murray River came the Onus and the Patten families – both from Cumeragunja where they too had histories of forthright outspoken criticism of the Protection Board. All of these families and individuals were seeking refuge from the coercive intrusions of the Board into their lives. Salt Pan represented freedom.

Another recently arrived family, the Groves came from Walhallow on the Castlereagh River. Led by Bob Groves, and including his son Bert, they were related to Tom Williams. The family was well remembered by all the younger men like Ted and Jacko because they moved into the house where the Campbells had lived, once they eventually moved just a little further away in 1932.

As Jacko and Ted recalled the atmosphere of the later 1920s and early 1930s, there was always talk of politics:

> JACKO All them old fellas used to live out there, the Pattens and all them others. You'd see them old fellas sittin' around in a ring, when there was anything to be done ...
>
> TED They were well educated! They could talk on politics!
>
> JACKO They always DID! ... Around the kids! ... No matter where they went! ... 'Specially when there was anything to do about the Aborigines Protection Board! There was talk about writing a petition. That was always goin' on! Joe Anderson said he'd be talking to the Duke of Gloucester!

So the Salt Pan Creek community was a vibrant and active place in the 1920s and even in the hard years of the Depression in the 1930s. The area was in uproar during those years, as the landlords of many rented houses forced evictions in working-class suburbs, and particularly in Bankstown. As the numbers of evictions escalated, the people affected began organising, often with the support of the Communist Party, to challenge the police when they came to throw people out.

One of the well-known Communist families most active in these eviction battles, in Bankstown and elsewhere, was the Aboriginal Eatock family, originally from Queensland and then living in inner-city Glebe. One family member in particular, Nobby Eatock, was a key organiser in the Bankstown conflicts, heavily involved in the eviction struggles and eventually arrested with great violence, making his case a *cause célèbre* throughout the area and in the wider press.[22] The

Aboriginal role in these early 1930s local conflicts must have resonated throughout the suburb. It was undoubtedly discussed among the Salt Pan Creek camp members, especially considering Charlie Leon, another member of the Communist Party, used to stay there when he was in Sydney.[23]

Jacko Campbell remembered that many of the Salt Pan Creek men would take the opportunity to 'spruik' during their trips to Paddy's Market selling gumtips and busking.[24] A well-known member of the Aboriginal community, Monty Tickle, was a nightwatchman at the markets and he made sure that Jacko got 'to see these fellas on the butterbox' down there:

> JACKO Every Friday night they used to be spruiking at
> Paddy's Market. Jack Patten, Bill Onus, Bob McKenzie from
> Woolbrook, old Joe Anderson, they all lived at Salt Pan …
> They'd only be spruikin' on land rights, that's all, on land
> rights … You know: 'Why hasn't the Aboriginal people got
> land rights?' That was always the [thing] … That paper come
> out, the 'Aboriginal War Cry'. It was the first and then the 'Abo
> Call'.[25]
>
> HEATHER They wouldn't have used those words would they?
> Did they actually say 'land rights'?
>
> JACKO They actually said: 'The Aboriginals cryin' out for Land
> Rights' and they called it the 'War Cry' …
>
> HEATHER What sort of land were they asking for?
>
> JACKO Aboriginal land! They were asking for the land they
> were on! That's when they were chuckin' 'em off. There's places
> round Nowra, 'bout 35 or 40 acres, 60 acres, what Aboriginal
> people was ON. And they [whites] went into 'em, run their
> cattle through 'em, mob of cattle through 'em, through their
> crops and that! They only had dog-leg fences then. That was
> the Stewarts and Bollaways at Tullanger … They was pushin'

[NSW Premier Jack] Lang at that time for Land Rights. That's
was what it was all about. And to break up the Aborigines
Protection Board!

For the youths of the Salt Pan Creek community, this was a powerful induction to the world of political activism. Later in the 1930s, two
of the Patten sons, Jack and George, made interstate headlines when
they challenged the Protection Board and led the protest walk off
from Cumeragunja. Bert Groves later became the quiet and powerful
leader of the Aboriginal political movement through the tough years
of the 1950s and 1960s. During the 1960s, Charlie Leon was a tenacious activist in south-western Sydney and across the state, battling
the government's assimilation policies – which had replaced protection and segregation. By the 1970s, Tom Williams had become a stalwart organiser in the La Perouse and wider Sydney communities, while
both Guboo Ted Thomas and Jacko Campbell became key figures in a
renewed national and state land rights campaign into the 1980s.[26]

But for Joe Anderson, his time was to be there and then.

The challenge to the
Salt Pan community

Fuelled by the Protection Board's 'dispersal' program, and then by the
Depression – when Aborigines were routinely refused the new Unem-
ployment Relief rations and work in many areas – the numbers at
Ogilvy Street increased further. Some of the men found they could get
government-paid relief work putting the railway line through to East
Hills: Jacko Campbell's older brother, supporting the family of 16, had
two weeks on and one week off. (A single man only got one week on,
three weeks off.) Men of the Mackenzie family found similar relief
work at Sandy Beach. But at least at Salt Pan Creek they were safe from

Board intervention, and the children could be sent to school. David Cross, who had been a pupil at Peakhurst Public School, remembered the influx of new Aboriginal faces at this time. The sense of increasing turmoil was reflected in his uneasy memories that these new pupils 'were regarded as outsiders ... not merely by the white kids by also by the black kids'.[27]

The rising Aboriginal population in the area was by no means welcomed by all their white neighbours. This was precisely the period when local Anglo-Irish community organisations were emerging and seeking to shape the suburb's social and physical environment. The Salt Pan Creek Progress Association (later to call itself Padstow Park, as a less 'detrimental' name for such a 'promising and beautiful' suburb[28]) was already organising in 1913; a Progress Association had formed at Kogarah Bay in 1921; as had one at Lugarno in 1922 and another at Herne Bay well before 1930. (A fifth local group, the Sandy Point Progress Association, did not form until 1951, reflecting the lower population and slower growth on the southern side of the river.[29]) These groups were forming in the heyday of local and regional public use of the river frontages for picnics, swimming, boating, fishing and many other forms of leisure. The many private pleasure grounds were still operating and the public was increasingly using the few public parklands which had been reserved over the previous decade or so. The slow extension of the rail network was bringing more Sydneysiders to the rivers on weekends and holidays. Rivers were seen as places with an endless variety of holiday and leisure pursuits, from enjoyment of the native environment to the razzle-dazzle and the dance pavilion. The local Progress Associations along the Georges River hoped to take advantage of the high and growing interest in river activities to expand their communities and to enhance their economic and cultural opportunities.

The associations were both expressing and shaping the views of these emerging communities and of what they understood to be 'the public'. There was a strong and vocal contingent of local businessmen, including both the established market gardeners and poultry farmers and the storekeepers in the developing shopping centres which were growing to meet increasing suburbanisation. The Depression slowed this process of community formation and assertion, but it was to re-emerge strongly by the later 1930s. It was a sense of community which was racially limited and defined by class, with the Anglo-Irish component of the population self-consciously beginning to flex its demographic strength to exert control over their suburb's directions.[30]

There had been complaints made by local white residents to Hurstville Council in 1926 that the Aboriginal community at Ogilvy Street was unsanitary and its residents were creating a disturbance in the area. However, the council's health inspector had found little to condemn in the Anderson's sturdy weatherboard cottages, with their 'surprisingly clean and well-kept' interiors and 'tidy' surroundings. He argued that since the Andersons and Rowleys owned the blocks, it meant there was little the council might do without more substantial cause.[31] However the community's defence was about to disappear. Hugh Anderson died in July 1928 and by November 1930, under Depression pressures, the Andersons had sold their Ogilvy Street block. This forced Ellen Anderson and her community of around 40 people to move deeper into more secluded bush close to the creek and on to land over which they had little or no tenure.[32]

The family was still well known among whites in the area. It was sympathetically depicted in the Sydney newspaper *The Sun* in January 1931, doing everyday things at this new, temporary camp site: chatting with the local bakery delivery man, for example, and patting their kelpie dog. The headline on the page was romantic fantasy: THE CONTENTMENT OF NATIVE LIFE. One of the captions read: 'Next to Nature and content with his simple native philosophy – Joe Anderson at the Peakhurst Aboriginal camp'.[33] The reality was a long way from contented.

King Burraga
speaks out

The pressure had begun again immediately after they had moved. A rowdy Christmas, leading to police visits at the new camp, coincided with more formal resident protests. The Herne Bay Progress Association wrote to Hurstville Council complaining not only about unsanitary conditions and noisy disturbances at the camp but about the inappropriateness of having 'a blacks' camp' in this 'growing district'. The residents' organisations, failing to understand the long-established relationships with the area held by the people who formed the nucleus of the camp, argued that the residents 'were not the original ones who had camped at Peakhurst, but were newcomers from Wollongong, La Perouse and other places' and that they should be 'removed to the compound at La Perouse' where they could be properly 'supervised' and 'protected'.[34]

With Ellen's death in May 1931, Joe was left to defend the community as the senior member of the Anderson family. He had been passionate in his opposition to the evictions and dispossessions he had seen happening to his countrymen over the last decade. As Jacko Campbell and Ted Thomas remembered, he had been active in the wider political movement at the time. But now he saw his own community at Salt Pan Creek facing the same challenge.

In casting around for new ways to raise his urgent concerns, Joe turned to the very new and modern media: the 'talkies'. Picture shows were crowded all round the country in the depths of the Depression, as everyday Australians tried to forget their worries by escaping into the movie fantasy world. The silent movies of the 1920s had drawn big crowds, but when sound was introduced in 1929, the new 'talkies' brought even bigger audiences. Filmmakers scrambled to find content for the B-film and newsreel footage which showed in all the cinemas before the featured film, so there was plenty of interest in unusual themes or images. The Australian film industry was burgeoning, despite the Depression, and directors were looking for extras, including those of Aboriginal people in films with rural or Pacific themes – of which there were many made in the 1920s and early 1930s. Joe's good-looking brother Jack had already been employed in a number of these roles as an extra.[35] So Joe began to cultivate the film connections his brother had, and before long, they bore fruit.

Joe finally had his chance to be heard when he was filmed by Cinesound News in 1933 at Salt Pan Creek.[36] Unlike his brother and other Aboriginal extras who were given scripted lines – if they talked at all – Joe Anderson spoke his own words. He drew on the authority of his land, calling himself King Burraga after his grandfather Paddy Burragalung, and so using a name that resonated through Dharawal and Gandangara country. Speaking directly to the camera and the audience beyond he said:

> Before the white man set foot in Australia, my ancestors had kings in their own right, and I, Aboriginal King Burraga, am a direct descendant of the royal line ...
>
> The Black man sticks to his brothers and always keeps their rules, which were laid down before the white man set foot upon these shores. One of the greatest laws among the Aboriginals was to love one another, and he always kept to this law. Where will you find a white man or a white woman today that will say I love my neighbour ... It quite amuses me to hear people say they don't like the Black man ... but he's damn glad to live in a Black man's country all the same! ...
>
> I am calling a corroborree of all the Natives in New South Wales to send a petition to the King, in an endeavour to improve our conditions. All the Black man wants is representation in Federal Parliament. There is also plenty fish in the river for us all, and land to grow all we want.
>
> One hundred and fifty years ago, the Aboriginal owned Australia, and today, he demands more than the white man's charity. He wants the right to live![37]

Evicting A King

KING BURRAGA, of the Thirroul
tribe, who has dreams of a double
coronation.

Burraga, King of the Thirroul
aboriginals, is to be evicted with
his people from their huts at Salt
Pan Creek, Peakhurst.

Daily Telegraph
28 August 1936.
Joe Anderson was
shown carving
mangrove root
boomerangs at Salt
Pan Creek. He
continued to fight
the pressure to evict
his family and the
broader Aboriginal
community. The use
of the township
name 'Thirroul'
misidentified the
affiliation Joe and
his family had
as members of the
Dharawal language
group with the
Georges River.

Spectacular as this appeal on national media was, it could only stave off the pressure for a short while. By 1935, Hurstville Council had decided to evict the Anderson family network from the public land on which they were now camped. They were given a 12-month eviction order, but again Joe refused to accept this quietly. He once more began recruiting support, inviting the press for an interview and photography session. He was again photographed in his camp, rugged up against the winter weather, carving mangrove boomerangs as he explained to the reporters that his family had a long-established right to keep on living on the Georges River.[38]

Again in his role as King Burraga, Joe then wrote to the newly appointed governor of New South Wales, Sir David Murray Anderson, requesting intervention and support from the representative of the King. He wrote as well to the Society for Protection of Native Races, at that stage chaired by the up-and-coming policy broker, AP Elkin, to whom he pleaded his case for support against eviction. Joe's letters to them, just like his appearance on Cinesound footage in 1933, stressed that there were resources for all to share equitably and that Aboriginal people needed to have justice, not charity.[39]

Joe kept on organising, and linking up with the emerging political movement led by his young friends Jack Patten, Pearlie Gibbs, Bill Ferguson and, as a young supporter, Bert Groves. Joe attended the 1937 hearings of the state government's Select Committee into the Aborigines Protection Board, mixing with the new leaders and, as King Burraga, meeting white supporters like Joan Kingsley Strack – who was delighted to receive a carved hatpin in the shape of a boomerang.[40]

This campaign was possible for Joe Anderson because he was old friends with the people who were its organisers. The Day of Mourning, which more than any other event has symbolised the tenacity and courage of Aboriginal resistance against the Protection Board, was planned by many of the activists with Salt Pan Creek connections.

The photos of the event on Australia Day 1938 show just a few: notably Jack Patten and Bill Onus from Cumeragunja, and Selena Avery from Grafton. But we know that there were veterans from the 1920s campaigns of Fred Maynard in the crowd as well, and that there were also the younger activists who would take up the struggle in the next decade, like Bert Groves. So many of them had shared the camaraderie and the debates around Ellen and Hugh Anderson's campfires at Salt Pan Creek.

Once the Depression was past and people were looking to the future, the local white residents organisations again began to demand that the camp and its community be removed. By March 1939, their complaints had expanded from the allegedly poor hygiene, noisy disturbances, and the needs of the 'growing' suburb. As the health inspector understood it, they wanted to move the camp because its residents 'were spoiling the beautiful bush area'.[41]

This brief reference to native bushland suggests white residents were claiming authority as managers of the environment, usurping Aboriginal people's position. It also gives us a clue about how to interpret a puzzling newspaper item about Joe a year before, in January 1938. The pictorial magazine *Man* carried a photograph for which Joe had obviously posed, carrying a dead wallaby over his shoulder and armed apparently with a bow and arrow – which are not traditional weapons. The text indicated that Joe had been prosecuted for killing a wallaby which a local white resident had claimed to be his 'pet' but which Joe had disputed. In the absence of any other formal protection for native wildlife at the time, the RSPCA had carried out some sort of punishment on or issued a caution to Joe, and had 'caned the King's ankles for killing it'.[42]

There are many unanswered questions here. There is no doubt that white residents had joined Aboriginal people in hunting swamp wallabies since the first European settlement over 150 years before. There had not been any notable accounts of white residents prosecuted for

Joe Anderson, from the curious Man magazine article, 1938. The story and photo were the result of conflict with local white residents and Progress Association.

BURRUGA, King of Thirroul aboriginals, N.S.W., at right, bow-and-arrowed a "kangaroo." A local resident claimed it was his pet "wallaby." The king stood on his dignity, said, "My great-grandfather shook hands with Captain Cook when he landed at Kurnell, so I ought to know if it is a kangaroo." The R.S.P.C.A., rather tended towards the "wallaby" theory, caned the King's ankles for killing it, anyway, whatever it was.

Man, January 1938, Mitchell Library, State Library of NSW

killing native species, even in the recent depths of the Depression when whites in that area had been living in deep poverty. But the unnamed resident's sentimental claim to have tamed a native animal is consistent with contemporary nationalism which celebrated native environments but domesticated and trivialised native plants and animals. The complaint that the Aboriginal man had killed what was now a pet positioned the white community in the role of protectors of 'native' species and environments, as the same time as it accused Aboriginal people of being predators and exploiters who were less able to care for the nature all around them. It is hard not to see the complaint as symptomatic of the attempt to drive Aborigines out of the area, by suggesting firstly that they were not 'native' or local but 'from somewhere else', and then by accusing them of not knowing how to protect the now domesticated 'native' environment. It points also to the increasingly intrusive surveillance to which the Aboriginal community had been subjected.

Once we start exploring the memories of both Aboriginal and non-Aboriginal residents we find more traces of the story. Shayne Williams, a young member of Joe Anderson's family – and Ellen's great-grandson – unearthed this newspaper report recently, and is aware of a longer family story about the wallaby hunting having somehow been the cause of the community's removal. But it is not only within the Aboriginal community that this event has been associated with the removal. Bob Haworth, now a geographer, grew up around the eastern side of Salt Pan Creek and remembers his father spending a lot of time knocking around with the area's Aboriginal population through the 1930s. Bob's father told his family that the Aborigines had been pressured off the land because they had been wrongfully blamed for hunting wallabies.[43]

The endangered status of the wallaby had little to do with Aboriginal hunting. It had everything to do with increasing urbanisation and the rapid and ongoing changes to the environment. It is a bitter irony that the intensifying pressures on the environment were used as one of the tools to force a free Aboriginal community away from their country and into incarceration under the Aborigines Welfare Board (as the old Protection Board was now called). Joe died soon after this marsupial incident and within a year the remaining camp members had been forced out of Salt Pan Creek, against their will, to the La Perouse reserve to live under the manager.[44]

Still plenty of
fish in the river

This forced removal to La Perouse could be seen as an end to the story of Aboriginal landowners on Salt Pan Creek. For white settler Australians there has been after all a strong preference for sentimental 'last of his tribe' stories. While these stories seem to be sympathetic to a noble Aboriginal presence, at the same time they serve to confirm the disappearance of Indigenous people from the present and future. But this was not the end of the Salt Pan community, because that community had never been tied to only that one locality.

Through its history as a campsite, Salt Pan Creek had drawn a society of Aboriginal people from all over the south-east of the continent. Precisely because it was never under government control or surveillance, Salt Pan Creek had offered a place of safety where people could gather their strength for resistance. Joe Anderson was certainly linked strongly to people like Biddy Giles, his grandmother, who belonged to that country and who had known a time before British or Irish settlers dominated the landscape. He had chosen the name King Burraga to emphasise just that connection when he was filmed challenging the attempts to force his people away. Yet Joe was also directly connected to people from the Murray River, the Castlereagh River and the southern coasts. King Burraga in fact exemplifies not any mournful 'last of his tribe' but instead the resilience of local Indigenous societies who creating new and rich communities in the challenging conditions of the invasion and the city.

While the Anderson family's eventual departure in 1939 did leave a gap in the Aboriginal community on Salt Pan Creek, it was not by any means the end of the network which had been building there over many years. One of the ways that group was sustained was in the many families who continued to live in the area – like the Campbells from the Macleay valley who lived in Padstow, and the MacKenzie and Williams families in Peakhurst.

The Salt Pan Creek camp had not, in any case, been the only one on the river during the 1920s and 1930s. In the wide sweep of the river above Holsworthy, there were still more families living in a range of conditions. Some lived informally, in the undeveloped areas around creeks and waterways. There are memories of Aboriginal people living on Prospect Creek near Fairfield, for example and at Cabramatta Creek, just to the west of the Georges River near Warwick Farm, until well into the 1960s.[45]

At the other end of the scale were the few families who held freehold land, like the Andersons and Rowley's had done for a while at Salt Pan Creek. One of these landholders was Clarence Henry Hannah, who had come to the city from Coolah in the 1930s and bought 50 acres (20 hectares) at Rex Road, Chester Hill. Here he ran a farm which employed a number of immigrant families over many years. Many more Aboriginal families lived in conditions somewhere between the informal camps of the small creek valleys and the substantial land holdings of Mr Hannah. Some rented and some had small blocks, although their names are hard to trace as they were scattered across the area. And many Aboriginal people were married to non-Aboriginal partners, creating the complex web of relationships which can be traced by family members but which are hard to explore otherwise. One such family was the Perrys, related to Clarence Hannah's children by marriage, with one woman married into the Pike family and said to be living at Holsworthy into the 1940s.[46]

Robyn Williams' family history reflects this pattern of long-established residence in Sydney, with a family background which spanned her Wiradjuri roots from the family of her father, Wally, who had come from west of the mountains, to her links to the Irish and Scots ancestry of her mother Kath. During Robyn's early childhood her parents had lived in St John's Park, which was then a semi-rural area near Cabramatta just to the north-west of the Georges River.

After Kath and Wally divorced, Kath remained in close contact with Wally's mother, sisters and extended family when she took her daughters to live in Moorebank, south of the river between Liverpool and Voyager Point. Robyn remembers continuing influences from the Scots, the Irish and the Wiradjuri sides of her heritage. Kath later married again, becoming the wife of Dom Syme – the Moorebank activist and egg producing chicken-farmer who has been an outspoken advocate for working-class and small-businesspeople for many years. All of them, Wally, Kath and Dom were members of the Australian Communist Party – the only political group which Robyn remembers to have stood up for Aborigines in those days.

So Robyn and her three sisters all grew up immersed in both the hard work of looking after the chickens for the egg farm and the excitement of political debates and campaigns. They swam in the creeks (not the shark infested river!), collected oysters and caught eels. The river was a place of resources still, as it had been for King Burraga, and as it had been for many before them:

> And there's some great spots up along William's Creek and in
> the creek that comes in there at Sandy Point. They're all tidal.
> There's beautiful eels. Fresh water eels.
>
> Or up in the top end of them creeks where there is fresh
> water, when they stop being tidal. There's yabbies – and fresh
> water fish, you know.

I don't know if other families went and got all that stuff, but our family did it. And there was always a big mob of us. We'd go out – We'd say, 'Oh, we're going over to swim over here and have this big feed'. People had row boats that lived right on the river, but you had no way to get it to the river, so unless you lived right on the river you didn't have a boat. You just fished from the side.

There was always good oysters. And you could eat the fish. The water was pristine that used to come down from Campbelltown way and all over the back. ... The George's had beautiful pristine water. [47]

Many people continued to live along the river after Joe Anderson's family had been forced out. Even those who moved away in the next few decades – like Jacko Campbell who went to live at Roseby Park on the south coast, Tom Williams junior who moved with his family to La Perouse, from where his sister Ellen later moved to Blacktown – retained a vivid memory of those formative years in the vibrant community at Salt Pan Creek. Each of them was to come back into the story of the Georges River in ways which sustained its tradition of resistance and resilience. So King Burraga's death and the departure of the Anderson family in 1939 did not mark the end of the long-established Aboriginal presence on the river.

There were to be still more people to come. The post-war period saw a further major expansion of the Aboriginal population of the Georges River and particularly along Salt Pan Creek itself. These greater numbers of people, both long-time Aboriginal residents and newly-arriving Aboriginal migrants from rural areas, were faced with a river which was itself under intensifying stress. This river was less and less able to offer the resources and the secluded environments that it had done for so many decades. But it continued to offer two things: an avenue of mobility and, in some ways, freedom.

SEVEN

The river under challenge: defending Goggey's victory 1950s

World War II brought dramatic change to the river and the lives of the Aboriginal people who lived beside it. It was the conflict around these changes which created the archives and memories that allow these stories of sustaining lives and networks to be told. In particular, the aftermath of the war allows us to better understand Goggey's victory at Voyager Point in 1857 and its implications.

With its tidal waters, its steep cliffs, sandy soils and swamps, the Georges River had created the possibilities that Aboriginal people would still have spaces along it long after the invasion began. World War II began to change that. Many Aboriginal people enlisted. Among the Salt Pan Creek community alone, both Jack Patten and Bert Groves became well-known for their army careers. But the places where they had lived on the river began to feel the impact of war as well. The expansion of military bases and later the intensifying industrialisation of the post-war city began to cut into the free spaces where Aboriginal people had been able to hold land.

Yet the river was to remain the key to the ways in which Aboriginal people have made sense of *being* Aboriginal in a rapidly changing environment. This was no easy or simple journey. Aboriginal people had to fight to make a new sense of identity and community at the same time as they were under intense pressure to 'assimilate'. The government wanted them to disappear into the emerging 'modern city' into which Sydney was trying to transform itself by the 1960s.

The pressures
of war

One of the spaces on the river where Aboriginal people lived until the war was Doctors Bush. This large area of undeveloped open land was north of Ellen Anderson's block on Salt Pan Creek. It stretched around the eastern side of a tiny inlet called Herne Bay – which gave its name to the surrounding suburb and then, in 1932, to the railway station on the line running from the city to East Hills. Doctors Bush lay between that railway line and Canterbury Road. It had remained low wetland and brush-dotted grassland, although it had been increasingly affected by the siltation coming down the river from clearing and farming around Bankstown. Many Aboriginal families had lived here at different times, all of them part of the extended network of people linked to the Salt Pan Camp but spread across the area. Some had been passing through, but others were longer-term tenants who had been evicted in the insecure 1930s, as the Williams family had been. Doctors Bush had also been one of the 'happy valleys' which had sprung up all over Sydney, offering temporary shelter for unemployed workers and evicted families, both white and black, when they were forced out of their jobs and homes.[1]

The war brought new demands to the whole river, expanding

military facilities into what the government saw as 'empty' spaces. Many military sites were already on the Georges River: the Holsworthy army base to the west of Williams Creek was one example, housing Australian troops and used for weapons testing since 1912. At Milperra, the Bankstown civil aerodrome, which had been planned since 1929 but delayed by the Depression, suddenly became a reality in 1940. The Commonwealth purchased about 600 acres (240 hectares) and finally began to build the runways, initially to meet the needs of the Australian Air Force but then to meet those of the United States. In 1942, the operational base of the whole massive US Pacific military force was transferred to Australia after the Japanese advance. Australia needed to house and support not only the American servicemen and their equipment but their wounded soldiers as well.

These impacts were felt all along the river, but Doctors Bush was one of the first places to feel the changes. The Aboriginal families living there in 1939 had disappeared entirely in 1943, leaving no record to suggest where they had gone when Doctors Bush was turned into an enormous American military hospital.[2] The Aboriginal families had apparently moved on, perhaps to other places near Salt Pan Creek, but the campsites were diminishing rapidly.

Along the coast, to the north and south of Sydney, the same military pressures were being felt. Hill 60 near Port Kembla was particularly important for the Georges River families, because it was part of the Five Islands where Biddy Giles had lived for many years and where her daughter Ellen had grown up. It was home to a continuing strong community and was an accessible camping area to many among the Georges River network, like Jacko Campbell and Ted Thomas as well as the Anderson family, who all travelled frequently between Georges River and the south coast.[3] It had much evidence of long traditional occupation in its middens and hearth sites, but this Aboriginal community also had a history of its men working in the unionised heavy industries of Port Kembla and Wollongong.[4]

These twin sources of strength had for many years allowed the Aboriginal community to fend off the pressure from encroaching military and local government interests, but the war finally made such resistance impossible. In September 1942, the Hill 60 Aboriginal community was pushed to the small patch of more remote reserve land at Coomaditchie.[5] Hill 60 itself became the site of heavy fortifications, honeycombed with tunnels and bunkers to house large guns for the protection of the steel works and loading facilities at Port Kembla.

The war deeply eroded the areas where Aboriginal people were free to live without interference. Some people, like those of Hill 60, had been promised that the land would be returned to them once the military no longer needed it for the war effort.[6] But the shocks of World War II also pushed the Commonwealth government to decide that it must strengthen Australian self-sufficiency, and it wanted to expand the country's faltering industrial production, which had barely got started before Depression. The government planned to increase migration dramatically to boost the workforce for the newly planned factories. Much of the change was expected to take place in the large cities like Sydney and the New South Wales government hoped to manage this process with careful planning. In the meantime, the many hurriedly constructed wartime buildings – like the hospital wards at Herne Bay or the military huts at Holsworthy – were turned to a range of temporary uses. After delays and confusion, the strategy for Sydney was finally announced as the Cumberland County Plan in 1949.[7]

The impacts of
post-war planners

The government's program aimed to benefit the whole city when they planned the intensifying residential and factory activity. But the projects to build many more factories and house many more people were carried out almost entirely on the Georges River in the 1950s and the 1960s.[8] This deepened the damage to the river, which had already been harmed by the wartime escalation of the numbers of troops housed nearby. Their rapidly built and poorly serviced accommodation had added to the burden of sewage and other waste pouring untreated into the river.

An essential part of the social democratic philosophy which guided the planning for the new city was that low-income families would be relocated from inner-city areas, which were regarded as crowded and unhealthy, to newly constructed suburbs built by the State Housing Commission. The public housing areas were intended to share the same spacious living areas, wide streets and healthy atmosphere as any privately owned suburban housing area in order to build an egalitarian society. While the Housing Commission had been established with a strong commitment to providing rental accommodation for low-income earners, after the war it began to pressure tenants into purchasing houses. The protected tenancy system in the inner-city meant there was little incentive to landlords to continue renting properties and so they increasingly turned to selling them at low rates to residents. The result was that there was less rental accommodation, especially in the inner city. What remained was available only at soaring rents which became impossible for low-income earners to meet. This contributed to the pressure for people to move away from the inner city as well as to turn, wherever possible, to home purchase.[9]

The Cumberland County Plan was supposed to manage this major spread of the population from inner city to outer areas by carefully controlling the locations where residential and factory areas were to be sited. As well, it aimed to retain and even expand agricultural areas around the consolidating residential areas, and to protect the existing parklands within already developed areas. Together this was meant to keep a 'green belt' at the same time as ensuring an equitable distribution of subdivision and new housing. This blueprint, published in

1949 and endorsed by the government in 1951, was a template for the new city which was supposed to guarantee an equitable and healthy environment for all citizens.[10]

Ideal and reality diverged. Local government endorsement was necessary to turn the plan into law in each area. So the local councils became the targets of lobby groups of many kinds, from factory owners and real estate agents through to local Progress Associations, all pushing the local councils into 'development'. In particular it was pressure from local community 'gentrification' advocates which forced out the remaining poor and aberrant populations – Aboriginal people in camps, like the Andersons, or squatters in areas like One Tree Point. When the alternative was new and 'respectable' housing developments, it also undermined the councils' support for the maintenance of the 'green belts'. Much less open land was actually preserved than had first appeared on the Cumberland County Plan in 1949.[11]

Across the whole city, it was the power of established wealth and of emerging industrial power which won out in most cases. One way this was achieved was through the location of zoned 'residential' areas. Once a 'residential' zone had been declared, there could be no factories or commercial premises established within it. While the zones had to be proposed by local councils, the approval had to be finalised by the state government. In the contest between big industrial and middle-class interests, there was virtually no land zoned residential in the working-class south-west of the city. Instead, the vast majority of the approved residential zones were in the wealthier North Shore and Eastern Suburbs areas. This meant that most of the new, large factory developments occurred in the areas where least residential zoning had been declared. From the 1940s into the 1960s, these areas were along the Cooks and the Georges Rivers, concentrating factories in this area.[12] From 1945 to 1965, the proportion of all factories located in the inner city declined from over 68 to 32 per cent, while those in the 'South' region – predominantly Bankstown – increased from 9 to 20 per cent.

This led to major industrial pollution of the air and soil, as well as the river, and severe health hazards for local residents. When the degree of industrial pollution was finally measured in 1971, it was found that the Georges River came second only to the Cooks River in toxicity level and, given its far higher population and longer length, this meant it was overwhelmingly more badly affected than any river in the city.[13]

The demands for raw materials, spurred on by post-war expansion of the modernising city, also damaged the river. Building materials for houses, roads, electricity, transport and other services meant that the river was dredged for sand and its banks quarried for stone. This had a concentrated effect on the Georges River which was seen to have more resources and more 'vacant' space than other parts of the city. Areas which were to become parkland under the Cumberland County Plan and might later have become part of the Georges River National Park, like the Lewis Gordon estate at Picnic Point, were turned over to use for electricity production so that the new houses and factories could all have 'modern' electricity and appliances.[14]

Population pressures were also felt around the Georges River, where both the baby boom and a post-war influx of migrants and rural-to-city migration meant dramatic increases in numbers of people living there. Many of the unskilled migrants were housed close to new factories in army buildings left empty after the end of the war and which were then converted to hostels. Nearby areas were subdivided and converted from farms to housing lots.[15]

With such a sudden expansion, a lack of proper sewage processing and connections led to effluent flowing into the river. By 1959, Bankstown municipality had the lowest rate of houses connected to a sewerage system (only 31 per cent) of any major residential area in Sydney. The sewage came from private homes with septic systems but even more from the major government facilities like the hostels and army bases where frequent overflows and run-off occurred.[16]

These broad government-initiated decisions had a big impact on people living in the area and as well as those moving to it. Yet working people had their own plans, whether they came from the inner city or from the communities along the Georges River itself. These personal and local plans intersected, challenged, collaborated and undermined the grand schemes of the Cumberland County planners and politicians.[17]

Aboriginal people and
a river under challenge

What did these wider changes mean for Aboriginal people who had been living on the Georges River for generations, or for the increasing numbers of them moving in to the city?

The pressures for them were somewhat different from those on working-class white Australians. All country people were faced with rapidly changing rural conditions, with mechanisation reducing bush jobs even while it seemed to be strengthening the rural economy. But Aboriginal workers were often disadvantaged because the least skilled jobs disappeared first. Both country and city Aboriginal people had the same needs as white workers to find jobs to regain the lost years of the Depression and the war. Yet on top of the search for work, Aboriginal people in the country areas were bitterly disappointed with what they had hoped would be a new, more democratic world after the war. Instead, the modern innovations like swimming pools and picture shows were actually only ensuring more effective segregation. It was turning out to be far easier to control entry to the talking theatres than outdoor picture shows, just as it was easier to keep people out of fenced municipal swimming pools than off the unruly river banks.[18]

In response to all of these pressures, many Aboriginal people began moving towards the cities to seek out jobs in the new factories which the post-war world was offering and the better, more modern housing which the cities were supposed to allow.[19] Many came to inner-city Sydney, into suburbs like Redfern, Alexandria and Balmain where there had been some Aboriginal people living over many decades in older and low rental houses.

There was lots of work around too, as the newcomers were finding. Those people already in the city were able to establish themselves in steady work as the factories multiplied and expanded. Young Tom Williams, now living at La Perouse, was one of the many who were able to do this, and he began his early work career at Boral, the British oil refining company on Botany Bay, where he worked for many decades. There were other Aboriginal workers there too and they were part of the company's social activities which formed a common part of post-war industrial management. They were even able to assert their Aboriginal identity, as this photo (overleaf) of Tom Williams suggests.

At the same time, the government had decided it would use the growth in city jobs to develop new strategies to change Aboriginal people's behaviour so that they would become more acceptable to conventional Anglo-Australian society. Such policies in the 1940s involved intensifying the surveillance and interference in Aboriginal people's lives – by increasing 'inspections', on and off government-managed 'reserves' and by continuing threats to remove their children. Then in the 1960s, policies changed again, shifting the management of many Aboriginal-related services like housing into mainstream organisations but in a way which focused even more on Aboriginal people by separating them from each other. These policies aimed to disrupt their sense of collective identification as Aboriginal, and subjected them to constant scrutiny and judgment about how well they were meeting the requirements to be 'respectable' and 'just like white people'.[20]

Aboriginal people were trying to chart their own ways through

Tom Williams (right) with Roy
Simon playing gum leaves alongside
workmates in the Boral Jazz Band's
performance for 2UE in
the 1950s.

the maze of changing conditions, yet were often caught up in these policy shifts in erratic and unexpected ways. Many of these Aboriginal people came to the Georges River either directly or from the inner-city, where rising rents were forcing people to move. Out on the Georges River, however, they found they had to deal with heavier government policies at the same time as living on an increasingly poisoned river. For them, 'community' had to be created all over again.

The industrialisation of the Georges River had direct effects for Aboriginal people. The invasion of the remaining Aboriginal spaces, beginning during the war, was to continue. The military establishments were not dismantled – as had been promised to the Hill 60 people – but were instead turned over to become temporary low-income hostel housing, which was what happened at Herne Bay. Land was needed rapidly to build cheap hostels for factory workers and immigrants, and it was gained in part by expanding further still, which meant displacing the few remaining independent Aboriginal communities. This takes us back to Holsworthy and Voyager Point, at the intersection of Williams Creek and the middle Georges River, the land which Jonathon Goggey had fought to save for his family in 1857.[21]

After his 1857 petition to stop white neighbours forcing them off their land at Voyager Point, no further correspondence with government seems to have survived. But no records did not mean that nothing was happening. Goggey must have been successful in defending the land against the pressure from his neighbour across Williams Creek, because there was also no record of 'improvements' on the land. There had been no attempt to alter the title from the original large grant given to Lieutenant Williams, and there had never been any subdivision. Although the blocks to the east and south were gradually broken up into two or three smaller blocks, Portion 53 – as Goggey's block was now designated by the Lands Department – remained unchanged.[22]

Jonathon Goggey's family was not the only Aboriginal family

around Holsworthy. Further upstream, Lucy Leane was establishing her farm with her husband William, beginning the large family with whom they would share their lives into the twentieth century. At about the same time as Lucy was making her claim on the Aborigines Protection Board for a boat to trade along the river, in 1893, her son Edmund was marrying Ellen Pike, from another local family, and apparently settling around the Liverpool area like some of his brothers and sisters.[23] Edmund and Ellen had a large family too, and their children, sharing Edmund's Dharawal heritage, also continued to live in the area, no doubt in contact with the other Leanes and Pikes from both sides of the family. One of their children, however, moved further way: their son Leslie married Edna Kennedy at Chatswood and so established a hub of this large family on the northern side of the Harbour. Some seem to have stayed around Liverpool. In this way, the wider community networks of Dharawal people who would have known about Goggey's land, and the group of people living on it, would have been extended among Aboriginal people all over the area.

Rumours circulated that this land had been set aside as an Aboriginal reserve and these appeared to be confirmed by the continued presence of Aboriginal residents.[24] These rumours would have seemed even more likely to be true after the government established the Aborigines Protection Board in the 1880s. In many other areas along the coast and to the west of Sydney, the Board actually did respond to Aboriginal demands to classify the Crown land on which they were living as reserved for the use of Aborigines. Yet by the early twentieth century, Voyager Point had become more of a backwater than it had been early in the nineteenth century when shipbuilding and quarry work occurred on the river and agriculture close by. By the 1920s, the area had declined economically, with the point itself becoming quiet and undisturbed. Certainly, Portion 53 itself, with its substantial areas of mangroves and swamp as well as wide flat areas along the saline river frontage, did not prove attractive enough to invite any further attempts to subdivide it. So Aboriginal families seem to have continued to live there undisturbed.[25]

When the Trainer family purchased Portion 68, the block on the eastern side of Portion 53, the new owner took his son Ted to visit the neighbours, and they found at least one Aboriginal home on the Williams block. (Ted Trainer has continued to live on Portion 68, which runs along the Georges River to Pigface Point, where he has developed an extraordinary teaching site to demonstrate socially and environmentally sustainable strategies for cities.) Ted vividly remembers the neighbour's house on Williams Creek and has a clear memory of the Aboriginal woman who lived there standing in the door of one of the houses as he and his father walked up to introduce themselves.[26] We know from government inspectors a few years later that there were five homes on the block, described as 'very old shacks', and a small cultivated area of 7 acres (2 hectares) with about fifty trees in an orchard.[27] We have no details of other residents or of this woman's name, but Ted's meeting with her confirms that Goggey's family and then the Aboriginal community network had not only won that battle in 1857 but sustained their relationships to that corner of the Georges River ever since. This was about to change.

Defending
Goggey's land

Although the war had not shifted the Aboriginal people on Goggey's land directly, it brought the army right up to the southern boundary fence of Portion 53 when the Commonwealth expanded the Holsworthy base in 1943. They remained there in fact until 1949, but this was when the final axe fell. The war was over, but the battle to industrialise the city had just begun. For this the Commonwealth urgently needed housing for factory workers, and in particular the thousands of European migrant workers it hoped to recruit from among the displaced people left by the war. The new Army huts at the Holsworthy base were expected to be adequate to provide one of the many hostels for migrant workers which would be needed. Yet when the Department of Works and Housing inspected the site, they realised there was not enough flat land to allow for rapid and, above all, cheap construction which would 'accommodate considerable numbers of migrant workers in this locality'.

The solution, so the Commonwealth decided, was simply to resume all of Portion 53 because at least some of its area was flat land. As the secretary of the Department of Labour and National Service wrote to the Department of Immigration in February 1949, after inspecting the sites:

> The prime considerations in this programme are speed and economy. Wherever possible, the Department of Works and Housing propose to lay down bitumen based floors by grading and preparing level ground on a more or less mass production continuous process which will save time and vast quantities of timber. Only part of the land already made available by the army lends itself to this process, and the 100 acres in Portion 53 will be ideal for the extension of the scheme.[28]

Not only did the Commonwealth know of the common belief that this was an Aboriginal Reserve, but it was also aware that this area had been zoned 'Green Belt' in the Cumberland County Plan as the New South Wales government had prohibited it from being subdivided into blocks smaller than 2.5 acres (1 hectare).[29] As well as acting to undermine these constraints, this resumption decision would mean displacing all the families living on Portion 53, even though the government only wanted the part of the block which was flat.

Nevertheless, the Commonwealth agreed that the migrant workers' hostel was their priority. The Department of the Interior issued compulsory acquisition orders, informing the startled residents that, although the owners would be paid for their land, they had to vacate the property. The problems with this were that the people living there already did not want to move and that the title of Portion 53 was completely unclear – except that it did not in fact reside with the Aboriginal occupants in any formal sense. Implacably, the Commonwealth moved to establish what it called a 'fair price' for the land and to identify the owners so it could pay up and get on with its 'mass production' laying of bitumen.

Then in May 1949 the managing authority, the Migrant Workers' Accommodation division of the Department of the Interior in Sydney, received a visit from Joseph Henry Pike, who had been identified as 'one of the possible owners' of Portion 53. Joe Pike was beginning his tough battle to win back this land, in an echo of Goggey's battle 90 years before. The details of this 1949 conversation and the many others which followed are scanty: the documents never reveal specifically whether Joe Pike was Aboriginal or not. His name is not well known among Aboriginal people in the area today, but there are fragments of memory and documents which allow parts of the puzzle to be pieced together.

When Lucy Leane's son Edmund married Ellen Pike in the 1890s, he brought the Pike family into the Dharawal network. They may have been Aboriginal or maybe they were not. Yet whether her siblings were Aboriginal or not, Ellen Pike's children *were* Aboriginal and her Pike nephews and nieces were her children's cousins. One of Ellen and Edmund's sons married in Chatswood in 1927.[30] When Joe Pike was forced off the Williams Creek land in 1949 and had to search for shelter, he found it at an address on the eastern edge of Chatswood – suggesting he may have had family there with whom he could stay.[31] From a different source altogether, Fran Bodkin, a member of the Perry family in the Liverpool Dharawal community, who was born in the 1940s, remembers an uncle with the surname Pike although she was very young when she met him. All of this suggests strongly that Joe Pike was Aboriginal or closely identified with the Aboriginal community. Could Joe Pike have been the partner of the Aboriginal woman whom Ted Trainer remembers seeing as she stood in her doorway in 1941. Was she the member of the Perry family who was married to a Pike?[32] Whether he was Aboriginal or not, Joe Pike's increasingly passionate correspondence with the government suggests a man who deeply identified with this place and who, by 1954, had repeatedly called it 'my land'.

The Department ordered compulsory acquisition on 7 December and began surveying. Pike however was not dissuaded. He protested about the compulsory acquisition in May 1950, and then formally requested the return of a portion of the land in May 1951.[33] He held little hope by then of reversing the Commonwealth's acquisition and so now offered to buy a 15-acre (6-hectare) segment of Portion 53 along Williams Creek: 'I wish to make application to retain or buy the low-lying portion of the above mentioned land'. The area Pike identified on his sketch map was north of the fence line for the migrant workers' hostel, running along the bank of Williams Creek and on to its junction with Harris Creek as if flowed to the Georges River. Much of the 15 acres Pike was prepared to buy was covered in swamp.[34]

Within a few weeks, however, he realised he had forgotten to indicate how he would access the land, which was surrounded on two sides by water (Williams Creek and Harris Creek) and on the other sides by what was now Commonwealth-owned land. In his next letter he requested permission to have a right of way to and from 'my land'.[35] This letter was annotated within the department with 'R[ight] of Way appears to traverse Hostel area'. The Taxation Office valued the land Pike wanted, including the easement, at a 'fair market price' of £635. This was just under half the initial 1949 valuation of £1600 for the whole 100-acre (40-hectare) property, which had included the 'flat land' which the government actually wanted. This would have been

Joseph Pike's sketch map of the land he wanted to reclaim after the compulsory acquisition at Voyager Point. The part he identifies is the same area where Ted Trainer remembers meeting an Aboriginal resident in 1941 and is where Jonathon Goggey and his family were living in 1857.

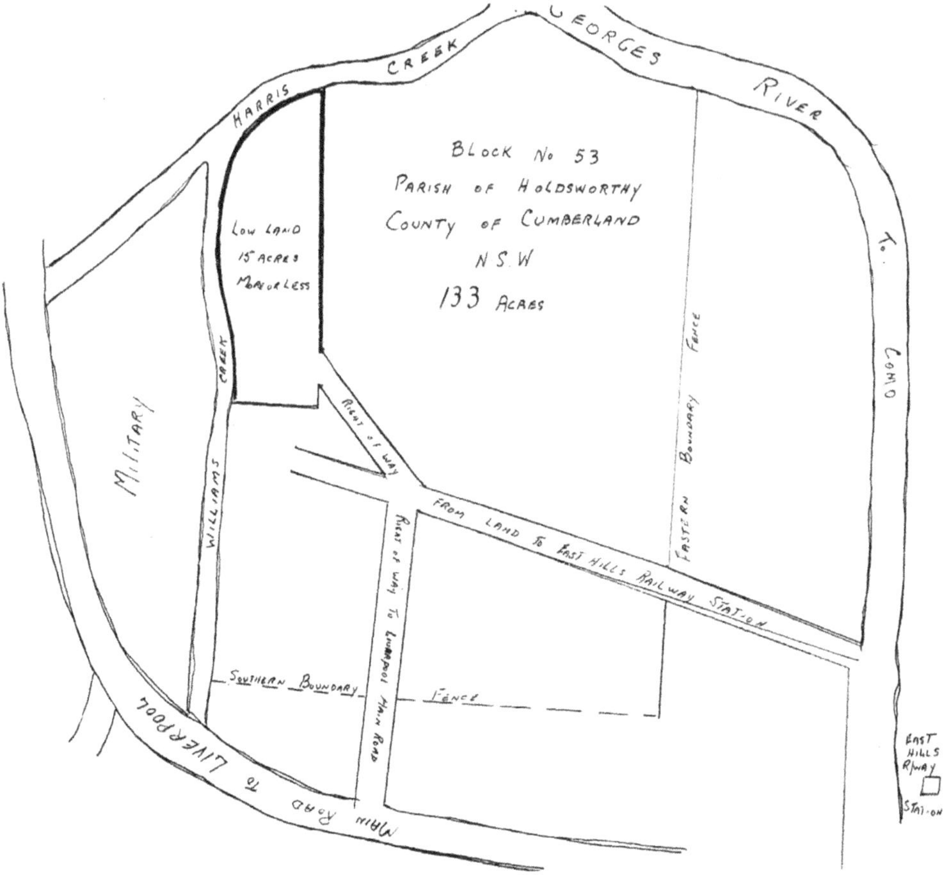

BLOCK No 53
PARISH OF HOLDSWORTHY
COUNTY OF CUMBERLAND
N.S.W
133 ACRES

LOW LAND
15 ACRES
MORE OR LESS

paid as the 'fair price', had it been able to identify an owner. In 1951 however the Taxation Office appeared to be prepared to approve the sale at the amount of £635. Yet the Department of the Interior decided that a right of way across the hostel property was not acceptable. In December 1951 it refused Pike's request.[36]

Pike made one final attempt in 1954. He had clearly been watching the developments on the land and in a moving letter he argued his case:

> Re my land acquired by the Department of the Interior
> 20.5.50, Block No. 53. Georges River and William's Creek
> Holdsworthy [sic].
>
> I made application on the 29.5.51 to purchase the low portion of the land, my application was not approved by the Department of the Interior.
>
> I again wish to make application for the same portion of my land, or any other portion not required by the Emigration Department.
>
> I don't think the portion I wish to have will ever be of any use to the Emigration Department as it is low lying land, and they seem to be keeping to the high land.
>
> The loss of my land has been a great inconvenience to me, I must have some where to live.
>
> I sincerely hope the Department of the Interior will grant their approval to this application.
>
> Yours faithfully
> Joseph H Pike[37]

The Department did not. Pike must have been saddened to read in its reply that it was perfectly happy to sell him the 15-acre strip he wanted, but was not prepared to allow him to have any right of way from the main roads across the Commonwealth's migrant worker hostel property.[38] This finally ended the long and, to that date, successful struggle

Bert Groves (in uniform) on the
Australian Aboriginal League float in
the May Day parade of 1947, protesting
about the continuing discrimination against
Aboriginal people.

by Aboriginal people to live securely on this bend of the Georges River. It closed a chapter which Jonathon Goggey had opened with such determination in 1857.

But there were many other bends of the river. The other major ways in which the war and the river's industrialisation were linked to Aboriginal people were to have very different outcomes. While the Aboriginal people at Voyager Point seemed to have disappeared without trace, there were many who would not go away. Bert Groves returned from the army after the war to live once again near Salt Pan Creek. He soon found that his army service overseas was treated with contempt because it meant nothing: he was still subject to the patronising exclusions and discriminations of the Aborigines Welfare Act. By 1947 he was so angry that he was appearing in his old army uniform to condemn the Act.

As he became more and more vocal in his protests, he became a major figure in the renewed Aboriginal campaign for civil rights. Before long, he was joined by the many Aboriginal people who had come looking for work and hoping to rent a house among family in the inner city. Instead, they were increasingly pushed out on to the Georges River, ironically filling up the spaces like Goggey's land where Aboriginal people had so recently been forced away.

EIGHT

Herne Bay to Green Valley: Judy's river 1960–1980

It was not only the migrant workers' hostel at Holsworthy which displaced Aboriginal people. The wartime intrusion into Aboriginal spaces continued. At Herne Bay, the US Army hospital huts were simply turned over to the Housing Commission for the low-income hostel once the war ended.

That same hostel, like the one upstream at Hargrave Park, came to be the home of many Aboriginal families who had come to the city from rural areas, hoping to escape the dwindling employment, the poor health and education facilities, and simply the racism of the bush. In only a few short years, the wheel had ironically turned full circle and Salt Pan Creek was once more being populated – rapidly – by Aboriginal people. This chapter and the next will follow one of those families, that of Tom and Sally Smith, and particularly two of their daughters, Judy and Janny (Janette).[1]

Moving to
the city

The Smiths and their three youngest children moved to Sydney from central western New South Wales in 1960. Sally (née May) was from a Wiradjuri family and had married Tom, a white railway worker in Wellington, before the war. While Tom was serving in the army in New Guinea, Sally had lived with her older children close to her relations on Nanima, the long-established Aboriginal reserve just outside Wellington on the Macquarie River.

After the war, Tom, Sally and their growing family had lived in Wellington itself, until Sally suffered two severe strokes, forcing her into a long rehabilitation in which she virtually needed to learn to speak again. With Sally's stroke, life had become harder. All her sisters and aunties rallied around to help look after the children so Tom could keep working. Judy remembers having to transfer from the primary school in town to the frustrating 'special' school for Aboriginal children on the reserve. This school had a far more restricted curriculum, with mixed age groups all being poorly taught in a single classroom. The decision to move to Sydney was forced on the family by the need for better medical care for Sally, but it seemed sensible as well for the children's education and to allow Tom more available employment. Once they arrived, Tom found work in the Corning glass factory on South Dowling Street, Redfern, and was able to begin paying off the home which the family bought in nearby Caroline Street.

Judy came to the city, aged 10, with mixed memories of Wellington. She had a strong awareness of her family's connection to the country at Nanima, as well as having known the frustration of limited schooling there. Judy, her older sisters Kath and Janette and her brothers had each spent much time with relations on the reserve and in the countryside, and especially on the Macquarie River, growing up learning about Wiradjuri land and river history from Sally's parents.

But the family was haunted by the loss of a child to the Welfare Board's removal policy:

> And I can still remember when the family would get together for Christmas dinner there was always one spare place set every Christmas, and I didn't know until I got a little older that my auntie had been actually taken away. And we've just found her after 57 years and it's really sad because all her brothers and sister are dead and her mother and father, there was one brother and he was very sick, he didn't know anyone, he was very old and he died soon after.

In many ways then the legacy Judy brought with her from her Wiradjuri childhood was a mixture of pride and confidence on the one hand and anxiety and frustration on the other.

Although Tom had found work nearby, it was not long before this security dissolved. He had an accident travelling home from work, and the resulting unsuccessful surgery cost him the use of his arm. Now unable to work, Tom could no longer keep up the mortgage payments and the family lost their house. Facing overcrowded living conditions with relations in Redfern, the family had few options but to turn to the new public housing authority, the Housing Commission, which offered them space in the hostel it had established in the old army buildings at Herne Bay.

Herne Bay
in the 1950s

There were many other Aboriginal families living at Herne Bay. Some had come back directly to the Georges River – as Bert Groves had done. Even as his rising political activities took him across the state and then the country, in 1954 he was still giving his address as Lupin Street, just on the edge of the hostel.[2] Others had been drawn into

Sally Smith, (right) with daughters Janny (left) and Judy, and son Johnny and Auntie Rose, at the Wellington Show on the Macquarie River in the mid-1950s.

Judy Chester and Janny Ely family collection

the large-scale relocation of working-class inner-city families through the state's major program of post-war reconstruction. This first stage involved clearing as many families as possible out of the inner city and into temporary public housing hostels like those at Herne Bay or Hargrave Park at Warwick Farm near Liverpool. This process was occurring in tandem with managing the inflow of 'migrant workers' who were also being loaded into temporary hostels in rural and urban areas, with the latter often intended for single men separated from their families, who were supposed to stay in the rural camps. Virtually all of the urban migrant hostels in Sydney were on the Georges River, in places like Chullora, Bankstown Aerodrome, Villawood, East Hills and Heathcote Road.[3]

The pressures on the river during these years were increasing exponentially. As we have seen, infrastructure like sewerage which had been set up hastily to address wartime urgency had been inadequate even then, and it proved even less equipped to deal with longer-term residence by an increasing number of people. With more houses built in Sydney immediately after the war than in the previous 150 years, and a major proportion of them within the Georges River catchment, the backlog of unsewered dwellings in the area spiralled upwards between 1946 and 1956. The only alternatives were poorly functioning septic tanks in unsuitable soil and the continued unchecked dumping of untreated sewage into the river. As late as 1962, and indeed well beyond this, it was the government sites – both military and public housing managed by state and Commonwealth governments – which were pouring the greatest amount of untreated sewage and other liquid waste into the Georges River. Yet the broader picture of failed alternatives, as well as delayed infrastructure, meant the burden of high nutrient load on the river was escalating.[4]

The state government depicted the 'upgrading' of the army buildings to house the new families as the heroic work of building a new society. But the reality was more grim. The migrant hostels have been

Not quite the great Australian backyard: the Herne Bay Housing Commission hostel in 1946.

described elsewhere and there was mutual recrimination about whose conditions were worse, with migrants often feeling that the 'old Australian' public housing tenants had better conditions.[5] But it seems that conditions were appalling for everyone. The hostel at Herne Bay was very similar to Hargrave Park, just up-river at Warwick Farm, with both Anglo and Aboriginal public housing tenants rather than migrants. Robyn Williams, who continued to live at Moorebank in the 1950s, remembers the neighbouring Hargrave Park hostel:

> They were Army huts, only two or three metres between them and roads between were just dirt. In the rain it was all mud … they would go for miles, the huts, and nowhere for kids to play. Nothing, except on the bank between the end of huts and the Cabramatta Creek.[6]

John Lennis was at Herne Bay as a child in the mid-1950s.[7] He remembered the one- or two-bedroom flats inside the long huts, so cramped that although the families would eat and sleep in there they tried to do everything else outside. Kids felt such constraints in particular ways: you couldn't play loudly outside without disturbing other families. Some kids would get into the ceiling crawl-spaces and run along the whole length of the huts – but that would earn you a whack. John recalled that even running up and down along empty hut verandahs was likely to get you into trouble because the huts were so close that the noise echoed into everyone's rooms. John remembered that in such close quarters, everyone knew everyone. This was a bonus for kids, it had a sense of comfort: it meant you ate dinner with the family of whichever friend you were playing with each evening and when you got home your family didn't have to feed you. John remembered that the food would be gone by then anyway. But it had its disadvantages too: 'Nobody was an individual. You belonged to the collective.'

In the wider area, the kids from the Housing Commission hostels were picked on – and it bred a fierce loyalty: 'The housing commission kids stuck together – we were looked down on as scum'. The rapid imposition of thousands of inner-city families into the hostels along the already poorly resourced working-class suburbs of the Georges River led to tensions which flared up in the hostility and name-calling that the hostel kids had to face. The hostel was regarded as bringing an 'unsavoury' reputation to the area, and by 1958 the local progress associations had succeeded in having the suburb renamed 'Riverwood' in an effort to dissociate themselves. Yet the old name kept hanging around: very few of the Aboriginal people we interviewed called it anything other than 'Herne Bay', no matter how recently they had lived there.

Children
and the river

The place these children went for a real escape was the river. Many of the remaining bushland areas along the Georges River had become parks under local government control by the 1940s. After much local campaigning, some of these were gathered into one and named a 'National' Park in 1961, but this remained firmly under the local control of a Parks Trust. There were no changes to the parks' accessibility, which remained much as it had been for Ellen Anderson in the 1920s – although the overall bushland area was being reduced by encroaching residential subdivision. Interestingly, none of the Aboriginal people interviewed for this study talked about using the National Park, although they moved freely through it to get to the water. But they all remember the river!

John Lennis has memories of swimming spots along the Georges River itself, like Revesby Beach, Lambeth Street, East Hills and Picnic Point. Despite the rising concerns about pollution in the river through the 1950s and 1960s, the Aboriginal people coming onto the river were not well informed about its problems. But they posed a major challenge to people who had come from country rivers where the water still ran freshly. The Georges River was increasingly showing the burden it was carrying – the wire netting around the swimming enclosures was pulled down, the water in the creeks looked dirty, and often it simply stank. Yet children in particular were still eager to be in the water. There was a footbridge across to what many, including John, remember as the East Hills 'refugee hostel' on Portion 53 at Voyager Point and to the Holsworthy Army base. This bridge was a good place to jump off into the river below.

Salt Pan Creek was used less for swimming, but it was where they would go for crabs, prawns and fishing. John remembers older people warning kids against swimming in Salt Pan, although he was unclear about their reasons. He later put it down to its importance as a fish breeding spot, because he remembers it as so important for fishing and gathering. His family took fishing in the river there very seriously. His father taught him fishing along all this length of the river and creek – showing how to throw some fish back in, not only if they were small but even the good sized ones who could be breeding. But he also remembered the kids did end up swimming in the creek, and his memories line up with others. As he explained it, 'Georges River was the playground'. For many, Salt Pan Creek as well as the surrounding river offered a way to escape the pressure of the hostel.

Even into the 1970s Jason Groves, Bert Groves' grandson, remembers the river for the pleasure it offered in fishing, gathering and even sometimes for swimming.[8] It is not clear, however, how much of the river's catch was actually eaten. Bert was still living there in the 1970s, and Jason remembers Salt Pan Creek fondly as:

a place where I grew up when I was a kid, and did most of my exploring and playing and catching crawchie or yabbies in the creeks. Also we used to catch ducks as well … being young Koori kids, we basically had free range to run amok, and enjoy life and experience ourselves and our culture. And a lot of that stemmed back from growing up on Georges River.

Jason was born in Bankstown Hospital in 1970 and his family was in the hostel they still called Herne Bay until he was three or four, when they moved to Panania. But he still had relations living in Herne Bay, so it remained:

> always a point of picnics and family gatherings and stuff like that. And from Herne Bay obviously there's Salt Pan Creek. There's Revesby. We used to call it Revesby Beach. The bottom of River Road on Georges River. There was a massive parkland, a play area for us kids. And massive amounts of exploration spots.[9]

The experience for girls may have been different if they had less freedom than boys, but the river was still a key memory. Judy and Janny Smith had only recently come from a Wellington childhood, in which the Macquarie River at Nanima had played a large part. Arriving at Herne Bay in 1960, Judy found she enjoyed the challenging syllabus at her new school at Beverly Hills, but the hostel itself was cramped and restrictive. Both girls found the creek at the back of the hostel was a welcome space to get away from the crowded hostel and to begin exploring this new place: 'we swam in the river at Nanima, we swam in Salt Pan Creek and we swam in Liverpool weir – we were *river* girls!'

Like the boys, they have no memories that the bush they were using to get to the river was National Park. They tried to ignore the pollution in the water which was becoming more and more evident. Instead, the muddy banks were favourite places to play. Just as interesting were the mysterious underground tunnels. Like many of the non-Aboriginal kids growing up in the area at the same time, Judy remembers being fascinated by these long tunnels, built during the 1930s, which connected suburb to suburb for a drainage system that didn't in fact function until the 1970s. The kids from the hostel spent long hours exploring these secret tunnels, creating for themselves an underground and invisible geography of their new place. Yet although both Aboriginal and non-Aboriginal children were exploring the river – and the tunnels – in much the same way at this time, there was less of the interaction and shared friendships which are such a feature of the 1920s memories from Salt Pan Creek.[10]

The realities of
hostel living

Judy's memories, however, are mainly of the people in the huts, many of them from Redfern like her own family, such as the Kennys and the Hickeys. She remembers especially well the Buttons, partly because they were such a large family that they were allocated a whole long hut to themselves, but also because they made a point of coming around regularly to help Sally, Judy's mother, in her agonisingly slow recovery.

Faced with the lack of rental accommodation in the inner city and drawn by the promise of a real house in the distant future, these Aboriginal families had all agreed to move to the crowded hostels to wait their turn in the long queues for homes. If they could afford to purchase a Housing Commission house they knew they would only have to wait for four years. If they wanted to rent – as many had no financial alternative but to do – and if they were able pay normal market-level rent, they had to wait six years. But many more were not even in this favourable position. If they needed their rent subsidised, they faced a wait of eight years or longer. So the crowded hostels, which might have had few real advantages over the inner-city slums from which families had been moved, were nevertheless home for the duration.[11]

The developing suburbs around Salt Pan Creek were rife with class and factional disputes. Although there had been examples of friendships across racial lines in the 1920s and 1930s,[12] the suburban middle-class interests which had forced the Andersons out late in the 1930s had only been strengthened by winning the local battles to wind back the Green Belt in the 1950s. So the initial placement and then the growth of the Housing Commission hostel at Herne Bay was not welcomed by the progress associations and others.[13] Name-calling did not end after the re-naming of the suburb Riverwood in 1959. Aboriginal residents of the hostel, like John Lennis in the 1950s and Judy in the 1960s, remember their home being called 'Hoon Bay' – it was rarely even Herne Bay, and never Riverwood. They were very aware of the stigma clinging to hostel residents throughout the area.

As the hostility intensified, the Smiths received an unexpected escape offer. They had only been in the hostel for two and a half years, and while other families were there for much longer, it was perhaps because of Tom's war service that the family was told in 1963 that they could move. They were eligible for a new and permanent home being built by the Housing Commission on one of their development estates on resumed farming land further away from the inner city. The families in the hostel were all eager to get out, so the Smiths didn't raise too many objections to whatever they were offered, but they had to decide between a house in Blacktown, on the Parramatta River, or one in the very new development at Green Valley just to the west of Liverpool – on the Georges River.

'Broken from the group': assimilation and the Housing Commission

The Smiths had to make their decision in a context which was very different to that today. By the 1990s, there were such substantial concentrations of Aboriginal people in areas like Blacktown and Mount Druitt that it was easy to assume that these far western areas were the only centres of Aboriginal residence in the city apart from the most easterly areas of the inner city and La Perouse. This was not, however, the early pattern of the changing urbanisation in the post-war period. Although these Aboriginal communities in western Sydney had their own long history, in the 1950s and 1960s many people from the inner-city Aboriginal populations and from rural areas moved instead towards the Georges River and Liverpool. These places already held a nucleus of similarly long-established populations and were closer to the inner-city areas in which rural Aboriginal families had initially settled.

This is clear from the movements of the Herne Bay families. Many who had first come under pressure to move from the inner city out to suburban Housing Commission accommodation had gone first to the Georges River hostels like Herne Bay and Hargrave Park. Their next move was still on the Georges River which allowed them to maintain at least some of their developing social networks when they went into the public rental houses being built on the huge Housing Commission estate at Green Valley. Some went later to the public housing estates offered even further up river, at Campbelltown and Macquarie Fields, heading south rather than west, and in doing so maintaining geographic and community connections along the Georges River.[14]

These Aboriginal moves into public housing, although often unavoidable, came at a high cost. The Housing Commission, although it had initially focused its offers of homes towards 'white' Australian low-income families and to migrant workers, had begun to offer homes to selected Aboriginal families from early in the 1960s – as public pressure mounted to 'assimilate' Aborigines into the wider population. This was only after the Aborigines Welfare Board had attempted to settle Aboriginal families in mainstream accommodation in rural towns. The Board's attempt at 'assimilation' in rural areas had foundered in the 1950s because white landowners and real estate agents acted in concert to block attempts at housing Aborigines away from Aboriginal reserves.[15]

The State Housing Authority had, since its formation in 1941, adopted stringent and intrusive moralistic criteria into their selection process for white low-income applicants to ensure only 'respectable' and deserving families received the limited number of houses it had to offer.[16] The state government increasingly 'mainstreamed' Aboriginal housing into the wider housing programs, applying similar tests of morality and respectability to Aboriginal applicants. This operated to enforce severe cultural change, demanding families isolate themselves from their communities and turn away relatives who might come seeking short-term accommodation.

When Aboriginal families were first offered homes by the Housing Commission in 1962, they were spread out, with one family roughly in every two streets – in a strategy called euphemistically the 'salt and pepper' or chequerboard approach. State intervention into Aboriginal lifestyles through housing escalated even more rapidly in 1969 with the 'Homes for Aborigines' program. More homes were set aside for Aboriginal recipients, but they were still carefully isolated from other Aboriginal housing, scattering the Aboriginal families widely apart throughout the new suburbs.[17]

In 1962 the Aborigines Welfare Board proudly showcased the new access to Housing Commission accommodation for Aboriginal families, who were being directed equally to Green Valley as well as to the far western suburbs like St Mary's. 'Four Aboriginal families', the Board boasted, had been selected 'to be the models in a new phase of assimilation'.[18] The Welfare Board went on to argue that it was bringing families currently resident in rural areas to the city – although much of the evidence of memory suggests the families involved were already in the city, having earlier made their own decisions about heading for urban conditions.

The key goal, as far as the Board was concerned, was to isolate these families from their communities:

The purpose of this experiment in success, however, is to establish for the Aborigines themselves that they can break away from the group when opportunity opens to an entirely new and stimulating atmosphere.

The Board wants these families to show the way out of the social inertia which so often envelops groups of Aborigines on the fringes of our community, in places where there is little work or hope for them … This is perhaps the most important test of our policy of assimilation: that the aborigine broken from the group is fully assimilable given the self-respect that comes with a good job, a good home, the example of those around him, a awareness of his social responsibilities and reasonable hope for the future.[19]

This moral pressure on Aboriginal families to 'lead the way' by cutting themselves off from their communities was an attempt to obscure the fact that the rural rehousing attempts had foundered only because of hostile white residents' refusals to co-operate in land sales throughout the 1950s.[20] There were clearly very different agendas motivating Aboriginal families on the one hand and government departments on the other. This government view of Aboriginal families who were moving into Housing Commission homes in the mid-1960s was completely at odds with the way Aboriginal people themselves remembered their own goals.

The personal experiences
of assimilation

The Smith family was just one example of these very different Aboriginal perspectives, and the decision that Tom and Sally Smith faced was a difficult one. Yet with no financial alternative to public housing, they had to make a choice. Blacktown had a terrible reputation in the press at the time, Judy remembered, of having 'too many Bodgies and

Widgies' – referring to post-war youth gang culture. In the end her parents made their decision based not only on their familiarity with the Georges River but because they thought it was going to be 'too rough' for their kids at Blacktown. So they chose Green Valley. Little did her parents realise, Judy laughed, that Green Valley was 'as rough as any area you could ever move to'. And perhaps if they had seen the way the land development had taken place, they would be been less confident in their choice.

Robyn Williams was a teenager living at Moorebank near Liverpool through the 1950s and early 1960s, and she had watched the neighbouring estate at Green Valley take shape. The Housing Commission transformed the former dairy farming area, selling off the rich topsoil and leaving the area bare:

> It was just left with just clay! And then they built houses on the clay for all these people that were put out of places like Herne Bay at Peakhurst, Hargrave Park at Warwick Farm. A lot of Aboriginal people lived in those places because there was no housing. And then they built Green Valley and moved the people from those places, Herne Bay and that, into there.
>
> But there wasn't even a blade of grass or any topsoil left. And you know what clay's like when you walk on it? It sticks to your boots. So people would have all this clay on their boots. And they were stuck out in the middle of nowhere. There was no transport – I mean, they wouldn't do it now. The places today come all lawned and gardened and top soil and turf.
>
> But then people were just stuck out there with all this clay and you couldn't grow anything except roses – no backyard gardens. Roses are all you grow in clay. Who could afford roses in those days?[21]

The Smiths moved to Eureka Crescent in Green Valley soon after in 1963, when Judy was 13. They lived in a rental house just a few streets away from the McLeods – one of the 'model' families installed there by the Board in 1962. The Smiths found that apart from the bare house, there was absolutely nothing: no public transport, no shops, no community services and just scoured infertile land.

But these were not the most powerful memories for Judy. What angered her was the isolation forced on individual Aboriginal families by their separation from other Aboriginal peoples' homes, which had been placed no closer than two streets apart. Even worse was the treatment of the family once their neighbours realised they were Aboriginal. Judy felt it most keenly on behalf of her mother. Still sick, Sally was almost a recluse, and yet the family was met within weeks with a hostile petition from their neighbours:

> I didn't like my white neighbours, that's the reason I became
> political. When we first moved in, Mum never left the house.
> But we were only there two weeks and they had a petition
> out to say that she was going to bring the value of the houses
> down. There were Two-Pound Poms next to us! And everyone
> was RENTING! Everybody in Eureka Crescent was in public
> housing and they still had a petition out!
>
> Dad told us to laugh it off – he said 'You OWN this country!
> Don't worry about them other fellas out there!'
>
> There was two people in the street that didn't sign it,
> and that was the people that lived on the other side who were
> Catholics – quite nice people – and there was a man up the
> road who I found out a few years later was Aboriginal. And
> he said to me he wouldn't have signed it even if it had been
> against a white family – 'You just don't do that! We're all
> WORKING class!'[22]

For Judy, her sister and brother, the racial tensions in high schools posed as much of a problem as those within the housing estate. Judy had been happy in her two years at Beverly Hills High while she lived at Herne Bay, but she found her experiences in Bonnyrigg High and Ashcroft High to be either unwelcoming or deterred by the hostility of

Sally Smith with Janny (left),
Judy, now taller than her older sister,
and Johnny, just after they moved into
the Housing Commission Estate at
Green Valley in 1963. Note the barren
landscape with only a few remaining
trees in the newly constructed
estate streets.

Judy Chester and Janny Ely family collection

some teachers who demonstrated contempt for her Aboriginal background. This was a recurrent problem for the family: with a non-Aboriginal father and some children fairer than others, assumptions were often made by teachers and others that the family was white. This made their racial hostility even more evident when the family's Aboriginality became apparent. Judy was angered by having to deal with such fluctuating attitudes: she'd felt that although she didn't 'yell it from the balconies or let everyone know' about her Aboriginal identity, she had 'always taken on the issues at school'. And, as she pointed out, 'I'd be too scared to deny my Aboriginality, my mother would have killed me!'

At the same time, Aboriginal people also had to deal with the stigma – from both Aboriginal and non-Aboriginal people – against those Aborigines with white partners. There were many avenues for this issue to be discussed at the time, including films beginning to come from the United States with underlying civil rights themes. Judy remembers her mother and aunts 'seeing *Imitation of Life* about 30 000 times'. It was a disturbing film released in 1959 about the pain an African-American mother faced when her daughter, with fair-colouring, repudiated her.

> That movie was on for a week in Wellington and my Mum and
> my aunties went in on the bus everyday – it was nearly eight
> miles into town – and saw that movie and came out crying
> every day … They wouldn't let us walk two paces in front or
> two paces behind them – they were frightened that we were
> ashamed of them!

To add further to these problems of interactions with the surrounding white communities into which they had been scattered, families like the Smiths had to cope with the intrusive surveillance of the Housing Commission itself, which was constantly evaluating Aboriginal families' 'respectability' and 'suitability'. Aboriginal people who lived in Housing Commission homes frequently remember feeling intense pressure, not only because Commission staff could visit day or night to inspect and directly criticise. They also feared their white neighbours were watching them too, on behalf of the Commission, and were always eager to report them if they 'lapsed'.[23]

Ruby Langford was just one of the many Aboriginal people like the Smiths who lived in a rented Housing Commission house in Green Valley during the 1970s. She had waited ten years, and once she had moved in, she felt the intense isolation of the commission's policy of separating Aboriginal families: 'I used to die to see another black face like mine. I got so lonely, I'd keep coming back to the city, to Eveleigh Street [in Redfern], to see my daughter and friends.' Ruby too felt constantly under surveillance from neighbours, whom she suspected to be reporting any visitors staying overnight and any rowdy children 'misbehaving' in the backyard. Her children had a difficult time at school too, with her young son feeling discrimination and being constantly challenged to fights 'because the kids were ganging up on him'.[24]

Charlie Leon: making community

Not all the relationships with white neighbours were so negative for the Smiths and other families. As Judy had pointed out, no-one at Green Valley had much of anything at all, and there were no civic services for anyone, black or white. Bonds with working-class whites strengthened as families struggled to provide social and community structures for their children. Sporting teams, for example, became an important meeting ground. It was the hard work of many residents of Green Valley, white and black, in the tuck shops and raffle drives to support the sporting teams in which their children were playing, which slowly began to build up a sense of community after all.[25]

Yet there were two important ways in which Aboriginal families in Green Valley began to emerge *as* Aboriginal, despite the pressure of the Housing Commission and the Assimilation policy. Firstly there were the growing networks between them which were built up by their own attempts to find their own people, in defiance of the state's policy of isolating Aboriginal families. This was done informally, as people found their way around the streets and schools, but some people took key leadership roles.

The person most often and most fondly remembered in this regard is Charlie Leon, who had been one of the people living at the Salt Pan Creek camp in the 1920s. He had been born in Forster and lived in Taree in the 1920s, until he left to be first a labourer on the Cotter Dam near Canberra. He then travelled with his vaudeville troupe, living in Salt Pan Creek when he was in Sydney. Leon became involved in the 1920s Australian Aboriginal Progressive Association with Fred Maynard and others from the north and south coasts. He remembered, when few others did, that Maynard had been influenced not only by union ideals but by his contact with the calls for African American unity and activism of Marcus Garvey in the United States.[26] Then during the Depression, Leon worked as a travelling showman, organising a vaudeville troupe called 'Leon's Entertainers'. But he had continued his political activity by connecting up with Bill Ferguson and the Progressive Association.[27]

Over these two decades, Leon had travelled widely, learning about conditions in many different types of rural areas as well as in cities. He worked on the wharves in Tasmania and in other jobs where he had intensive contact with unionists and political activists. His convictions led him to join the Communist Party and although he left it 1958, he continued close friendships with many party members like Helen Hambly.[28] He attributed his political determination to his experience in both Aboriginal and Communist politics: 'They taught me that if you stood up and fought hard you would win in the end'.[29]

Charlie Leon, in 1974,
during his period as elected
Aboriginal representative on the
Welfare Board and later the
Advisory Board.

Leon and his wife Peggy had settled in Sydney by the 1950s and were living either on or near Herne Bay, using Riverwood as their postal address. They continued to be in close contact with other activists including Bert Groves, to whom Charlie was related by kinship as well as by political ties. In the mid-1950s, Groves invited Leon to join the Aboriginal Australian Fellowship, initiated by Pearl Gibbs and Faith Bandler not so long before, and Leon succeeded Groves as president of the Fellowship in 1958.[30] He explained later that he decided then to leave the Communist Party because 'the Fellowship started doing those things that the party was [just] talking about'.[31]

During that decade, Leon and his wife had been active not only in the Fellowship but in wider Aboriginal politics, holding meetings in their home and, when they eventually had a backyard, using it to host fundraising barbeques.[32] In 1960, Charlie Leon stood for and won the 'part-Aboriginal' seat on the Aborigines Welfare Board – previously held by Pearl Gibbs among others – which he held until 1964.[33] After his election to the Board in February 1961, he issued a press statement which was distributed widely to the city and rural press. It included the eight-point program Leon had developed in collaboration with the executive of the Australian Aboriginal Fellowship which set out a clear program demanding an end to legislative discrimination and the achievement of full participation of Aboriginal people in policy, an urgent increase in funding for Aboriginal housing and health, and the encouragement of Aboriginal-controlled co-operatives.[34] His press statement ended with a powerful denunciation of the Assimilation policy as it as being implemented by the Aborigines Welfare Board: 'Finally, I stress that "assimilation" must not mean the scattering of Aboriginal people and the loss of their identity; it must be an integration where they can keep their group identity if desired'.[35]

By the early 1960s, the Leon family had been trying anxiously for some years to move away from Herne Bay, and finally in November 1962, they were offered a home on the housing estate which became

Green Valley.[36] By 1963, Leon was on an aged pension and living in Ashcroft, one of the Green Valley suburbs. Rather than retiring, he escalated his public work, in his role as president of the Australian Aboriginal Fellowship and in his active involvement with bodies like the Co-operative for Aborigines which was based at Tranby in Glebe.[37]

His active role in organising both national and state-wide conferences won him great respect throughout the 1960s. He drew on his wide rural and urban networks to foster situations where, rather than having the Welfare Board or other white officials lecture Aborigines on what they should do, he created opportunities to have Aboriginal voices heard, to have Aboriginal people from all over the state come together to discuss what they wanted.[38]

He also continued to champion the cause of Aboriginal people who were seeking security on land they could call their own, in a home in which they could be secure. In 1969, as the Aboriginal Fellowship voted itself out of existence in favour of the Federal Council for the Advancement of Aborigines and Torres Strait Islanders, he delivered an address to its closing session. After praising the Fellowship's contribution in difficult circumstances, he warned about deteriorating current conditions:

> But, friends, in my opinion the trouble has not started yet.
> Reserves have been taken. The Housing Commission is taking
> over La Perouse ... Judging by the evictions in Green Valley
> alone, this is food for thought. If these evictions occur to white
> people, what chance will Aboriginal people have? ... So we
> can only see shanties going up again on the riverbanks unless
> something is done now. Every Aboriginal would like to own
> his own land and have land reserves restored back to him; this
> is what they want most of all.[39]

Charlie Leon had therefore had a formidable political career, but it wasn't for these public roles that people in Green Valley remember him. Instead, it is for the warmth, effort and patience which he put into finding people, scattered across these new and barren suburbs around Liverpool, and spending time getting to know them and bringing them together. Judy Chester remembers her family's first months in Green Valley in 1963, and how she was able to build up her knowledge of where Aboriginal families were:

> There was this old man, old 'Pop' Leon. Charlie Leon used to go around and make connections with Kooris. He used to come and sit down and talk to Mum for hours about what was happening. You know, Mum actually voted in that board election! – I think she voted for Charlie Leon – but he was wonderful, you know?
>
> And that's one of the ways the word got around that Mum was sick and she couldn't get out. Then Mrs McLeod would just come around and have a cup of tea with her. So did Mrs McKenny and then we found a cousin of ours who lived down Ashcroft, she'd come down every fortnight and bring lamingtons down for Mum.
>
> So there was a lot of little links like that. And they sort of kept each other informed of what was going on. And they weren't political. It was their kids that went on to become political, you know?[40]

There is a revealing photograph taken in a modern home in Griffith during a Welfare Board rural fact-finding trip late in 1963. Leon, as the Aboriginal member, had accompanied the Board's secretary A Kingsmill and politician S Wyatt to visit Aboriginal people. These two white men are standing formally in the middle of a very tidy lounge room, on either side of the clearly uncomfortable Aboriginal housewife and tenant. Leon is relaxed and calm: he can be seen stretched out in a chair to the side, reflecting an easy informality and comfort in his relationships to Aboriginal people in their homes. In another photograph in nearby Condobolin, on the same trip but this time while visiting a tin house on the banks of the Lachlan River, Charlie Leon stands just behind and supportively close to the Aboriginal housewife and resident, while the white officials stand further away and again, more formally.[41] The body language in these photographs echoes the memories Aboriginal people still retell.

Robyn Williams, then still living at Moorebank just to the east of the Georges River and Liverpool, also remembers Charlie Leon's role warmly:

> At first there was just a big mob of our family all around, all
> through Lansvale and place like that. My father's family, the
> Greens, had come down for work. But main person that was
> the most significant influence then was Mr Charlie Leon. And
> I call him Mr Charlie Leon out of respect. Mr Charlie Leon.
> An absolutely amazing man![42]

These developing connections between people, nurtured by Charlie Leon and others, began to shape a new form of Aboriginal community despite the best efforts of the Welfare Board and state government to keep people apart.

Building relationships
with 'new' country

But there was another way in which Aboriginal people resisted the Housing Commission strategy to assimilate them into disappearing culturally into the more general working class. This was to begin to embed their emerging network into the new country into which they had all been thrown.

As 'wild teenagers', Judy and Janny Smith were not too interested in the details of the conversations about the Welfare Board their mother might be having with Charlie Leon, they were just relieved to feel she was no longer so isolated. They were also busy building their own networks.

In this way they met up with the other young people in the area, including the longer-term Aboriginal residents like Robyn Williams and her sisters – the Symes girls. From the 1950s, they had known the weir as a gathering place for young people and a way to explore new – and often exciting – relationships. The sharks made it dangerous to swim in the tidal waters downstream, so the weir allowed safer swimming as well as water that was fresh and deeper than on the tidal side. Robyn remembers the weir as even more a social space for young people who were escaping the surveillance that characterised the small, almost rural community there before the big developments took place:

> I think everybody – just about everybody in Liverpool in those
> days – went to the weir. There was no swimming pool then.
> There was nothing there … Opposite there was the saleyard.
> And every Tuesday there was a cattle auction, chook auction,
> produce auction.[43]

Despite there being 'nothing there', the weir was a rich and exciting socialising space. Many young people gathered there, even after a chlorinated public pools began to appear, because it was an informal and unregulated place for meetings and picnics as well as for more exciting rendez vous. Robyn laughed about the rumours which used to fly around, but 'the weir' was an important site for exploring people and places all around.

By the mid-1960s, once the Housing Commission estate was established, the population had soared and the tensions which had marked the Herne Bay hostel were starting to shape the way Green Valley people were seen and saw themselves. As Judy Smith commented: 'We just called it Dodge City! Or the Valley.'[44] This fragment from an interview with the sisters raises important questions about how the 'modern' city, which the government intended to be such a positive cultural influence, was in fact shaping the lives of the families from 'the Valley':

JANNY We used to walk to Liverpool. The railway line then had a ramp that went up and over and down towards the river side. So we used to walk up and over that and then spend our sixpence we had to get into the pool on hot chips. And then we'd go and swim in the weir!

JUDY All the kids used to swim down there. It was always the biggest mob of people down the weir.

JANNY That's where – if you wanted to meet anyone – that's where you met them, down the weir. We very rarely went to the swimming pool – 'the Baths' – did we? We all went to the weir.

JUDY So we stopped swimming in Salt Pan Creek, and started swimming in the Georges River at Liverpool. We were river girls!

JANNY And we used to dive off the old train bridge that goes through there.

JUDY Yeah. We were always climbing that railway bridge. I used to get splinters all over me.

JANNY And you look at those bridges now and you think, 'I must have been a bloody idiot!'

JUDY An idiot! It didn't seem like it was that high.

HEATHER [19]63? They just closed the river in '62. So did you know you weren't supposed to swim in it?

JUDY Didn't care. We didn't know anything about the environment. We knew there were a lot of factories and that all around that area.

JANNY And it was hot and it was a good place to swim.

JUDY And it was free! It was our little stamping ground. There's nothing much to do when you're poor. When you're poor you've got to make your own fun.[45]

The 'modern' facilities of the Olympic Pool were of little value to these teenagers because, even when they walked across county to Liverpool, they did not have enough money to pay for both pool entry and a snack. The best value they got from modernity was being able to jump off the train bridge. The real impact – pollution of the river caused by the massive sewage contamination from the hostels and new public and private housing developments, as well as the post-war increases in unregulated and toxic factory waste – was not passed on to teenagers. They were outside parental or official control and swam where they liked. In any case, they were much more interested in the excitement of meeting friends and exploring new relationships among their own age group and in seclusion or a party atmosphere, depending on their mood. Overall, the girls were building up a new way to understand the country they had come to: they were, after all, 'river girls'!

NINE

Finding Guragurang: caring for country 1980s

In the 1950s and 1960s, as the city was changing so rapidly, Aboriginal people had faced many pressures as they migrated to and through Sydney. They were pushed into the hostels and low-cost houses of the Georges River where industrial expansion was fastest but resources were least. At the same time, government policy had shifted to trying to separate and isolate Aboriginal families, undermining the very networks of community which might have helped people cope with these pressures of difficult migrancy. As the stories we told in the last chapter show, Aboriginal people responded – as best they could, family by family – by slowly rebuilding the networks between them and by using the environment of the river to find a familiar link to the land. They demonstrate the resilience which led to the re-emerging assertion of Aboriginal people in the city in the 1970s and 1980s.

The question for this chapter is how were those beginnings, those tentative new networks and relationships, put into practice? There was no easy or established pathway through which these Aboriginal people could express their emerging sense of either community or city–land relationships. It would have been much simpler to continue to focus on rural 'homes' than to try to express a new affiliation with urban land. To answer that question, we need to pull together the threads of urban and rural politics in the 1970s and 1980s, because many of them run right through the Georges River.

Linking the city
and the bush

The people themselves reflected the continuing links between urban and rural Aboriginal societies. As earlier chapters have shown, Aboriginal people living on the Georges River by the 1970s could often trace their family affiliations to one or more regional areas. Yet some of these families were also directly linked to the people who had lived on the river before the British came, such as, among many others, the Williams and the Simms families.[1] Others like Charlie Leon and Bert Groves had lived at Salt Pan Creek in the 1920s and 1930s, but still kept in close contact with the places they had come from, as well as those where they had travelled for work or politics. Both had sustained those connections when they were living through the Housing Commission hostel and estate days. Others again, like Robyn Williams, had been born on the river but retained links to rural family who continued to travel backwards and forwards over the mountains.

Then there were the many Aboriginal country people who had come to Sydney in the massive urbanisation from the 1950s and moved, like the Smith family, by force or choice, into those hostels and estates. From there they had continued to see their country families often, travelling to and from the bush and having family and friends frequently visit to keep them up-to-date on the news. And finally there were still more Aboriginal families outside the public housing sector, families who moved independently for jobs in the suburban areas, living in purchased or rented accommodation and staying there often many years before returning home. This was the pattern for many families originally from Brewarrina who during the 1960s and 1970s lived in and around Padstow, on the western side of Salt Pan Creek. They hosted other family members who came to the city for education or short-term work, and they had jobs in the light industries all around the area. Many returned to their home community in Brewarrina as they reached retirement.[2] So for all these people, any sharp distinction between 'city' and 'the bush' was artificial.

An Aboriginal
voice in policy

One of the key leadership roles played by Bert Groves and Charlie Leon through the 1960s had been to express the common anger of both rural and city people in their rejection of government interference and their loss of independent space. Leon had explicitly rejected the Assimilation policy in relation to both housing and land when in 1969 he equated the city evictions by the housing commission with the rural revocations of the remaining reserves.[3]

State policy was developing in two directions by the late 1960s. The New South Wales government was slowly responding to the rising pressure of its constituents to reform the laws which still discriminated against Aboriginal people across the state. Until 1963, Aboriginal people were still excluded by law from a whole range of civil rights, and the legal ban on access to hotels lasted even longer. The de facto segregation of swimming pools and, more importantly, of schools went on until the 1970s.

In 1969 the Aborigines Welfare Board was finally dismantled, in what seemed like a victory for the many Aboriginal voices who had spoken out against its power. It was replaced by the Directorate of Aboriginal Affairs, universally known only as 'the Directorate', which had a greatly cut-down portfolio and far less direct power. The previous Board's real powers, however, had been devolved to 'mainstream' government agencies, and the body which now loomed even more oppressively into most Aboriginal people's lives was the Housing Commission, as we have seen at Green Valley. In practice these changes led to increased pressure on Aboriginal people through housing from one body or the other. There was more 'salt and peppering' from the Housing Commission, for example, and more targeted pressure on rural community leaders to move to the city as the Directorate immediately began its Family Resettlement Program – known universally as 'relocation'.[4]

The Directorate was launched, however, with promises of a new start because it was accompanied by a newly created Aboriginal Advisory Board composed entirely of Aboriginal members. This important breakthrough allowed a number of Aboriginal people who were already active in the community to speak more directly to the State government as it went about formulating new policy. Some of the people who took up positions on the Advisory Board were senior activists, including Charlie Leon. Others were younger but one, like Leon, had close connections to the Georges River. Tom Williams (junior) was by then a community leader at La Perouse. While working at Boral in Matraville,[5] the young Tom Williams had begun to play a role in community life, including in the early years of the Foundation for Aboriginal Affairs, an organisation established in 1964 by Ted Noffs and Charlie Perkins. Funded through donations from eminent members of Sydney's middle class and professional establishment, it offered welfare support and a space to build social networks among Aboriginal people moving into the city in the 1960s. In 1969 Tom Williams also stepped into the role of manager in the foundation when Charlie Perkins left to take up work in Canberra.

As these changes were occurring in the Aboriginal policy area, the state government established its first National Parks and Wildlife Service (NPWS) in 1967. Its brief was to focus on the questions being raised in public debate: the severe pollution in Sydney's industrial environments, like the Georges River; and the need to protect native environments by expanding the National Park system, and using emerging scientific approaches like ecology to manage those parks. The government initially saw these two emerging policies areas – Aboriginal welfare and environmental management – to be completely unconnected, but they soon came to have a direct relationship. Initially the NPWS was concerned only with the protection and management of flora and fauna and, more broadly, of iconic natural environments. This focus on the world was abruptly challenged within months of its formation, when NPWS was given responsibility for the care and protection of Aboriginal relics. The NPWS expected to be conducting strictly scientific surveys and reporting, but its role was significantly expanded in December 1969 when it became responsible not only for the conservation of Aboriginal cultural heritage within its parks' boundaries but also for the management and protection of Aboriginal relics found in sites anywhere across the state.

So by 1970, both the new Directorate and the Aboriginal heritage components of NPWS were in place. Each, for different reasons, was largely directing its attention away from the city and towards rural areas. And there were new pressures developing in the bush as the focus of the popular forms of white Australian recreation shifted to coastal beaches.[6] The secluded sandhills on which Aboriginal people had been continuing to camp had been free of settlers because they were of no interest to farmers and because, before World War II, white Australians had travelled to their holidays by train and spent their leisure-time fishing and boating on rivers, inland from the coastal dunes.[7] The 1960s witnessed dramatic changes in these patterns, as proliferating car ownership revolutionised the family holiday, and

Charlie Leon, here (third from left) at a meeting of the NSW Aborigines Advisory Council. Leon was an active leader in the growing Aboriginal representative bodies of the 1960s and 1970s. He was soon joined by, among others, Tom Williams (second from right, and chair of the council), a fellow Salt Pan Creek activist.

Australians' leisure interests turned from rivers to the surf beaches now made suddenly more accessible.[8]

This was being felt keenly by Aboriginal people who lived in Sydney but came from those coastal areas – like Charlie Leon from Taree. Among these coastal Aboriginal communities, on the other hand, there were people in leadership roles who had grown up on the Georges River. Ted Thomas for example was a man from Wallaga Lake, although he had lived on Salt Pan Creek in the 1920s and had worked on the Warragamba Dam construction in the 1950s. Jacko Campbell too, a Dhungati man from Kempsey on the north coast originally, had lived at Salt Pan Creek in the 1930s and later spent much time on the south coast. He eventually settled down there, marrying Nan, a Jerinja woman, with whom he raised their family at Roseby Park near Nowra. He still stayed in close touch with his Kempsey family, and he travelled constantly up and down to Sydney. So all of them were aware of the way tourism and beach culture was putting more and more pressure on coastal Aboriginal communities. This was giving an urgency in their rising demands for secure tenure over old reserves and traditional lands on the north and south coasts of the State.

Ted Thomas and Jacko Campbell were a generation younger than Charlie Leon and Bert Groves, but they also had sustained close links with the networks of Aboriginal people on Georges River, even as they were fostering community activism over land in their south coast homes. Each became more prominent in the community organisations of the mid-1960s, pushing for recognition of Aboriginal traditional rights to land as well as an end to further revocations of reserves. So rural issues were a high priority in the minds of Aboriginal people in the city because of their own continuing connections and the attention of the new agencies, as well as urgent new pressures.

'Making locality'
in Green Valley

While sustaining their links with rural communities, city people were also becoming more deeply committed to the Georges River land and its communities. This was a common element in expressions of resilience, but how were these Aboriginal people actually making the new landscape meaningful for themselves? How were they 'making locality' in the city?

We can return to the stories of the Georges River families – in particular to the Smith girls Judy and Janny and to Robyn Williams, all living around Liverpool – to follow the process more closely.[9] Each of these three grew up to marry, have children and make adult homes for themselves in the area. Janny moved to nearby Busby, Judy stayed in the family home in what was now called Sadlier, and Robyn moved from her parents' home in Moorebank to Edensor Park near St Johns Park where she had lived as a child.

For each of them as young mothers, the questions about housing continued to be intrusive and oppressive. This was related to the continuing pressure on Aboriginal families through the Housing Commission 'Homes for Aborigines' program and the even more intensive 'relocation'. Both policies tried to push Aboriginal families towards cultural assimilation by making them conform to an imagined working-class culture and separating themselves from the Aboriginal community, including their own family and limiting visitors. It encouraged them to accumulate possessions and keep 'tidy homes' and steady jobs.

There were other sources for this focus on housing, however, particularly in its impact on women. It arose in part from the self-imposed pressures of a wider social conformity to an idea of 'home-making' which, ironically, was exactly what the Welfare Board had tried to impose with its housing schemes. This locked women into providing an unquestioning self-sacrifice for working husbands and school children, even in the poorly serviced conditions of the new suburbs of the Green Valley estate. Janny had married before Judy and moved a short distance away begin to raise her children. Even in 1970, as Judy remembered:

> There was nothing. We had a bus service into Liverpool. That's all. We didn't have a shopping centre at Green Valley, we had a couple of little stores but you had to actually get a stroller and these kids and lug them on this bus into Liverpool. Thank God they had home deliveries for groceries because if you didn't have a car you were up the creek.

Janny was able to have the family car on occasional days, so the two sisters would try to do their shopping in between taking the kids to sports training.

Judy was aware of the pressure on women not only from the surrounding society but from the older generation of Aboriginal women. After Tom Smith died in 1968, Judy's mother Sally lived with her in the family home in Green Valley. 'My life revolved around rearing my kids, looking after my husband and I just accepted that', Judy explained. 'And my mother never questioned it either, she accepted it and she thought that that's what women had to do. And I did, I accepted it for 20 years!' Finally, in very real economic terms, rental housing continued to be in short supply across the city throughout the 1970s, and so these pressures of grim economic reality were never far away from the minds of women caring for young children.

Yet there were also reasons why the Housing Commission goal to 'assimiliate' Aboriginal families did not ultimately succeed. Firstly the society into which the government wanted to make Aboriginal people disappear was not a simple one. Trying to create a community to offer facilities for children in the barren unserviced wastelands of Green Valley was the motive for much of the hard work with both working-class white and Aboriginal families put into the area of Green Valley in its early years. Judy lost track of the numbers of tuck shops and sports fundraisers she cut sandwiches and sold raffle tickets for. She served up tea and soup for endless winter morning games and sat through hours of netball and hockey practices waiting for her kids. In the process she made strong links across the working-class networks of the area, contributing to a rich web of community there which had turned 'Dodge City' back into Green Valley by the late 1970s.

A diverse working culture surrounded people in the Georges River suburbs around Liverpool or Mortdale. In both these areas, long-established Communist Party members and active Labor Party groups had been fostering relationships with Aboriginal people. The large Sydney Youth Carnival in 1952, for example, sponsored by the Eureka Youth League and the Communist Party and attracting many international guests, celebrated the final day of its 100 events by drawing 30 000 people to Hollywood Park in Fairfield, where one of its key items was an Aboriginal talent quest with 30 acts.[10]

One of the people most active in support for Aboriginal causes and left-wing local politics was Dom Syme, by this time an alderman on Liverpool Council, as he continued his battle against the price-fixing of the Egg Marketing Board and on behalf of small chicken farmers. His step-daughters Robyn, Lynne and Wendy were themselves active in a range of left-wing political movements, from the rank-and-file union activism of the Builders Labourers' Federation to local women's movements. Robyn in particular, now married and known as Williams, sustained her links with her Aboriginal relations and wider networks, partly through the connections with the Aboriginal communities of the inner city and south coast with whom she had built alliances in her time as a builders' labourer. She worked with the union's Aboriginal organiser, Kevin Cook, who was from Wollongong originally and was closely related to families who had lived at Hill 60 and Kiama as well as further down the coast.

The other reason the Assimilation goal failed was that the networks of Aboriginal families kept on operating, keeping people in touch with everyone's doings in the city but also back home. As Judy said of these connections: 'It worked for a long time there, even when I had my kids. We still had that little Koori network even when Mum died.'

In this setting, Judy began reflecting on her own sense of belonging in the area. Building on her teenage years at the weir, Judy got to know the area and its people in a deepening way through the proliferating network of places which her children drew her to: sports venues, school performances and children's friends' homes. After a while, she became aware that her feelings about the place had changed from thinking of Green Valley as 'Dodge City':

> I suppose, I didn't really feel connected to it until I had the kids. But see my kids were born and reared there and I thought, 'This is our country, it's where my kids were born'. And then I started getting interested in who lived here before, and how we have to respect the sites and look after that land, and especially when I found out that the whole Gandangara nation was killed off, you know?
>
> I thought, 'Well, there's nobody from that country here to look after it so we as Aboriginal people have to look after this land for them'. I started to try to find out as much as I could about the sites and that in the area, and about the people, because I thought 'This is my kids' country'.
>
> I still have a soft spot for Green Valley.

As her children grew older, Judy became more and more interested in drawing on the networks among Aboriginal families in the area which had their roots in the work of Charlie Leon and others in the 1960s. Many other Aboriginal women experienced the same things – not only building up links with the local non-Aboriginal community but facing continuing racism and hostility – which meant that they valued the continuing links with the scattered Aboriginal families of the wider area.

'We're all strong
independent women now'

Robyn Syme had worked in the activist Builders Labourers' Federation in the early 1970s when it had pioneered the Green Bans movement and had supported Aboriginal housing and land rights demands.[11] After the union was destroyed by government and building company intervention in 1975, Robyn started work for the state government adult education body TAFE, turning for support to Tranby Co-operative College. Her fellow union member, Kevin Cook, had begun working there with the goal of building wider community-based Aboriginal education networks. Robyn's thinking about community learning contributed to the nucleus of a group among older women which she had begun to gather – the St Johns Park Aboriginal women's group.

Initially forming around common needs like organising playgroups, childcare and car pools for school and sport, women like Judy and Janny found in this group the combination of practical support for women looking after families and the inquiring focus on Aboriginality which they had both been missing. Judy's involvement with the women's group increased over the years:

> When all the kids were at school, and they starting growing
> up, then I started getting totally involved in those networks,
> setting up Aboriginal playgroups and things like that. We
> had our own women's group up there and it used to be just
> a pleasure once or twice a week just to get with them Koori
> women, you know. I always made sure I didn't have anything
> else on those days so I wouldn't miss out on it. And I started to
> question all that about just accepting what happened at home
> … started to develop just by hanging around other Koori
> women and I watched them develop … but we all grew up, we
> all developed and we're all strong independent women now.
> There's not one of us that's in an oppressed state any more.

This group drew in Aboriginal women from all over the Liverpool region, and further afield, from around Mt Druitt and Blacktown. They included Ellen James, Tom Williams' sister, and others who had lived either at Salt Pan Creek or at Herne Bay. They had bonds in common, Judy recalled, which related both to the country they had come from, in rural New South Wales or other states, but also to their shared histories on the Georges River and in the places where they now lived:

> When we all started getting together, we all learnt each others names and that and then all of a sudden we just got deeper and deeper, you know? Old Nana Latham came up and said to me: 'Where do you come from?'
> And I said: 'Wellington'.
> She said: 'Who's your mob?'
> And I said: 'My grandmother is a May'.
> And straight away she said: 'You're related to me'. She was my grandmother's cousin, she was a Carney. And she said that she'd been doing research.

As they became more confident, these women began to build up their relationships with the range of local activist groups and particularly those in the women's movement. One organisation they became involved with was the Liverpool Women's Health Centre, which first opened in 1975 and fostered new links between working-class white women's activities in unions and the many immigrant and Aboriginal people who lived in the area.[12] By 1981, the women from the St Johns Park group were marching on International Women's Day through the main street of Liverpool.

Janny Ely organising books and artwork
at the Aboriginal Women's group stall at
the International Women's Day fair in
Bigge Park, Liverpool, in 1981.

Judy Chester and Janny Ely family collection

Education
for change

Robyn Williams was working for TAFE at this time, but had also done some work with the National Parks and Wildlife Service. Increasingly she was able to draw the two together. In 1980 she was organising excursions for Aboriginal TAFE and university students. It was on a course like that this that one of us, Heather Goodall, met her. Robyn took our UTS applied history students along with her Aboriginal TAFE students to a number of places around Liverpool, showing us the traces of interaction as well as the sites of traditional society along the river. She was able to open up a new way for us to see these places, even those of us, like Heather, who had grown up there. The area began to look very different when we became aware of both the Aboriginal history – up to just a few years before – as well as the immigrant perspectives of the Irish, the Italian and the many other groups of the area.

The St John's Aboriginal women's group began to demand education for themselves too, but it wasn't easy. As Judy explained:

> our course got going at Liverpool because Robyn Williams was doing the outreach programs for TAFE back then and she said: 'Well what do you girls want?'
>
> We all said: 'Well we just want a taste of education!'
>
> We'd all been locked up with our kids for years, our self-esteem was down around our bootlaces!
>
> But we had to fight tooth and nail with the Aboriginal Education Consultative Group over that because they said it wasn't accredited! In the end we got it! It was called the Aboriginal Women's 'NOW' program, we were the pilot course.
>
> And now the NOW program is still going, it's for migrant women and for other women … it's just wonderful![13]

To shape the course, the women turned to the Tranby Adult Education Cooperative, especially Kevin Cook. He had by then become the co-op's general secretary and had fostered a number of community education courses, as well as strengthening Tranby College's more formal education programs. Kevin had worked closely with Jacko Campbell in the independent organising body, the NSW Aboriginal Land Council, which had been active since it was formed in October 1976 at a Land Rights conference attended by the many Aboriginal people from all over the state. The St John's Park women wanted some courses in basic skills, but mainly they were hoping to make Aboriginal Studies the centre piece of their program.

And it was here that the women's group became enmeshed directly in the past and the future of the Georges River. Through Tranby, Kevin introduced them to a range of Aboriginal educators like Terry Widders – a linguist from the Anewan community on the Northern Tablelands, then teaching the Aboriginal history of the early British invasion of Sydney at Tranby and at Macquarie University – and anthropologists like David Morrissey, who was already researching land history on behalf of Aboriginal communities.

Most importantly, they met up with Jacko, by then a key member of the Tranby Board. He and Ted Thomas were regular visitors to Tranby when they were in Sydney, and they were eager to take part in the local teaching in the suburban kitchens and community halls where the St John's women's classes were held. They were reactivating their own links as they did so and were able to introduce a whole new way to think about the history of the Georges River to the many Aboriginal people who were now living on it. Judy and Janny remember Jacko's sustained commitment to achieving active Aboriginal control over the places of importance to them, whether or not those places happened to be on land reserved for Aboriginal interests. Above all, Jacko wanted recognition of Aboriginal people's right to be acknowledged as owners and custodians of the land, its stories and its special places. Both the educational and community networks he and others had worked so hard to foster were instrumental in these aims.

Kevin Cook, general secretary of the Tranby Aboriginal Cooperative College, in 1982.

With permission Penny Tweedie: PXA 465 #9, Mitchell Library, State Library of NSW

Jacko Campbell at Tranby College, c 1981.

Tranby Aboriginal Cooperative College

Focus on
land

The New South Wales government had tried to stave off Aboriginal demands in the early 1970s by tinkering with the Directorate of Aboriginal Affairs so it appeared more responsive on the land issue. The Directorate managed the various areas of Crown land across the state which continued to be officially reserved for the use of Aborigines. These were only a small proportion of the land which had been set aside for Aboriginal use by the 1910s and they formed only a small part of the land Aboriginal people were now demanding. But the government chose to focus solely on these existing reserves. In 1973, it renamed the Directorate's Aboriginal Advisory Board, calling it the Aboriginal Lands Trust, and announced it would now hold title to all these existing reserves and make decisions about their future retention or revocation. This sleight of hand placed the many respected members of the Advisory Board, like Charlie Leon and Tom Williams, in the uncomfortable position of appearing to support the government's severe curtailment of Aboriginal demands. The tensions generated were to continue to cloud the issues for some years to come.

Jacko Campbell had no confidence in the Aboriginal Lands Trust, regarding it as little more than a rubber stamp for government decisions to continue revoking reserve lands. As a better way to place power over Aboriginal heritage into Aboriginal hands, he began trying to establish a training course for young Aboriginal people so they would be accredited to identify and advise on sites of significance to Aboriginal communities. He believed such assessment should operate outside the NPWS, which he also saw to be obstructing Aboriginal control with its narrow environmental focus and its retention of legal power over Aboriginal relics. Instead of either of these government structures, he wanted to encourage self-sufficiency and autonomy, and his key strategy for this was through Tranby courses.

He worked with Kevin Cook to get the course underway, as Kevin has explained:

> Jacko Campbell wanted us to train Aboriginal sites officers
> or rangers. He reckoned National Parks was insensitive and
> basically he wanted Aboriginal people to be able to run things
> themselves. We worked it out and organised it through Tranby.
> Jacko was the driving force behind it … We wanted to have
> laws that wouldn't allow the Department of Roads, or Telstra
> or anyone, to go anywhere without firstly going through the
> Land Council to find someone to check that what they wanted
> to do was all right in terms of protecting sites and important
> places. So that if there was a road to be dug, well that person
> would be employed, or the Land Council would be employed,
> they send out their sites bloke, and money should go back
> into the local Land Council or the Regional Land Council,
> whoever employed them, so that they can, you know, cover
> their wages.[14]

All this had a resonance for the connections Jacko and Ted had been rebuilding with the land along the Georges River.

The St John's Park women had not studied the whole length of the river in any formal sense, but they knew from their childhoods at Herne Bay and Moorefield that the river was rich in art sites, stone tools and their manufacturing areas, and campsite remains like hearths and shell middens. The poorly resourced efforts of the NPWS were most focused on rural areas, particularly those where strong, long-established and vocal Aboriginal communities demanded their attention, like the coastal community in which Jacko lived. And even there, the focus was on traditional 'relics'. The NPWS could pay very little attention to the many 'contact sites' which demonstrated Aboriginal community history after British settlement, even in rural areas, let alone to the urban sites like those along the Georges River for which there was as yet no strong community to speak. There was no longer even a National Park on the river, as it had been downgraded – over bitter local protests – to a 'recreation area' in 1967.

There was a very small number of committed NPWS staff like Sharon Sullivan and Horrie Creamer, who single-handedly documented both archaeological and 'contact' sites in many areas, and nurtured the training of Ray Kelly, the first NPWS Indigenous Site Recorder.[15] Yet there remained a myriad of known sites which were not officially recorded. Even if such sites were actually entered onto the NPWS database, it gave no assurance of protection. This was the situation which Jacko was seeking to challenge as he formulated the idea of Tranby running an Aboriginal sites recorders course in the early 1980s.

So the little course which the St John's Park women got started about 1981 was one among a cluster of programs, supported through Tranby, which were aimed at empowering Aboriginal people at a community level. Like the others, the women's course worked with Tranby to apply for funds from the State government as part of its adult education outreach policies. The course then drew on Tranby teaching staff to introduce both the skills and the cultural components. What began as an short 'pilot' course opened up an unexpected and wide range of activities for the women involved. They learned some literacy and some numeracy, practised writing CVs and held endless roleplays about applying for jobs – about everything from typing to camel driving. But much of what they learnt involved finding out about the history of the Georges River and the people who had owned the land.

JANNY We read about the massacres and that, and we didn't think there was anybody else around that was going to protect it.

JUDY And we considered ourselves – the carers. The caretakers. And it's the same as I don't like people touching sites up in my country either.

JANNY We're Aboriginal. It's not our country but it's our job to care for it.

JUDY They're still our ancestors. And it's still important country, you know, because there was important stuff happening out there back in those days. That's why they are sites, they're beautiful places, you know. They used to sit around – like you see all axe-making sites and you think, they must have sat around for hours, and it's beautiful isn't it Jan?

JANNY Yeah. And our kids grew up in that country.

For many of them, this research and learning for personal interest then blossomed into activism around the recognition of Aboriginal rights to land across New South Wales. As they became more confident in their skills and knowledge, they became more outspoken in their advocacy for the services they and their families needed – like childcare and medical facilities – but also for the urgent need for land rights legislation. They marched, and spoke at community meetings, trying to reassure anxious white residents that their 'backyards' were not under threat.

The advent of Aboriginal Land Councils

The land rights movement across Australia had borne fruit by this time. The long years of campaigning had resulted in NSW in a series of inquiries and then draft legislation. This was limited in itself, and later substantially modified and distorted on the floor of State Parliament, but it finally became law in 1983.[16] The new Land Rights Act required initially a short-term body, known as the Interim Land Council to work with Aboriginal communities all over the state to set up a three-tiered structure in which Local Land Councils – which were to include every Aboriginal person within defined boundaries – would hold the title of all acquired land. The Local Land Councils would collaborate and plan collectively in one of 13 Regional Land

Councils, which would provide each of them consolidated legal, economic and planning skills to acquire land in the interests of the local people. The Regional Land Councils were to send delegates to confer on a State Aboriginal Land Council, which would derive its authority from the Regional and Local bodies. This structure was intended to ensure that decision-making power rested with the Local and Regional Land Councils.[17]

All of this meant that the Local Land Councils had to be set up by having boundaries drawn up and then the Aboriginal residents of the whole area informed and signed on as members. This process occurred differently in each area, but the general pattern was that it tended to draw on existing, interested groups who acted as the catalysts for the necessary recruiting and organising to form the local bodies. At La Perouse, for example, Tom Williams decided to take an active role in organising the Local Land Council, later becoming its chairperson.

In the mid-Georges River area, it was the St John's women's group which became the nucleus of the newly formed Gandangara Local Aboriginal Land Council. They were eager to do it. Janny and Judy explained that they had two aims. The first was to ensure that the land acquired would lead to the recognition and protection of the Aboriginal history of the area. But perhaps their greatest hope was that it would achieve decent housing, so that young people just starting out with new families would not have to face the pressures and frustrations they had faced in trying to find a house to rent or buy. Even in the process of building the membership lists for the new council, they found that the Housing Commission policy of scattering families – and the fear of surveillance and eviction by the commission – still haunted fellow Aboriginal residents of the area.

The women built on the skills they had just been learning about in their NOW course, but with virtually no other resources. Everything they did was voluntary, and they refused to draw on any of the initial set-up funding available to local councils – which they insisted should be kept for land purchase. Instead, they set up the first council office in Janny's front room, and looked around for alternative ways to raise money for some part-time positions to begin organising. For example, they applied for funding grants from employment and training projects, some designed for Aboriginal recipients and others for the general population. To find Aboriginal people to discuss membership of the Local Land Council, the women's group laboriously contacted everyone they could find from personal knowledge and from Housing Commission lists. They used a battered old typewriter, the one photocopier they could access in Liverpool – which was in a chemist's shop – and an old car to do letterbox drops, even roping in their kids to help out!

Kevin Cook and Pat Stewart, members of the Interim Land Council, also visited the St John's women's group to talk about how to set up the Gandangara Local Land Council. Kevin remembered being worried by the absence of men in the organising group, explaining to them that they needed to involve a broader range of people from across the community. 'You can't run ahead of them', he told them, 'you have to bring them along slowly'.

The women agreed, but had found doing so was challenging. The bonds they had built up between the women in the learning group had offered a useful starting point, partly because men were often at work and unable to take part in the earlier processes. But as well, many of the Aboriginal women in the area were married to white men, limiting the presence of Aboriginal men in the initial organising group. One of the men who joined early however was Wayne Dargan, drawn in like many others through the bonds of friendship and community networks. He had been born in Kempsey, but grew up with his grandparents at St Peters in inner Sydney, before moving to Herne Bay to 1963 and then to Green Valley. Wayne, like Judy and Janny, was part of the network which had developed among the people from many different areas who had been thrown together in the hostels and housing estates along the Georges River.[18]

Ultimately, the membership broadened, after continuing visits around the area and by rotating the meeting locations, one month in Bankstown, then Revesby then Guildford and so on. The visits to encourage people to join were always lengthy. The women were asking people not only to enroll for the Land Council elections, but to sign up for the full electoral roll so they could vote in municipal, state and federal elections. They encountered much anxiety about completing forms among people who deeply distrusted the government. So the women explained the processes to people carefully and thoroughly – and as many times as necessary – and many more people enrolled to vote:

> JUDY And we got a lot of people on the electoral roll, didn't we?
> We didn't have to get people on those other rolls to be on the Land
> Council roll, but it was just a process that we wanted to do for our
> Land Council, get them on all the electoral rolls. To get people
> involved in – politics! … We wanted them to know the importance
> of being heard, you know. People have to be on the electoral roll to
> vote. Most people wanted to vote but they were just a bit scared …
> As soon as they realised it wasn't as scary as what it had been made
> out to be, then they wanted their whole family to vote.
>
> JANNY They wanted their say in who runs the country.

Surveying sites on the Georges River

At this time, Tranby was developing its independent course for Aboriginal site recorders and was seeking participants from among the newly forming Local Land Councils. As Tranby implemented Jacko's vision, Kevin explained:

> each Regional Land Council employed two people and gave
> them a Toyota and an office to work out of and so on. Some

of them were actually working for the Local Land Council, like La Perouse for example, where the Regional Land Council wasn't organised enough to do it yet, so La Perouse took it up as a local issue. Some of it worked out and some of it didn't.

Wayne Dargan was interested and became one of the students enrolled in the first course in 1983. He enjoyed learning and travelling with the other Land Council and community students, who came from a range of different rural communities. He found common ground among those other students: 'there were lots of blokes on the sites course doing the same as me ... trying to find out what was there and trying to protect it'.

As well as learning about sites and community goals in all those areas, Wayne became better trained to identify sites in the Georges River area where he felt he had really grown up. As he remembered it:

> During the Tranby course, I became aware of the issues:
> if nobody else does anything about it, then who will? I
> thought if I could find the sites, then I could get someone to
> do something about it. Some sites were already recorded by
> NPWS but some weren't. But even the ones that were recorded
> were not protected! Logged but not protected back then.

Wayne was working from NPWS grid maps which contained some indication of site locations, but as he pointed out, at that time the recording process in the poorly resourced NPWS guaranteed no protection for sites, only documentation at the most cursory levels. He became aware, for example, of a large rubbish dump being built over recorded sites, but as he repeated in frustration, 'there was no NPWS protection'.[19]

Wayne focused on the less built-up southern side of the river, to the east of the Holsworthy military camp, where much bushland remained from around Mill Creek, across Alfords Point to Illawong. Often he travelled by road, but he also used a boat at times, puttering

Wayne Dargan (centre),
in a class training Aboriginal site
recorders at Tranby College, Glebe,
in the mid-1980s.

along in a tinny because he found that from the water it was easier to see the midden shells glistening clearly on the shores and to pick out the promising overhangs where campsites might be found. He began to uncover the evidence of traditional Aboriginal residence along the river, as well as the sustained traces of the post-invasion, continuing presence we have been discussing throughout the chapters of this book. He found too the presence of the white hermits and eccentrics who still inhabited the river bank, appreciating the Aboriginal spaces even while they compromised their records of Aboriginal living:

> I'd found a couple of old rock shelters that I was certain were [originally] Aboriginal sites but they had been taken by squatters and people living in the shelters … there were newspapers … there was one old fella I bumped into – a hermit – he'd occupied some of the bigger shelters and had half destroyed them – near Mill Creek. But one of the shelters near Alfords Point Bridge had a small handprint in it … And there were axe grinding grooves near Menai in four or five different sites.

The numerous pre-invasion Aboriginal sites which Wayne was seeing along the southern bank of the river were still there because much of this large area had in 1912 been protected by the Holsworthy military reservation of nearly 18 000 acres (7200 hectares) for training and weapons testing. Some blocks there had been granted in the early nineteenth century but, like much of the lower Georges River, they had been left undeveloped. Since 1912, all outsiders have been prohibited entry because of the dangerous unexploded ordinance scattered across the range. So this area has been left largely as it was in 1912: an extraordinarily precious area because it shows not only what Aboriginal life may have been like before the British arrived but, just as importantly, what all the river must have been like just one hundred years ago. This was what it looked like when Biddy Giles was travelling over it and indeed for over 20 years after she had passed away.

Within the restricted zone, there has been little disturbance except for occasional ridge top use in the military exercises. The rugged topography has protected many of the 503 known, and at least 500 more predicted, sites from damage. Wayne's estimate of the types and frequency of these sites is consistent with the work of the Sydney Prehistory Group from a nearby area to the south-west.[20] In 1996, the Tharawal Local Land Council had the opportunity to become involved in the environmental impact assessment for a possible airport at Holsworthy.[21] The Council organised 20 members to assist in surveying the military range for a number of weeks. Their results were so compelling that the Aboriginal people themselves then mounted an application to have the whole massive area nominated for the National Estate, something they achieved in 1998.[22] It is named for the Dharawal clan group, whose country was Cubbitch Barta in the Holsworthy area.[23]

Summarising the findings from the surveys, Tharawal Local Aboriginal Land Council quoted the statement of significance for Holsworthy:

> The large number of sites and the stories they may tell form
> a landscape in which Aboriginal life prior to 1788 is recorded
> without the large scale impact of European settlement. There
> is also a high density of sites ... This is particularly important
> because sites are found in groups or clusters with their
> relationship to one another largely intact.[24]

The area is also unique for its remarkable range in the depiction of figures and styles in the artwork in the caves and along the flat rocks throughout the area. In one of the Tharawal Council's contributions to the environmental consultation, chairperson Cliff Foley explained what this meant:

> Aboriginal people maintained a traditional and custodial
> link through their association with Land, the environment
> and its natural resources.

There is evidence throughout the area of the Holsworthy Army Base of that relationship between Aboriginal People and their Land.

This evidence is laid bare on the creek beds that contain hundreds of axe grinding grooves; and across the rock platforms with engraved motifs, animals, figurines and their tracks ...

Images of stencilled hands, feet, fish, animals, birds and boomerangs festoon the rock shelters and large rock galleries.

The Artists walk with you. And expose their works at their contentment; and conceal them in their fright.

The land is pristine. A time capsule of the Sydney Basin – protected by unexploded ordinance.[25]

Wayne Dargan had been able to identify the edge of this extraordinary place in 1983 and 1984. He was building up his recording work at the same time as the Gandangara Land Council widened its membership. So he made a point of taking young men from the community with him on some of his trips as he combed the region along the river for sites.

Over the same time, the women from the St John's group remained active in trying to consolidate the early land council organisation. They had been talking around in the area to both Aboriginal and non-Aboriginal communities about land and community responsibility for some years by then, and had become known as people to contact about places of possible Aboriginal significance. So in 1984, just as the new local land council office was being set up, it was Janny and Judy who got the news about a site near Barden Ridge which was being threatened by development on the escarpment between Mill Creek (Guragurang) and Alfords Point, near the Lucas Heights nuclear reactor. The experimental reactor had been set up in 1958 in an area which was almost completely unalienated bushland at the time, far from any permanent houses and run by the Australian Atomic Energy

Commission. But through the 1970s, the State's Lands Department had been releasing land for private housing developments which were edging closer and closer to the reactor site. In 1984, after the release of yet another block of Crown land for a private residential development, the bulldozers had arrived to clear the bush.

The people who contacted Janny and the Gandangara Land Council were not the scientists. They were the workers in the waste disposal section – not the nuclear waste disposal section, but the everyday rubbish disposal workmen. They had frequently been out in the surrounding escarpment and creek areas monitoring the bushland and waterways to avoid the effects of rubbish disposal. They had become aware of many Gandangara camps, hearth sites, tool-making areas and art-filled overhangs. These white men had watched the fences for the development zone go up alarmingly close to what they could see was an important site. So when the bulldozers arrived, they rang the land council to suggest some urgent action.

JUDY There were a couple of blokes. And I thought that was really fantastic of them, you know. They were really concerned and then they came to us and so we said 'Yeah, we'll try and get them protected'.

JANNY So we were there for about half a day, in front of the bulldozer, until the National Parks got out there. And then they put a stop to the work. Once they came out it became official.

JUDY They already had the bloody housing and that going up, and you couldn't stop it. And they said they would put a fence around it, and we said it's not going to stop dogs and kids and that from getting in and destroying it.

JANNY Yeah, it's housing around it now … right up to it, which is really sad. But some of the other stuff is down in thicker bush. That's why we had to get land claims onto it, but it took a while for those land claims to actually come through. That's why we had to rely on people like National Parks and Wildlife to come to the rescue while the claim was in. In the end it belonged to the Land Council. So, Landcom had no control over that.

Reclaiming Guragurang

There were other incidents like this in the early days of Gandangara Land Council which pushed the women and the first group of Local Land Council members into deciding to try to claim land – although none of them expected that it would come to much. A decade later, the Commonwealth's Native Title Act would impose a set of eligibility criteria on hopeful Aboriginal claimants which are almost impossible to meet in urban communities. Native Title claimants must prove, for example, that they have direct links to the pre-invasion landholders and must demonstrate that they have sustained continuous and culturally traditional relationships with the land under claim since the invasion. (As we shall see, one of the few groups in New South Wales who have been able to meet this criteria is in the upper, freshwater section of the Georges River.)

But the 1983 NSW Land Rights Act did not set such exclusionary criteria for eligibility. Any Local Land Council could lay claim to land within its boundaries, but only if it was 'vacant Crown Land not wanted for a future, essential public purpose' – a phrase which could mean many things. The government had recognised that early grants and sales of land would have left little that could be defined as 'vacant Crown Land' in any urban setting. And it was expected that heavy mortality from early epidemics and frontier violence would have made it difficult to demonstrate continuous traditional connection. So the NSW Act had established a fund in order to purchase land on the open market. Yet it also stated simply that if Local Land Councils could find any vacant Crown Land inside their boundaries, it could be successfully claimed on grounds including historical association and economic need.

It was unlikely, so anyone believed, that any unalienated Crown Land could be found within the city boundaries. There had after all been massive alienation of land along the Georges River, as we have seen in earlier chapters, in the first years of settlement. The inter-war years and then the post-war city expansion had filled up the few remaining spaces so it seemed the only areas where land could be claimed would be rural areas in the state. Judy remembers they were not optimistic about making successful claims:

> And it was so important to us out there. When the Land
> Rights legislation came in, because we lived in a developed
> area, we were thinking we're not going to get much out of
> this in terms of claims because there wasn't much land in the
> Sydney basin at all. We're thinking anything we get is going to
> be fantastic, you know. If we get anything at all.

Given the knowledge these St John's Park women and others in the area had been developing of the sites like that at Alfords Point which were under threat, they were determined to explore the possibilities of claiming land. As they became aware from studying the Land Rights Act, they just had to identify unalienated Crown Land and then put the claim on. They were most concerned to protect culturally rich sites, but they had been deeply distressed by the way the Alfords Point site had been so tightly hemmed in by the encroaching housing development, even with NPWS protection. So they were hoping for land which would be large enough to protect sites but also allow plenty of surrounding space to give privacy, protection and environmental amenity at the same time.

In the end, it was Janny who found the land. Despite having barely any secondary education, and working from the things she'd learnt in the NOW program, Janny put together a wage from NESA

– a short-term Commonwealth grant for 'new employment starts' to train Aboriginal people. She was to be formally employed by the Land Council, and trained through Tranby, which allowed her to use a proportion of the small wage to pay Tranby for their teacher in accounting, Sidney Wells, to teach her how to manage the paperwork. Then she set about learning how to find land to claim:

> Cookie [Kevin Cook] put me in touch with Colin Clague who worked at the Lands' claim office, and I marched in there one morning and introduced myself. I just knocked on the door – this little black woman – and said, 'Cookie sent me'.
>
> And I said 'I'm here to find out how to …'. Well, I didn't tell him I wanted to learn how to do a land claim … I just asked him how I could tell by looking at maps what was Crown land and what was not Crown land.
>
> So I spent a week in there and he was sort of training me and giving me all these maps. And while I was in there I was making sure I was getting all the maps of Gandangara's area. So that way I was looking at what was Crown land.

Janny and Wayne Dargan worked closely to consolidate all the information they had been gathering. Although they did not know about this detailed history, many of the areas they had identified, either in Wayne's surveys or in Janny's painstaking searches of the maps, were in the vicinity of Mill Creek. Guragurang had been Biddy Giles' river in the 1860s and is still one of the most effectively conserved and complex ecosystems along the whole esturarine Georges River.

Once they felt they had as much as they could identify, Janny, Wayne, Judy, Robyn and others in the Land Council began to formulate the claim. As Janny remembers:

> I took copies and notes of all of it home with me and worked on it there … I sorted out where there *was* a lot of Crown land that we could claim. But then we put a blanket claim over an

even bigger area ... We did it because there were Aboriginal sites on it – it was *significant* land to Aboriginal people. That blanket claim was because we thought it was really important to make sure that all those sites came under what we were claiming, and they were all going to have that ongoing protection.

So anyway, the claims got up!

There is both irony and a certain symmetry in the fact that these claims were all so close to Biddy's home and to the country she travelled over so freely. That the claims had been made at all was remarkable: they had been painstakingly researched and documented by people who had faced years of discrimination at school and in employment. Janny, Wayne, Judy and Robyn had all been been poorly equipped by the educational and cultural processes of Australian society to navigate the complex, arcane New South Wales land law, let alone the contested and contradictory elements of the Land Rights Act.

Yet they found the land, filled out all the forms and submitted the claims in 1985 and 1986. And they had done it so well that, despite it taking many years of deliberation, they made them stick. The claims were granted in 1988 and made public in 1991. This unexpected success gave the Gandangara Land Council the largest holding of land of any of the Local Land Councils in the metropolitan area at that time, and it secured – for what they all hoped was perpetuity – the safety of so many of the rich sites they valued.

TEN

Resilience on
a city river
1990–2008

We return now to our first questions: how have Aboriginal people on the Georges River *made* their locality? How did people like Joe Anderson turn the spaces of the changing and damaged river into meaningful *places*, and make those places their own?

Salt Pan Creek continues to be important in Aboriginal people's stories and in their memories – even though the creek is overgrown with mangroves and the Aboriginal blocks are hard to find today. All that is left of the Anderson and Rowley homes is a thin strip of overgrown land beside a gully, hemmed in by subdivisions and gentrifying villas, on the edge of the National Park. Yet together – through the 1920s and 1930s – the river, the gully, the beach with its midden, the sandstone on the shoreline and the flowers on the ridge had all played a part in the way a group of people from many different places had come to understand themselves as a community. This community had fostered the political passions which so many of its residents carried with them over the years wherever they went, in turn linking Salt Pan Creek with the places of their later lives.

There are many other important places like Salt Pan Creek. Some were bends of the river with a camp, from Liverpool weir to Voyager Point to Weeney Bay. Some were rocky overhangs or sandy shores or mangrove swamps. People have created meaningful bonds with and in these places. They have anchored their experiences of those places to their memories of the other places to which they remained connected. This capacity contributes to what we have called 'resilience' – the process of regrowth which takes account of the current changed conditions but draws its roots from a rich heritage.

Although it takes sustained searching through archives, images and many discussions, it is not difficult to see how places were being created by Jonathon Goggey, Biddy and Billy Giles, or Ellen Anderson and William Rowley. During the nineteenth century on the river, many of the spaces which allowed Aboriginal families and communities the resilience not only to survive but to develop remained accessible. But the middle years of the twentieth century brought even faster change: damaging the river environments and encroaching on the spaces which Aboriginal people could use in ways different from the mainstream. From the end of World War II, industrialisation and a massive influx of new people and their impacts on the area seemed to have undermined the Aboriginal hold on the river altogether.

Yet what seemed like destructive change revitalised the process of 'making locality', as the Aboriginal immigrants began trying to relate to this new home with the same sorts of models they brought with them from rural birthplaces. Aboriginal memories of these years share common themes: grappling with the disorientation of moving many times; fending off intrusive surveillance by the Housing Commission or the Welfare Board in unfamiliar new environments; coping with the loneliness of 'salt-and-peppered' estates and hostile neighbours; looking for work in unstable industries. Yet such memories also share similar themes of exploring these new spaces, looking for 'country' close to the crowded huts and the mud and clay of the barren new estates. Often they were looking for rivers which allowed them some of the freedom they remembered from home. Most of all, people recall building up connections: making new communities from the changing present-day Aboriginal populations around them at the same time as they were learning about those pre-war generations who had sustained their networks on the river.

Much of this process found expression during the Land Rights campaigns of the 1970s, which reflected this emerging city consciousness of land relationships *in* the city, as well as the more commonly recognised concern with land relationships in rural and more 'traditional' areas. How have these Land Rights movements worked in practice? Did they fulfill the hopes of the 1970s? More broadly, have the policies and legislative outcomes of those decades enabled the continuing processes of 'making locality' among Aboriginal people on the river today?

Within this chapter we find some of the people who have continued to make the river into a significant place for themselves and their communities into the twenty-first century. Two key organisational structures were evolving over the 1980s through which Aboriginal people tried to express their interests in land and water. These were the Land Councils and the National Parks and Wildlife Service. Each of them has offered both opportunities and obstructions to the goals that Aboriginal people have expressed. Within each of these organisations we can see important individual and collective approaches to keep on making relationships with places, to *make* 'locality'. Yet there have been many limitations. These organisations have also been frail and unpredictable. Aboriginal people have tried to chart their courses independently and to draw on organisations only where needed. And Aboriginal people have not fitted easily into a simple definition, continuing to come from diverse backgrounds and to have very different personal goals.

There are three stories in this chapter. The first is about the conflict around the partially completed sale of Gandangara land. The second records Lew Solberg's advocacy on behalf of the Local Aboriginal Land Council as an expression of his long involvement with fishing and his sense of responsibility. The third tells the story of the youthful Towra Team's mission on a National Park marine reserve at the mouth of the river. Together, they trace out some of the strategies of resilience occurring within the current constraints on Aboriginal people on the Georges River.

The Aboriginal Land
Council system

The Gandangara Local Aboriginal Land Council, like its neighbouring Tharawal and La Perouse Local Aboriginal Land Councils, had been set up after the passing of the state's Land Rights Act in 1983. They were entirely Aboriginal-controlled and their membership was mandated to be all of the Aboriginal people living within their boundaries.[1] The Act established a three-tiered structure in which Local Land Councils sent representatives to Regional Land Councils, based on long-standing and functioning cultural and political affiliations. These were expected to give a collective voice to local communities and consolidate resources for advice and policy arising from local experiences. The State Land Council was established as a formal umbrella body to reflect the views of the regional councils, through their representatives who comprised it.

Land could be claimed by the Local Land Councils on the basis of historic associations and economic need as well as – or instead of – 'traditional' affiliation. The land available for claim was only what could be designated as Crown land 'unwanted for any public purpose'. This was a catch-all phrase inserted by rural politicians into the Act in last minute Parliamentary debates. Opponents of Aboriginal claims did not have to prove land had been earmarked for a specific public purpose, merely state that it would have one in the future, in order to obstruct any land claim. This clause has often been used to limit the amount of land open to claim.[2]

However, land which was successfully claimed, along with other land purchased or declared to be 'Aboriginal land' under this Act, became inalienable: it could not be sold under any circumstances. Inalienable title had been a non-negotiable goal throughout all the long Aboriginal campaigns for recognition of their rights to land in south-eastern Australia, from the 1860s onwards. It became a central element of the 1983 Land Rights Act. It was widely supported among Aboriginal people, as they demonstrated in numerous Select Committee hearings around the State, and in other statements and claims. The bitterness over the revocations of so many of the temporary reserves created in the nineteenth and early twentieth centuries remained uppermost in discussions among Aboriginal people when the 1983 legislation was being enacted.[3] So the inalienability of land under the new Act was seen as a safeguard against a similar piecemeal loss of any land acquired under successful land claims or further legislation.

The unexpected success of the claims to the Georges River, lodged after the research done by Janny Ely and Wayne Dargan, had made Gandangara the largest landholder among the Metropolitan region's Local Land Councils, and in fact the largest overall landholder, black or white, in Sutherland Shire. Open to every Aboriginal person in the area, the Local Councils offered a new structure through which Aboriginal people on the river could express their concerns about the land and waterways. The substantial land holdings of Gandangara offered the potential for a real impact through environmental action. But the Local Councils were also inevitably the forum for anxieties about the pressing issues which had not gone away with the legislative recognition of Land Rights. These issues included discriminatory limitations on housing, employment and education, and a crippling lack of access to financial resources to overcome disadvantage and expand community development.

Through the later 1980s, Gandangara members struggled to come to terms not only with the land claims process but with the complex quarterly accounting procedures demanded by the Land Rights Act. Most land council members across the state had had little formal education, so these administrative requirements were challenging. Adult education bodies like Tranby College were increasingly called in to assist with training. The reporting demands became more complicated and intrusive after the 1988 New South Wales state election. The incoming conservative coalition government demonstrated its hostility to the Act immediately by attempting to seize the funds vested in the Land Councils to purchase land. On failing to achieve this, it forced through an amendment to the Land Rights Act, passing into law in 1991, which severely undermined the support which the Local Land Councils could receive from the Regional Land Councils. These changes did not assist local members to become more confident in administering the funds they now had to manage largely alone, nor to control irregularities or petty corruption among members. But most momentous among the amendments effects was its removal of the clause which prevented the sale of Aboriginal land.

Balancing financial need and concern for country

Pressure on Local Land Councils to make their land produce revenue escalated because of this key 1991 amendment to remove the inalienability of Aboriginal title to their land. Inalienability was replaced by the capacity for Local Land Councils to sell any Aboriginal land as long as some safeguards were fulfilled – essentially the requirement that all members of the Local Land Council approved of the sale.

The amendment opened up the potential either to sell some land as a one-off fund raiser or to mortgage the land to fund housing or some other form of development. It introduced very new tensions among members because it pitted the fears held by many Aboriginal people about losing what little land they had been able to win back against the anxieties of others about access to secure housing and jobs.[4]

The piecemeal processing of the Gandangara land claims, all submitted in 1985 or 1986, was extremely slow. One section, consisting of six to ten home sites plus four hectares of bushland at Alfords Point, had been approved just prior to the election, in 1988, but was not announced and so did not become public knowledge until 1991. The hostility of the conservative government was by then well known, and it found a ready echo in the response of local white landholders in the Menai area when they became aware of this granting of Aboriginal land claims near their properties. This 'wasn't about race' they argued, but the criticisms they launched against the Gandangara Land Council mirrored exactly those of the Progress Association neighbours of the Andersons in the 1930s at Salt Pan Creek.[5]

There could be no mistaking the racial tensions which were being exposed after Aboriginal people were recognised as legitimate residents and landowners. Similar public hostility emerged around the state as Aboriginal people were seen to be taking possession of what was in fact only a very small amount of land. (Very small indeed, compared to what they had pre-invasion!) The complexities of implementing the 1983 Act, with the added frustrations imposed by the 1991 amendments, led to a weakening of Labor support for the Aboriginal organisations. When the Labor party was re-elected into government in 1995 they failed to reverse any of the conservative amendments to the Land Rights Act. Indeed their own conservative financial approach saw the Labor government continue the pressure on Aboriginal people to raise the funds needed for community development from commercial exploitation of the small amount of land they had acquired through land rights.

Land claimed from the mid-1980s continued to be granted in small amounts through the 1990s, until a major block of around 750 hectares (2000 acres) of bushland at Menai was granted in mid-1999.[6] By then, leadership had changed hands in the Gandangara Land Council and, in a context where there were few alternatives, the executive bowed to government pressure to sell portions of Aboriginal land to create 'development' funds. Severe conflict occurred within the organisation as the Aboriginal population divided over the issue of whether any land should be sold for short-term income. A formal development plan was researched and the Land Council proposed to the authorities to excise 750 hectares at Windle Place – now a row of ten housing blocks above a small stream flowing into Mill Creek.

Numerous Aboriginal members of the Land Council objected to the sale, and in 2000 the Sutherland Shire Council, for very different motives, tried to block the development application on what the Land Council argued were the spurious grounds of bushfire and traffic concerns.[7] The Land Council had undertaken the development itself, to be drawn from its own funds and so there was no middle-man involved to reduce its profits. The Labor government very strongly backed the sale plans, seeing it as a strategy to generate funds for Aboriginal community employment and possibly for housing.

With the mounting government enthusiasm – and pressure – along with an active housing market, the approval process was pushed through and development began early in 2002.[8] The Land Council announced the sale had netted $1 million to be used to employ permanent staff. The Land Council proceeded with a second development, excising a larger piece of land called Barden Ridge higher up towards the Lucas Heights facility. This was to be subdivided into 41 new house blocks, with another hectare of land adjoining it set aside as a conservation block – as had also occurred with Windle Place. This was expected to produce a $6 million profit, this time to be used to funding the employment of Aboriginal rangers and trainees for future land management.[9]

Again the membership was bitterly divided and conflict continued as well as concerns being voiced from outside about the procedure for achieving the formal approval for the sale. Ultimately, this second development plan was only partially realised: the courts found that the land transfer had been legally unsound, with a failure to secure full approval from Land Council members being one of the factors contributing to the collapse of the process.

Despite the difficult circumstances of the attempted land sale, there were important elements of sustained concern about country demonstrated in the development plans. With the Windle Place plans, the Land Council insisted on a structure for the development which was quite different from usual suburban development plans in the area – in which the primary goal was the maximisation of profit. In what became known as the Gandangara model, the sales involved a series of environmental protections. These included land titles with covenants requiring that stormwater and domestic waste run-off was strictly controlled, and either retained or treated on site, to ensure minimal damage to the river system below. The native bushland around the housing blocks, including the habitat of specific species, was to be protected. The impact of the housing was to be minimised by providing Land Council subsidies and cash-back inducements to buyers who undertook further energy efficiencies and landscaped the sites according to the development guidelines.[10]

At least some of these goals seem to have been fulfilled in the ongoing use of the sites by land purchasers, but the questions around how effective the incentives to responsible environmental behaviour have been is yet to be seen. Within a short time, the strong tensions over land sales and other issues resulted in a change in Gandangara Land Council leadership. Relative stability has returned to its management, yet the troubled dilemma over the need to find development funds within severely restricted budgets continues to challenge the membership, at the same time as they have continued to work on innovative land management strategies for the land remaining in their control.

Gandangara Land Council today

The debates within Gandangara Land Council have been painful for many people, but they have also demonstrated the strength of debate and democratic processes within the community. Throughout these difficult times, a recurrent theme in the interviews we conducted with Local Land Council members was the hope for an overarching claim over the whole river to demand action to restore its environmental health. Some saw such a claim being perhaps framed collectively by all the Local Aboriginal Land Councils along the river as a Native Title claim.[11] Although such a claim has not been mounted to date, the idea of restoring Aboriginal management to achieve river health has been a strong one.[12]

There has remained room for diverse roles within the overall Land Council structure for a range of people. Janny Ely has continued to be involved as an active member of the Local Land Council, as well as graduating with a Bachelor of Education and working in TAFE in the Aboriginal education program. Others like Wayne Dargan remain members and take a role when possible in their own busy work schedules. Gandangara Land Council itself has focused its recent attention on developing active training programs for its younger members, fostering employment in environmental restoration work. Their most recognised achievement has been in the combination of history with place, demonstrated in an award won in 2007 for an environmental project at Mount Annan Botanical Gardens which protected sensitive environments at the same time as commemorating the Stolen Generations.[13]

Some people have moved to different Land Council areas, and are now active in other organisations. Judy Chester moved to the inner city where she became an organiser for the Public Sector Union and has remained active in the Metropolitan Local Land Council. Robyn Williams moved upstream on the Georges River and has been active in the Tharawal Local Land Council, as well as teaching in a wide range of subjects in the education and Aboriginal studies programs at TAFE and the University of Sydney.[14]

Jason Groves (Bert Groves' grandson) and John Lennis, who both grew up at Herne Bay, are just some of the people for whom an involvement in land and water in the area has been expressed through Gandangara Land Council work as cultural officers. Today Gandangara runs an environmental development team which mobilises young people to undertake site surveying for the area as a necessary part of the all development impact assessments. These roles are reminiscent of the vision for recognition of Aboriginal culture and ownership which Jacko Campbell had fostered.

Lew's
story

There are Aboriginal people on the river, however, whose lives cannot be easily fitted into the narratives of contemporary Aboriginal organisations, family and community. Some have lost contact with the Aboriginal community because they were drawn into the well-known apparatus for removing Aboriginal children from their families.[15] They have often found it was a painful path to find their way back into the community. There are many other Aboriginal people in city areas who were not removed from their families through these policies, and who do not identify themselves as members of the 'stolen generations'. Instead they have been part of the major dispersal of Aboriginal people over many decades into the wider population. This happened perhaps because individuals have married outside the Aboriginal community and then no longer acknowledged their heritage. Sometimes children of fair skin-colour have had their ancestry hidden from them because of prejudice, shame or to protect them from removal. During the later years of the twentieth century there was a rising public appreciation of Aboriginal culture – sometimes romanticised but still a very new phenomenon in Australia. This encouraged some people to search out the background of family members whose Aboriginal connections they may have ignored in the past. The new funding for housing and education that was offered to families recognised as Aboriginal from the early 1970s, modest though it was, enticed others. The burgeoning public genealogical movement gave them all some more tools to find out just what those links were.

Many of these people had lives which ran parallel to those of the Aboriginal community. Sometimes as friends and workmates, at others as uncomfortable neighbours, they had lived on the same river in working-class families, facing very similar frustrations around housing, work, environments and street life. Their transition into stronger relationships with the Aboriginal community has been not been easy either: there have been tensions and suspicion on all sides which have made building relationships slow and the results fragile.[16] Yet some people have embraced their Aboriginality wholeheartedly and have sought out organisational links like Tranby College and the Local Land Councils, not because they offered any advantage but because they offered opportunities to learn. Slowly they have formed stronger attachments to Aboriginal people and to the country they share. Every one of these stories is different, but together they have expanded still further the numbers of Aboriginal people on the river.

Lewis 'Lew' Solberg, born in 1938, has such a story.[17] His mother

Elise came from a well-known Aboriginal family from Yass, the Bells, and had married a second-generation Norwegian immigrant, Lewis Solberg senior, in Baradine in north-western New South Wales in the 1930s. Lew's father never encouraged his children in any recognition of his wife's Aboriginal connections. Although Lew was aware of his Aunty Janet's darker colouring and their rural background, he had grown up without any understanding of what this meant for his mother's family. As a fair-skinned child he had never faced any pressure at school or in the streets to acknowledge his background consciously.

Yet all his life, Lew and his family had lived in close proximity to Aboriginal people. His parents had moved to Redfern in 1942 when Lew was a baby, where they had struggled to maintain a foothold. They were finally forced out by rising rents in 1950, moving into the low-income hostel at Hargrave Park near Warwick Farm on the Georges River. Just like Herne Bay, this hostel was composed of converted army huts for homes, crowded together and uncomfortable. By 1949 already a thousand people had been crowded in.[18]

Lew lived at Hargrave Park from the age of 12 until his family moved to Strathfield three years later. After he married in 1957 he moved to Chester Hill, again close to the Georges River just north of Chipping Norton. At school and in each of those homes, he had had Aboriginal neighbours and friends. His home life had been like many of those of working families with low incomes and living under high pressure. His father was a heavy drinker who had slid into alcoholism, becoming increasingly unpredictable and eventually violent and abusive to his children and his wife. Lew's mother had been the person who held the family unit together, sustaining her children through a difficult childhood and allowing them to share the support of her sister Janet, by then living in Erskineville, and of her other relations whenever possible.

For Lew the greatest joy of his childhood was at his Norwegian grandparents' home, right on the banks of the Georges River near

East Hills Park. He and his brother found respite there from conflict at home. They spent endless weekends mucking around on the rocks, catching crabs and prawns, swimming in the wire-netted pool, exploring the inlets and the bush on both banks of the river in little boats, fishing from Blackwall just downstream, learning the river by heart. His father's brothers and sisters were often there too, and enjoyed taking the children fishing, offering some support building the boys' confidence in the river as their real home.

At Hargrave Park too, Lew kept in close touch with the river, like the other kids at the hostel:

> I used to swim in Cabramatta Creek every summer. The creek
> was great! You had two places, one was called The Punt and
> the other was the Pilot Hole. In winter time they were just
> about always full and crystal clear. Summer time after we
> started swimming they were all muddy – that's when the mates
> and I would play underwater chasings.[19]

Lew grew up to have a busy working life, installing TV sets in hospitals for much of it, but continued to explore the river as much as he could between working and raising a family. Only in 1988 did he finally have time to explore his family history, and it was then that he discovered his Aboriginality:

> I say I'm not one of the stolen generation, I'm one of the lost
> generation. I missed out on knowing about my Aboriginality
> …
> I found out in 1988 about my Aboriginality and I've always
> had a feeling for the place, for our land and I didn't know how
> it came about, but now I know why.
> My two sisters started [researching], then I recollected
> my mother's [sister] we always knew her as Auntie Janet, she
> had a very broad nose and dark eyes, dark hair … Then my
> sisters found this book about the Bush family which stated

... that John Bell, my great-great-grandfather was a half-caste Aborigine, he was born in Yass area, his parents came from Braidwood ... I've met the Bush family, they've welcomed me with open arms as a cousin.

Apart from archival research, Lew and his sisters asked his mother many questions as she was approaching death and found out more. He was thrilled to find out about the Aboriginal connections in his family: 'I felt great. I still do. I get a bit of ribbing from my mates because I [look] white, [and have] blue eyes ... I'm just proud to be part of this land, from my ancestors for thousands of years.'

Lew and the Catchment Management Authority

Lew's rediscovery of his Aboriginal family led him to some immediate steps. One was establishing active contact with his Bell and Bush family relations in Yass, with whom he has continued to be in close touch, visiting them with his wife Bernadette and uncovering still more branches of this old family –identifying themselves as both white and Aboriginal. Another was that he tried to take up a role in protecting the river he had always loved: 'practically the day I found out [about my Aboriginality], I applied to become a member of Gandangara Land Council ... I wanted to look after our land.'

With his focus on the river, Lew offered to join the river's Catchment Management Authority on behalf of the Land Council, because there was then no Aboriginal representation. Lew felt this was a way of expressing his sense of *being* Aboriginal, which for him meant demonstrating the strong sense of responsibility he felt to look after his local environment. The government had set up 13 such authorities across New South Wales in 2003 in response to a worldwide movement to recognise the overall environment in more meaningful units. Rather than managing 'natural resources' within geometric lines drawn on two-dimensional maps, these were aimed at managing the environment within whole river catchments – wherever water ran over the landscape towards the same river. This would allow more effective water and land management by more sensible planning of the residential expansion, waste disposal and industrial pollution. If as the end result the river with its banks, wildlife and vegetation, became healthier, then the environmental conditions of the overall catchment would necessarily be working better.[20]

The structure of the catchment authorities was changed several times over the years, as the New South Wales government amalgamated groups in the complex riverine environment of the city. But each time there was a change, Lew involved himself in the Catchment Management Board most relevant to the Georges River.[21] He saw his purpose in joining these bodies as being about 'just trying to get the environment up and running', to clean and care for the river.

While the rhetoric of the authorities has promoted their consultation with Aboriginal communities and with the wider public, Lew came to feel that the role of public representatives on these bodies was marginal. In 2007, there was no Aboriginal representative on the Sydney Metropolitan Catchment Management Authority (which now manages the Georges River) but instead mainly local government councillors and former state government ministers. 'None of them are Aboriginal', as Lew reflected ruefully in 2007. There is only one Aboriginal staff member, a catchment officer whose role is to develop educational kits and liaise with the Aboriginal community. It's a far cry from the formal advice – and the votes – which might be delivered from membership of the Authority itself.

Lew has since moved into roles in the advisory groups for the Southern Sydney, Botany Bay and Georges River authorities, whose aims are to help develop a blueprint for care of the river and surrounding area. He describes his own role on these advisory committees as attending and observing meetings and seminars, where he tries to 'put across an Aboriginal perspective when decisions will impact on Aboriginal people's use of the river'. He continues to be frustrated. Often, he observes, members of the Catchment Authority had neglected to speak with Aboriginal stakeholders. He had had to remind them to consult with Gandangara Land Council because 'They hadn't even thought of it!'. He pointed out that the Authority has stated that one of their 'community engagement' goals is to consult with Aboriginal communities.[22]

As well as his growing knowledge of the Aboriginal organisation's perspective, Lew brought to his work on the Catchment Authorities his deep personal knowledge of the river, developed over a lifetime of continued fishing and observation. The members of the Authority, he explained 'hardly ever come down here [to the river]'. He felt that, because of his frequent visits, he 'noticed things, noticed changes in the river'. Nevertheless, despite his skepticism, Lew has valued the interactions he has been able to build up with all the Authority members and staff in their serious interest in solving environmental problems. He felt 'there's a lot of good people involved who really work for the environment' and who believed their work had contributed to long-term change in protecting banks and vegetation, and keeping rivers clean.

In pursuing his responsibility as a Land Council environmental representative, Lew has moved outside the Catchment Management structure and keeps in close contact with the 'River Keeper' – a position funded by Georges River Combined Councils Committee and NSW Maritime (the department which manages waterways). The River Keeper on the Georges River is like a ranger and advocate for the river, involved in environmental education, clean-ups and bush regeneration, drawing on volunteers but also often using weekend detention participants as workers.

Throughout all this, Lew's relationship with the Gandangara Land

Council has been strained at times, particularly over the issue of the land sales. His main concern about the Gandangara development was that it would increase the density of housing. He sees this damaging the river in a number of ways, such as by drainage of pollution into the river or by the massive clearing involved in large houses and paved groundcover, leading to siltation, freshwater pollution of the saline river and loss of habitat. Lew was appreciative of the Land Council's attempts at environmental planning in its development plans, but deeply troubled by what he saw as a distraction from the urgent problems of river and bushland health. Nevertheless, he has taken his role as a Land Council representative very seriously, seeing the Local Land Councils as one of the few voices heard on the various environmental authorities which are genuinely responsible to both local communities and to the river.

'The fishing …
it's in me'

Lew's passion for the river continues into retirement, but he worries about the river's future. He turns to the Land Council to investigate the environmental abuses he sees and to champion the needs of the river in fending off the sustained pressures of encroaching development. He has been hopeful that the Land Council would take an active role in drawing together all the Land Councils along the river to submit a Native Title claim over its whole length.

Lew has argued that everyone should have right-of-way on the water and alongside it. 'It's ridiculous', he says, 'to call it private property, it's everyone's.' It would stay that way, he believes, if the native title claim went through:

> I don't like it, any of that building. Because we should be
> able to walk all around our rivers, on the edges of our rivers,

Lew Solberg, at home on the
Georges River in 2004.

Photo Allison Cadzow

wherever possible, some of the landscape won't allow it, but we
should have access to all our riverbanks … and the foreshores
of Sydney Harbour, the beaches, the whole lot. We should
be able to walk around there and enjoy our land and our
waterways, it should not be 'This is private property, keep off'.

In 2004, during Lew's early participation in this project, he was optimistic about the Land Council's power. By 2007, he was more frustrated, aware of the difficulties the Land Council faced advocating for
the river against powerful developers. Yet he continued to keep a careful eye on any new building on the river and hoped to be able to support a stronger stand.

He continues to fish as often as he can, taking visitors like Allison out in his small boat to learn to fish (now strictly catch and release
only!) and to talk about his passion for the river. Lew is anxious about
the changes to water quality, vegetation, fish and birdlife in the whole
area. He has seen major species decline in the river over his lifetime –
from the 1940s until today:

> There were plenty of crabs, oysters on all the banks, mullet
> jumping all the time, day and night, you could hear them in the
> river … The water was that clear you could see the prawns on the
> edge, they were everywhere, all the time.
>
> When I moved to my house in Georges Hall in 1967, we
> had kingfishers sitting on the back fence because there's a creek
> behind our house. But today there's no more kingfishers, don't
> see any blue wrens which were there, don't see any bearded
> dragons and half the birds have all disappeared. We had finches
> all around the area in Warwick Farm, no finches anymore.

He draws on his sense of his own many heritages to explain his
motivations:

> I like to go down to River Road at Revesby, put my boat in the
> water and go up to Lugarno, to the Moons area and the Soily

Bottoms area, drift up and down the river whichever way the tide takes me …

I just love sitting in the boat, just relaxing, just waiting for that bite I really enjoy fishing, love the water, it's so beautiful, the colour of that water. The fishing … it's in me. A bit of Norwegian blood. The Vikings with the sea and everything.

Continually he returns to his Aboriginality as central to his narrative of environmental care, but his concern is also a result of spending time around the river as a child – his knowledge of it, and association of it with positive times spent there fishing at his Nan's place. On the river, Lew feels in his element: 'I love it, I love this land. Even as a kid, I loved this land, I just had a feeling for it, before I knew about my Aboriginality.'

What he enjoys now is to teach. Lew has found his role on the Land Council to be the way to express his concern for the river. His many activities in the Catchment Authorities and in the research for this book have all reflected his goals of fostering responsibility for the river. But perhaps more satisfying than anything has been his personal role. His Aboriginal grandson from Yass is 11 years old and comes up to stay with Lew for the school holidays. During one interview he talked about a recent visit when, he remembered, they had caught fish all day from 10:30 am onwards. Lew smiled as he explained how pleased he was that his grandson 'loves fishing'. Lew seems to relish his role as grandfather, sharing his knowledge of the environment with a younger generation in the hope that their care for the river will see the mud crabs and all the river life return and flourish as they did when he was young.

National Parks and
Aboriginal directions

While Lew has been generally happy in his relationship with the National Parks and Wildlife Service, his focus has been on the river itself, which continues to be largely outside the service's jurisdiction. Few of the people he knew in the Land Council used the Georges River National Park at all, implying that their resistance to paying parking fees reflected their more fundamental sense of being unwelcome in these areas.

Perhaps even more important is the fact that few young Aboriginal people in the city are enjoying the bush or the river as much as Lew's grandson does. The pace and thrills of city life offer more than enough distraction to keep many young people away from the remaining spaces on the river. The fact that many of these spaces have now been termed National Parks is no immediate attraction.

The areas which are now National Park are largely the sandstone country along the lower river. In the 1920s this was the landscape where Ellen Anderson had so actively gathered flowers and other plants, and Tom Williams senior and the young men from La Perouse had travelling along the lower river banks collecting mangroves for boomerangs and other artifacts. This wood was carved by all the Salt Pan Creek men, including Joe Anderson, who made not only boomerangs but also miniature boomerang-shaped hatpins and broaches.[23] While the river itself has remained accessible to people fishing, like Lew, the shoreline vegetation and the parklands on the sandstone have become much less accessible: the fences of encroaching houses and entry fees of National Parks alike seem to send 'No Entry' messages.

Tracy Banivanua-Mar has pointed out the highly politicised claim of National Parks in Australia – and other settler colonies – of protecting the characteristic 'nature' of the country for the good of the nation. She argues that at the turn of the twentieth century, the primary purpose of the declaration of National Parks in northern Australia was to secure 'waste' and 'vacant' land – marking it as unambiguously part of the settler nation state. This reflected anxiety both about external invaders and the internal assertions of Indigenous colonised peoples.[24] The political assertion of land as 'national' has closed off ownership and access to Indigenous people. This 'national' claim has been just as exclusionary as the better-recognised concept of the parklands as 'wilderness', untouched by any human society before the colonisers. More recently, the questions of both dislocation and exclusion of real people by conservation has been debated.[25]

Both the chauvinistic nature of the concept of a 'national' park, and the past and continuing exclusion of colonised peoples from the lands designated as 'national' wilderness park, are relevant to the parks on the Georges River. This has been complicated in two ways. Firstly, the National Parks and Wildlife Service has the dual role of the management of designated conservation zones inside parks, and of Aboriginal heritage – whether on or off-park. Secondly, the NPWS has just acquired the role of protector of marine conservation areas, now bringing its role in managing conservation zones on land into direct parallel with its role over protected areas in marine – and estuarine – environments.

The lands and waters which were accessible to Biddy Giles, Ellen Anderson, Judy Chester and, most recently, Lew Solberg are within what is now called the Georges River National Park, along both banks of the Georges River around Picnic Point and Mill Creek. The northern bank of the river from Picnic Point downstream to Salt Pan Creek had first been called a National Park when it had been clawed back by local working-class environmental groups from the threat of development in the 1950s. They wanted the park to reflect the interests of local people, with 'native' environments and spaces for relaxation and enjoyment. The Aboriginal residents of the Herne Bay hostel in the 1960s had shared the same easy access to the sandstone bushland which the Salt Pan Creek community had had in the 1920s for their wildflower gathering. The designation lapsed in 1967, but when the state took back formal control of these lands in 1992 it had defined them as National Park once again, and it began to manage them with the standard NPWS approach to protected areas, including strategies for the limitation of visitors and the strict control of their behaviour.

Despite increasingly tight management controls within the actual boundaries of the land declared to be National Park, the 1970s and 1980s had also seen complex interactions between Aboriginal people and the NPWS over Aboriginal heritage management all over the state. As discussed in the last chapter, these changes had been of great interest to many Aboriginal people on the river, both because of their city connections to land as well as their concern over their original rural homes. As there was no National Park on the Georges River at that time, the implications of the formal NPWS control over land had been less important to locals than this off-park role in the protection and management of heritage sites. Yet many city-based Aboriginal people knew that the NPWS had been facing strong pressure since at least 1983 from rural Aboriginal communities who were demanding that the ownership of National Parks be handed back to them, as had been done in a number of parks in the Northern Territory.

In 1992, when the NPWS resumed direct control of the Georges River parklands and renamed them 'National', the issue of Aboriginal control over land was returned to prominence, creating tension in the relationship between Aboriginal people and the NPWS on the river. This became even more important when the National Parks and Wildlife Service Act was finally amended in 1996 to allow the hand-back of National Parks to Aboriginal owners, even though it incorporated a mandatory commitment to joint management of the parklands.

More recently, in 2007 the area of the Georges River National Park was substantially expanded by extensions on the southern bank from Pleasure Point down to Mill Creek, meaning that it runs along both northern and southern shores of the Georges River.[26] This has raised questions such as who has authority over land which has been sequestered for conservation purposes? And who has control over the interpretation of events on those lands, particularly when they now encompass sites like the artwork at Sandy Point and the home of Biddy Giles on Guragurang, as well as approaching within metres of the site of the Salt Pan Creek camp itself?

While this might seem like an opportunity for joint management, the potential for such collaborative interpretation of these Georges River parklands has so far not been taken up by the NPWS. There is no formal co-management role for Aboriginal people in the Georges River National Park which would allow exploration of the complex recent Aboriginal histories all along the river. So once again, the lower estuarine Georges River is an unfulfilled blank page in terms of recognition of Aboriginal presence, past and present. The NPWS has changed considerably in the two decades since Jacko Campbell and others tried to push it further towards recognition of active, present-day Aboriginal people's interest in the lands it manages. There has been a major expansion of the numbers of Aboriginal people employed by the NPWS as managerial and research staff in its Culture and Heritage division, and as park liaison officers. But the joint management of National Parks has been put into practice only very slowly, and so far only in a few rural areas. These policies have not been completely satisfactory from the point of view of many of the participating Aboriginal communities. They have continued to campaign for a stronger managerial role and for firmer commitments from the NPWS to collaborate with them.[27]

Yet the jointly managed park arrangements demonstrate the possibilities for further developments in the Georges River parklands. Where the breakthrough initiatives have arisen, however, has been at the mouth of the river – with the Towra Team of young Aboriginal conservation trainees. Although there are two National Parks on either headland of Botany Bay, this collaboration between Aboriginal communities and the NPWS has not come about in relation to land, but to the new marine sanctuary at Towra Point – where the Georges River flows into Botany Bay.[28] This promontory includes Pelican Point, the home of William Rowley's mother, the Malones and many other Aboriginal families throughout the nineteenth century. William Rowley was born there. Before he moved to Salt Pan Creek, Rowley had not only fished commercially on Botany Bay, but had been caretaker of the oyster leases in the broad, shallow Weeney Bay on the eastern side of the Towra promontory. It is this unique area which is now a marine protected area.

The Towra Team consists of ten Aboriginal conservation trainees from the La Perouse community, the youngest only 15 when they began, but most in their 20s, all supported by two older Aboriginal mentors. The whole group is led by Dean Kelly, born in 1967 into the La Perouse community and now employed by National Parks as a community liaison officer. Kelly selected participants from all the families in the La Perouse, aiming to distribute opportunities evenly across the Aboriginal community there. Each of these young people was chosen because of their interest in learning and in the responsibilities for country which the job offered. As Kelly has pointed out, they had become separated from an active involvement with the land:

> These kids are very urban, their environment is [made of]
> concrete. A lot of them had lost that connection to country
> and bushland, even though it was so close, with our two
> National Parks there on the headlands of Botany Bay. They
> were pretty much disconnected from it and distracted by the
> bright lights that the city hosts.[29]

Although funded by NPWS, this initiative has succeeded because it sits to some degree outside the organisation. As Kelly describes:

> A lot of people say we should have followed the National Parks

The Towra Team, 2008: (back, l-r) Adam Russell, Sean Delsignore, Joanne Timbery, Natalie Timbery, Lindsay Holton, Merinda Davison; (front) Darren Cooley, Wayne Simms and Joel Kelly.

Act, but if I had I never would have done anything with this
project. So policy was something that was 'up there' and we
flew underneath it!

And the other thing that people need to understand is
where I sit amongst all of this. I'm like a big knot in the middle
of it, because I work for National Parks … and I sit on the
board of the Aboriginal Lands Council and I also do a lot of
other things in the community around sports. So I walk a very
fine line … One minute you're 'community' and one minute
you're 'department' … and it's very hard to find that balance.

The roles the trainees are fulfilling are formal and structured, allowing them to learn both the science and the politics of managing protected areas, such as the nesting places of migrating terns which are
also popular picnic grounds. Kelly explains that the young trainees
'never try to be police' but instead are increasingly successful in edu-
cating visitors about the impact of their presence. He sees the motivation among the young trainees to arise because the role is building
on their underlying 'sense of responsibility for looking after Towra'.

Their role is just as directly involved with cultural heritage management and in this Dean Kelly is in constant consultation with the
Land Council and through them the community:

The other thing is, within the same area, and only a couple
of hundred metres or so from where the birds nest, we've
returned in the last five years, approximately 70 Aboriginal
remains that came back from the museums, as part of the
Sydney Metropolitan repatriation program … So there you
are, there's another special area there that's very deeply
[important] to the Aboriginal community.

The role of the National Parks and Wildlife Service in heritage management is important in this process, but it is also limited. As Dean has
pointed out, there is conflict between the environmental conservation

imperative of the parks service and the broader Aboriginal understanding of environmental resources as reflections of culture. The
examples in this book show that the concept of nature *as* culture, as
well as being a body of resources for livelihood, has been sustained
by many different Aboriginal people along the river, despite changing economies.

Dean Kelly has highlighted two of the key limitations that he has
encountered in dealing with the NPWS on this issue:

> One problem with National Parks protecting Aboriginal
> heritage, was that they didn't look at it as holistic – it had to be
> something you could see, to protect it …
>
> The other problem was, they didn't recognise the
> Aboriginal [interest in] plants. There was no separation as far
> as culture with looking at land and at water. It was all one, and
> that's the way Aboriginal people looked after it, and respected
> it. Speaking to my community about boomerangs and about
> the mangroves, in 1967 the National Parks Act came into
> effect. They have had no boomerangs since that time, because
> now that plant becomes protected. And if you harvest that
> plant, regardless of what it was for – medicine, artefacts, or
> food – you would be charged and fined or jailed. So it's caused
> a whole lot of problems for our people. We are just trying to
> sort that out now, with access to country and use of natural
> resources.

Frustrations have remained with the structures for protecting heritage on the river arising from the State's National Parks legislation. The
questions raised by Dean Kelly and Lew Solberg point to the continuing pressures on the National Parks and Wildlife Service to respond to
Aboriginal goals – including demands that such awkward restrictions

are reshaped to meet the needs of today's communities. The major shifts that the Parks Service has made in the last two decades have offered some real hope that such flexibility might occur. These changes have come about as the result of constant pressure from Aboriginal communities. In each of the examples in this chapter it has been the interactions between Aboriginal groups – sometimes the Local Land Councils, at other times local families and individuals – which have pushed state agencies like Catchment Management Authorities and the NPWS into change.

ELEVEN

Reflections
in the river

The stories of these chapters, from Jonathon Goggey, Biddy Giles, Ellen Anderson and King Burraga through to Joe Pike, Judy and Janny Smith, Wayne Dargan, Lew Solberg and the Towra Team, all suggest different ways in which Aboriginal people on the Georges River over the last two hundred years have grappled with the challenges of initial colonisation and then an emerging modern city. As urban Aboriginal people, they have continued to be ignored both by many historians and by the planners of the 'modern' twentieth and twenty-first century city. Only with the massive industrialisation and urbanisation of 1960s were Aboriginal people suddenly noticed, although they had been there all along. Even then, city Aborigines have been collectively defined as uprooted and displaced rural populations, only 'Aboriginal' to the extent that they defined themselves by their old rural homelands.

Yet as this book demonstrates, living in the centre of the growing city, Aboriginal people survived the expectations that they would disappear. They have explored different strategies to rebuild communities from the fragments of early groups and the incoming travellers from across the eastern states. This has been the transformative process of resilience in conditions of stress, trauma and change: drawing on the past to create new futures.

Many of their individual and collective efforts have been aimed at challenging the attempts by the new nation to define them, to marginalise them and to exclude them. One manifestation of this has been the symbolic challenge to Australia Day celebrations on 26 January, which mark Governor Phillip's landing in Sydney Cove and the beginning of the long occupation of Aboriginal land with which this story – and many others – began. White Australia had developed an elaborate commemoration of this 'beginning' as the birth of the nation – and so the displacement of Aboriginal Australia. As early as 1938, Aboriginal people including Joe Anderson – King Burraga – and many others from Salt Pan Creek had challenged this way to understand the 'nation' in their Day of Mourning – an insistence that the invasion be seen as theft which continues to be mourned.[1]

This opposition was celebrated by a massive protest held in Sydney in 1988, the Bicentennial of Phillip's landing, when Aboriginal people from all over Australia marched through the streets of Sydney. They were supported by thousands of non-Aboriginal Australians of all backgrounds in rejecting the narrow sectional idea of the 'nation' which this celebration of the British claim had always been. Yet this 1988 'Long March' was not just a sorrowful memorial to theft, but a vivid celebration of the continuity of Aboriginal life – of 'survival'. This concept has been the one which has since become the motif for the regular Aboriginal day of celebration held on 26 January: sometimes called Invasion Day, it is now most often called Survival Day and, more recently in Sydney, Yabun. While this day celebrates Aboriginal communities all over the country, it has a special resonance in

Sydney – the start of the story of British invasion and the oldest city where now the largest urban Aboriginal population is living. Survival Day – Yabun – suggests the ways in which the revitalised and developing urban Aboriginal societies express their hopes for the future as well as their pasts.

The 1988 Aboriginal celebration to counter the Bicentennial finished not at Sydney Cove, but at Kurnell. The Aboriginal people who had gathered in the city in the morning decided collectively that the story had in fact started at Botany Bay, with Cook's landing at Kurnell in 1770. They chose to spend the long night, with supporters from the many non-Aboriginal communities who had shared the protest, around blazing campfires on that southern shore of Botany Bay, where the Georges River flows through to the sea.[2] Aboriginal people from central and northern Australia sang their songs of the ceremonies which tell about ancestral travels all the way across the country to the coast. As they sang them, they were bringing those story lines back, once more, to meet the river and the sea. As dawn broke, Aboriginal people from Sydney and the coast built cleansing fires, and invited everyone gathered there, black and white, to walk through the restoring smoke they had created.

That dawn was symbolic of many things about the transformative resilience of Aboriginal Australia. One of them was the centrality of rivers in the survival of the Aboriginal people in the city.

The story of the Georges River shows how the rivers on which Sydney was built played a crucial part in the way Aboriginal people could shape their strategies to meet the changes brought by the settlers and then their city. Rivers offered the mobility firstly to confront the settlers, but also to evade them. Then, perhaps even more importantly, the complex geography of Sydney rivers ensured the settlement could not spread evenly over the landscape. Instead the settlers leap-frogged from one patch of alluvial soil to another, leaving the many swampy flats, muddy banks, steep gullies and sandy ridges.

These remained accessible for Aboriginal people to live along the river and allowed them time and space to choose their ways to interact with the new economy and society.

It was the mobility offered by the rivers which allowed the emerging Aboriginal campsites to stay in contact with each other and to share knowledge and resources. These resources were many: the river's plants, fish, oysters and birds sustained generations of Aboriginal people well into the twentieth century. Together with the sandstone bush they offered currencies for trade, like fish, game, flowers and mangroves which could all be re-purposed from traditional uses to commodities to sell for cash for survival and in cultural exchanges with local whites. Yet the river also offered cultural resources because it had spaces which had not been conquered or taken over completely by settlers. So the gullies and swamps allowed continuations of the traditional stories to become entwined with the new lives that people were building for the future. In all of these ways, the river offered ways to 'make locality': to allow creative interactions which were shared among Aboriginal people – both traditional owners and newcomers – to make the available spaces into places which carried meaning, identity and connections.

The geographical spaces and the qualities of the river would not have allowed such resilience if it had not been for the flexibility of Aboriginal cultures. Despite the long traditions of endurance celebrated in much oral tradition – and misunderstood by the British as static timelessness – these cultures had the capacity to embrace change and negotiate new conditions. The emerging Aboriginal communities along the river survived because in those river spaces they were able to incorporate Aboriginal people from different areas and diverse local traditions. They could even include complete outsiders, like those white Australians such as Billy Giles and Tom Smith, provided they entered relationships with Aboriginal people with respect and appreciation. This complexity meant that the emerging city Aboriginal communities were changing, but it allowed those shifts to arise from the culture and conventions of past Aboriginal societies. In particular they drew on the processes of their cultural heritage to engage with their surrounding environments in order to forge an identity and to express adult responsibilities. Making these new spaces into meaningful places – being 'river girls' as Judy Chester saw it – was a central theme of all the changes we have traced through this book.

Tharawal Land Council members gave an insight into this continuing process in 2005 when they tried to stop the military from expanding its activities in the Cubbitch Barta National Estate area. A series of Land Council members – Glenda Chalker, Cliff Foley and Charlie Mundine – spoke at a Commonwealth inquiry.[3] First was Glenda Chalker, Land Council member and chair of the Cubbitch Barta Native Title Elders Group, whose family has long traditional roots in the Dharawal clans of the area:

> As a member of the Tharawal Local Aboriginal Land
> Council, I participated in the environmental impact study
> that took place for the proposed Sydney airport [in 1996].
> It gave the Aboriginal community a chance to have a look
> at the Aboriginal sites that are within the Holsworthy area.
> Over a seven-week period, it took about 20 of us to record
> approximately one-third of … the Holsworthy area … It is
> a very special place. It provides a connection for my family's
> history from a little bit further south through to the Sydney
> area. There is some stuff in there that is absolutely incredible
> that if you have not seen it you would not believe it.

Cliff Foley, then chairperson of the Land Council, had grown up in Nambucca Heads, before moving to Sydney. Foley had a keen interest in the evidence of Aboriginal people living on the river. He had worked with his partner, Robyn Williams, in the early 1990s to organise field trips to Sandy Point and other Georges River locations for students from TAFE Aboriginal studies and from UTS history courses.[4]

Even so, the cultural richness of the Holsworthy lands had been unexpected. At the hearing in 2005, he spoke about the impact which working on the project in 1996 had had on Land Council members:

> what shocked and surprised us – and what really created the
> urgency for us to have a presentation here today – is the pristine
> nature of those sites out there. Those sites are still untouched.
> We talk about our old people. Their tools and their materials for
> doing business are still there; they are still in the shelters. Our
> old people put them away and they are still where they placed
> them. There is nothing else like that in Sydney ... 90 per cent
> of the stuff out there is untouched ... Charlie [Mundine]
> and I come from up the north coast around Goombangaree
> country, but this place so close to Sydney is incredible. It is
> within our boundary and it is part of our responsibility as an
> Aboriginal land council to ensure that that area of significance
> and importance to our people is looked after and to provide the
> opportunity to explain that to the broader public.

The Land Council, Foley explained, had formally proposed the nomination for the National Estate listing and had strongly supported the Native Title group:

> We have done that and achieved that in our responsibility
> as Aboriginal people to maintain, protect and look after
> these places and to present evidence in appropriate forums to
> get that message across. Not just us as Aboriginal people but
> all Australians have a unique opportunity with something
> so close to Sydney that is pristine. Part of our brief and
> our responsibility as Aboriginal people and in our role with
> our land council is to raise this issue.

Then Charlie Mundine, another Land Council member spoke:

> I always look at [it] from the perspective of where I come
> from. My backyard is the Washpool National Park and I can

see similarities between it and this land. Also, I have been
through other lands such as in Arnhem Land, and everyone
raves about that. You have got it here, believe you me. Plus,
there are some animals, such as the frogs, which are never
found anywhere else. How do you look after them?

   We as Aboriginal people do not just look at it and say,
'These are our sites.' No, we have to look at it as the total care
of the land: how do we look after the whole lot of it?

For city land councils like Tharawal, Foley explained, this as a central
part of their identity and their role:

> All Aboriginal people within our boundary are entitled
> to be members of our land council. We have some 700
> members. Every adult Aboriginal person who resides within
> our boundaries is entitled to be a member of our land council.
> We consult widely. We have partnerships with our other
> organisations. The nature of the way we operate with our
> community business is that we are of the view that there is
> only one community on the ground ...
>
>   Cultural heritage matters are a part of our core business
> and responsibilities.

The sense of cultural responsibility to care for country is evident in
each of the speakers from the Land Council in this hearing, wherever their families had come from. Reflecting in 2006 on the Tharawal
Land Council's attempt to protect Cubbitch Barta, Foley reiterated:
'there's just one mob in Sydney. We started off saying that in all our
submissions ... There's inherent Indigenous responsibilities – Aboriginal cultural responsibilities – its not dependent on where you are.'[5]

   The questions around how the pressures of the present shape the
way the past is understood, are always complex. The present can open
valuable new questions, but can just as easily lead to the neglect of
important themes which do not fit into dominant preoccupations. It

has been particularly important that the long campaigns for recognition of Aboriginal land rights and heritage values have had to battle so hard against the Eurocentric denigration of 'nomadism', so that Aboriginal advocates have had to explain at length the close affiliations to particular places. This has meant they have often had to play down the important role of mobility in maintaining responsible connections to the many places of their country across wide areas. Once victories had been won in this struggle for the recognition of rights to land, the resulting legislative policy and legal systems have been cast entirely in terms of British Australian law, resting on property titles founded on assumptions of sedentarism and surveyed plots of land. Building on the older legislation of the National Parks and Wildlife Service and other heritage bodies to protect sites and places of significance to Aboriginal people, the new laws and the powerful ideologies which surround them have stressed fixed and bounded sites as the only way to recognise and honour Aboriginal meanings.

We have found from this history of Aboriginal people on the Georges River that movement needs to be acknowledged too in order to understand Aboriginal significance in land. The many ways in which Aboriginal 'sites' are connected across time and across space to the other places of significance in rural areas for Aboriginal people today has not just been a product of massive post-1945 urbanisation. Instead it has been a characteristic of Aboriginal history on the Georges River – and no doubt elsewhere – across the whole period of settlement. Aboriginal people have been mobile throughout this time. They have not travelled randomly. Some of the sustained patterns of movement has reflected traditional patterns of mobility, between the north coast and the estuarine rivers of Sydney and on to the south coast, or between the south coast and Sydney across to the Murray River. Other movements have reflected the widening networks of life under the new economy, like the network from the Castlereagh River to the Georges River, possibly established by Jimmy Lowndes in the mid-nineteenth century and certainly consolidated by Tom Williams senior and Bob and Bert Groves in the early twentieth.

Above all, the everyday practice of travelling along the Georges River itself, so marked a characteristic of the life of Pemulwuy, has continued to shape the way the Aboriginal communities and their places along the river have identified themselves and have built the relations between them. This has been a central element in nurturing the resilience we have described on the river. It has added a dimension of meaning to the significance of each of the individual places, the localities created by Aboriginal people at different times in the last 220 years, which might be now be identified along the river as evidence of those histories.

These histories have demonstrated as well the way resistance to colonialism and to injustice has contributed to the transformative qualities of resilience. From Biddy's subtle cultural assertion and Ellen's shrewd cultural exchange to Pemulwuy, Jonathon Goggey and Joe Anderson's direct challenges to injustice and displacement, resistance has been a recurring theme. It did not disappear with the confusion of the immediate post-war migration and industrialisation. Advocates like Bert Groves and Charlie Leon were able to link the displaced families who were scattered across the bare new suburbs not only to other incoming migrants but to the long-established families on the river. Jacko Campbell and Ted Thomas were then able to work with the younger generation of new citizens of the river to build innovative cultural as well as political strategies for the future. The political resistance demonstrated by all of these, and many other Aboriginal people in the city, was not a response which built only on a call for respect for the past. Instead each of these advocates was evaluating the changing conditions in which they were trying to build innovative strategies for the future. The river – and the mobility it has sustained – has been an important contributor in both the links with the past and the capacity to look to the future. In turn, these have comprised key elements of the resilience which Aboriginal city communities have shown in the face of continuing challenges.

To acknowledge the importance of mobility calls for a new way to understand recognition of Aboriginal heritage interests as well as ownership in public places. Rather than bounded 'sites of significance' being mapped and protected by the NPWS, for example, it is the whole river here, along with the capacity to move along it, which needs to be recognised. Perhaps this is the reason so many Aboriginal people expressed a desire to create a claim for the whole river, using the Native Title Act or whatever means was to hand, to draw together all the river's Local Aboriginal Land Councils. Such a claim would recognise the river as a sustained corridor of the mobility which has contributed powerfully to the resilience of Aboriginal contemporary cultures.

This could be a central element, for example, in the way in which Aboriginal co-management of the National Park at Georges River might be reconsidered, as having a riverine as well as a land-based component now that the Department of Environment and Climate Change has some responsibility over some waterways. It would allow a way to explain the significance of the many community sites along the river, like Goggey's land, Biddy and Billy Giles' farm, Ellen Anderson's and William Rowley's blocks and Pelican Point. It would position them as they always have been in Aboriginal eyes – as places along a continuous passage, given additional meanings because of their links to other sites up and down stream. Such recognition would challenge the orthodoxy that Aboriginal significance resides only in bounded sites and not in the pathways, songlines and waterways which enabled mobility and give wider meaning to the places people had made.

The mobility which the river has enabled has not only been physical. It has been most importantly the stories about places and people which the river has allowed communities to share. These too are a key element in resilience, allowing people to make sense of both the past and the present. These links between Aboriginal people, their family stories – wherever they came from – and the places they have cared about as they changed, were expressed eloquently in 2005 in the Tharawal Land Council's statement about Cubbitch Barta:

> Aboriginal significance gives an understanding of our past;
> enriches our present and continues to be of importance
> to our future ... The evidence of the manifestations of
> Aboriginal people's relationship with our country is displayed
> in abundance throughout the valleys and ridges of this
> landscape. Each Aboriginal site has its place; every Aboriginal
> place has its story in the life of an Aboriginal family. Country
> is alive with stories.[6]

Notes

Abbreviations

A&U	Allen & Unwin
AAF	Aboriginal Australian Fellowship
ANU	Australian National University
APB	Aborigines Protection Board
BDM	Register of Births, Deaths and Marriages (NSW)
CMA	Catchment Management Authority
DECC	Department of Environment and Climate Change (NSW)
DL	Department of Lands (NSW)
HRA	*Historical Records of Australia*
HRNSW	*Historical Records of New South Wales*
LALC	Local Aboriginal Land Council
ML MS	Mitchell Library, State Library of NSW, Manuscripts
NAA	National Archives of Australia
NIAC	Northern Illawarra Aboriginal Collective
NPWS	National Parks and Wildlife Service (NSW)
RAHS	Royal Australian Historical Society
SRNSW	State Records New South Wales
TAFE	Tertiary and Further Education
UNSW	University of New South Wales
UTS	University of Technology Sydney

1 Aboriginal people and city rivers: an introduction

1 'Australian royalty pleads for his people: Burraga, chief of Aboriginal Thirroul tribe, to petition King for blacks' representation in Federal Parliament',*Cinesound Review*, no 100, 29 Sept 1933. 'Thirroul' is another spelling of 'Dharawal', and survives in the name of the town near Wollongong, at the southern edge of the language group's range.

2 S Luthar, D Cicchetti and B Becker, 'The construct of resilience: a critical evaluation and guidelines for future work', *Child Development*, 71(3), 2000, pp 543–62.

3 B Walker, C Holling, S Carpenter and A Kinzig, 'Resilience, adaptability and transformability in social-ecological systems', *Ecology and Society*, 9(2)5, 2004: <http://www.ecologyandsociety.org/vol9/iss2/art5/>.

4 For Sydney people see KV Smith, *Eora: Mapping Aboriginal Sydney 1770–1850*, State Library of NSW, Sydney, 2006: <http://www.sl.nsw.gov.au/events/ exhibitions/2006/eora/index.html> (viewed 28 April 2009); V Attenbrow, *Sydney's Aboriginal Past: Investigating the Archaeological and Historical Records*, UNSW Press, Sydney, 2002; G Karskens, *The Colony: A History of Early Sydney*, A&U, Sydney 2009; D Foley and R Maynard, *Repossession of Our Spirit: Traditional Owners of Northern Sydney*, Aboriginal History Inc, Canberra, 2001; for the western Dharug see J Kohen and J Brook, *The Parramatta Native Institution and the Black Town: A History*, UNSW Press, Sydney, 1991; for the Dharug at Parramatta see M Flynn, 'Place of eels: Parramatta and the Aboriginal clans of the Sydney region 1788–1845', unpublished, 1995; for Gundungurra see J Smith, 'Gundungurra country', PhD thesis, Indigenous Studies, Macquarie University, 2008; and for Wadi Wadi see C Illert/NIAC, *Early Ancestors of Illawarra's Wadi-Wadi People*, C Illert, Wollongong, 2003.

5 F Merlan, *Caging the Rainbow: Places, Politics and Aborigines in a Northern Australian Town*, University of Hawai'i Press, Honolulu,1998; H Goodall, *Invasion to Embassy: Land in Aboriginal Politics in New South Wales 1770– 1972*, A&U, Sydney, 1996, pp 4–6.

6 M Langton, 'What do we mean by wilderness? Wilderness and terra nullius in Australian art', *The Sydney Papers*, 8(1), 1996; M Langton, Z Ma Rhea, M Ayre and J Pope, 'Traditional lifestyles and biodiversity use: Regional report for Australia, Asia and the Middle East', in *Composite Report on the Status and Trends Regarding the Knowledge, Innovations and Practices of Indigenous and Local Communities Relevant to the Conservation and Sustainable Use of Biodiversity*, UN Environment Program, 2003; Merlan, *Caging the Rainbow*; Kolig, 'Noah's ark revisited: On the myth-land connection in early Aboriginal thought', *Oceania*, 51, 1980, pp 118–32.

7 RF Ellen, 'What Black Elk left unsaid: On the illusory images of Green primitivism', *Anthropology Today*, 2(6), 1986, pp 8–12; RF Ellen, *The Cultural Relations of Classification: An Analysis of Nuaulu Animal Categories from Central Seram*, Cambridge University Press, Cambridge, 1993; VD Nazarea, 'A view from a point: Ethnoecology as situated knowledge', in VD Nazarea (ed), *Ethnoecology: Situated Knowledge/Located Lives*, University of Arizona Press, Tucson, 1999; B Moggeridge, 'Aboriginal people and ground

water', unpublished MSc thesis, Hydrogeology, UTS, 2005, pp 9–15; RH Mathews,'Some mythology of the Gandangara tribe, New South Wales', *Zeitschrift für Ethnologie*, vol 40, 1908.

8   *Yorta Yorta Community v The State of Victoria & Ors* [1998], FC-VG 600195, FC 1606, n 129: <www.austlii.edu.au/au/cases/cth/FCA/1998/1606.html>.

9   G Cederloff, *Landscapes and the Law: Environmental Politics, Regional Histories and Contests over Nature*, Permanent Black, New Delhi, 2008' pp 4–22.

10 F Berkes, *Sacred Ecology: Traditional Ecological Knowledge and Resource Management*, Taylor and Francis, Philadelphia/London, 1999.

11 H Goodall, 'Riding the tide: Indigenous knowledge, history and water in a changing Australia', *Environment and History*, 14(3), 2008, pp 355–84; Gamilaaray Community members, M Cotter and I Davidson, 'The Gamilaraay Resource Use Project', Australian Institute of Aboriginal and Torres Strait Islander Studies conference, Canberra, 22–25 Nov 2004; A English, *The Sea and the Rock Gives us a Feed: Mapping and Managing Gumbaingirr Wild Resource Use Places*, NSW NPWS, Sydney, 2002; P Thompson, 'Aboriginal cultural heritage', in Inverell Research Service Centre (ed), *Boobera Lagoon: Environmental Audit*, NSW Department of Land and Water Conservation, Inverell, 1993.

12 TG Vallance, TD Moore and EW Groves, *Natures Investigator: The Diary of Robert Brown in Australia 1801–1805*, Australian Biological Resources Study, Canberra, 2001, pp 445–46.

13 A Appadurai, 'The production of locality', in R Fardon (ed), *Counterworks: Managing the Diversity of Knowledge*, Routledge, London/New York, 1995, pp 204–25; A Appadurai, *Modernity at Large: Cultural Dimensions of Globalisation*, University of Minneapolis Press, Minneapolis/London, 1996; H Raffles, '"Local theory": Nature and the making of an Amazonian place', *Cultural Anthropology*, 14(3), 1999, pp 323–60; Cederlof, *Landscapes and the Law*, p 60.

14 Raffles, 'Local theory', pp 329, 324.

15 Berkes, *Sacred Ecology*; Raffles, 'Local theory'; Cederlöff, *Landscapes and the Law*.

16 M de Certeau, *The Practice of Everyday Life*, trans S Rendall, University of California Press, Berkeley, 1984; D Byrne and M Nugent, *Mapping Attachment: A Spatial Approach to Aboriginal Post-Contact Heritage*, NSW Department of Environment and Conservation, Sydney, 2004.

17 H Goodall, S Wearing, D Byrne and A Cadzow, 'Fishing the Georges River: Cultural diversity and urban environments', in A Wise and S Velayutham (eds), *Everyday Multiculturalism*, Palgrave, London, 2009.

18 Merlan, *Caging the Rainbow*.

19 Merlan, *Caging the Rainbow*; Kolig, 'Noah's ark revisited'; K Palmer, 'Migration and rights to land in the Pilbara', in N Peterson and M Langton (eds), *Aborigines, Land and Land Rights*, Australian Institute of Aboriginal Studies, Canberra, 1983, pp 172–79.

20 I Chambers, *Migrancy, Culture, Identity*, Routledge, London/New York, 1994.

21 L Malkki, 'National Geographic: The rooting of peoples and the

territorialization of national identity among scholars and refugees', *Cultural Anthropology*, 7(1), 1992, pp 24–44.

22 D Massey, *Space, Place and Gender*, Polity Press, Cambridge, 1994; D Massey, *For Space*, Sage, London, 2005; YF Tuan, *Space and Place: The Perspective of Experience*, University of Minneapolis Press, Minneapolis, 1977; T Ingold, *The Perception of the Environment: Essays on Livelihood, Dwelling and Skill*, Routledge, London, 2000.

23 In different ways, this approach is seen in both Merlan, *Caging the Rainbow*, and Cederloff, *Landscapes and the Law*.

24 TILCEPA was set up in 2000 by the World Commission on Protected Areas and the Commission on Environmental, Economic, and Social Policy of the International Union for the Conservation of Nature. This inter-commission initiative evolved from a Task Force on Local Communities and Protected Areas, created in 1999, which had a similar mandate.

25 W Cronon, 'A place for stories: Nature, history, and narrative', *Journal of American History*, 78(4), 1992, pp 1347–76; W Cronon (ed), *Uncommon Ground: Toward Reinventing Nature*, WW Norton & Co, New York, 1995; W Cronon, 'The trouble with wilderness, or, getting back to the wrong nature', *Environmental History*, 1(1), 1996, pp 7–28; 47–55; T Griffiths, *Forests of Ash: An Environmental History*, Cambridge University Press, Cambridge/ New York, 2001.

26 D Benson and J Howell, *Taken for Granted: The Bushland of Sydney and its Suburbs*, rev edn, Kangaroo Press/Royal Botanic Gardens Sydney, Sydney, 1996.

27 NG Butlin (ed), *Sydney's Environmental Amenity 1970–1975: A Study in the System of Waste Management and Pollution Control*, ANU Press, Canberra, 1976.

28 JF Bird, 'The nineteenth-century soap industry and its exploitation of intertidal vegetation in Eastern Australia', *Australian Geographer*, 14, 1978, pp 38–41; L McLoughlin, *The Middle Lane Cove River: A History and a Future*, Centre for Environmental and Urban Studies, Macquarie University, Sydney, 1985; L McLoughlin, 'Mangroves and grass swamps: Changes in the shoreline vegetation of the middle Lane Cove River, Sydney 1780s–1880s', *Wetlands*, 7(1), 1987, pp 13–24; RJ Haworth, 'Changes in mangrove/salt-marsh distribution in the Georges River estuary, southern Sydney 1930–1970', *Wetlands*, 20(2), 2002, pp 80–103; P McManus, 'Mangrove battlelines: Culture/nature and ecological restoration', *Australian Geographer*, 37(1), 2006. pp 57–71.

29 RJ Haworth, 'Bush tracks and bush blocks: The aerial photographic record from southwest Sydney 1930–1950', *People and the Physical Environment Research (PAPER)*, 49, 1995, pp 32–42.

30 L Head and P Muir, 'Nativeness, invasiveness and nation in Australian plants', *Geographical Review*, 94(2), 2004, pp 199–217.

31 McLoughlin, 'Mangroves and grass swamps'; McManus, 'Mangrove battlelines'.

32 RJ Kelly (Member for East Hills) and JB Renshaw (Deputy Premier/Treasurer/ Minister for Lands), *NSW Parliamentary Debates*, Legislative Assembly, 3rd

session, 39th Parliament, 22 Feb 1961, vol 35, pp 2555–56.

33 *St George and Sutherland Shire Leader*, 4 Jan 1967, p 13; 23 Aug 1967, p 2; *The Torch*, 23 Aug 1967, p 7; 29 Apr 1967, p 5.

34 T Banivanua-Mar, 'Carving wilderness: Queensland's parks movement and the unsettling of emptied lands 1890–1910', paper to Department of Modern History, Macquarie University, 2 Apr 2008 (publication forthcoming).

35 M Hitchcock, *Wattle*, Australian Govt Printing Service, Canberra, 1991; P Timms, *Australia's Quarter Acre: The Story of the Ordinary Suburban Garden*, Miegunyah Press, Melbourne, 2006, pp 170–89; L Robin, *How a Continent Created a Nation*, UNSW Press, Sydney, 2007, pp 13–18.

36 Tharawal LALC (signed by Cliff Foley, chairperson), 'Relocation of 171st Aviation Squadron to Holsworthy Barracks', submission to the Parliamentary Standing Committee on Public Works, House of Reps, Parliament of Australia, Canberra, 9 Nov 2005: <www.aph.gov.au/House/committee/pwc/ holsworthy171/subs/sub2.pdf > (viewed 8 Feb 2009).

2 Rethinking the river: Pemulwuy and beyond

1   'Australian royalty pleads for his people: Burraga, chief of Aboriginal Thirroul tribe, to petition King for blacks' representation in Federal Parliament', *Cinesound Review*, no 100, 29 Sept 1933.

2   KV Smith and A Bourke, *Eora: Mapping Aboriginal Sydney 1770–1850*, State Library of NSW, Sydney, 2006.

3   Compare K Willey, *When the Sky Fell Down: The Destruction of the Tribes of the Sydney Region 1788–1850s*, Collins, Sydney, 1979; M Flynn, 'Place of eels: Parramatta and the Aboriginal clans of the Sydney region 1788–1845', unpublished, 1995; J Brook and JL Kohen, *The Parramatta Native Institution and the Black Town: A History*, UNSW Press, Sydney, 1991; M Nugent, *Botany Bay: Where Histories Meet*, A&U, Sydney, 2005.

4   Shayne Williams, pers comm; JL Kohen, 'The Dharug of the Western Cumberland Plain: ethnography and demography', in B Meehan and R Jones (eds), *Archaeology with Ethnography: An Australian Perspective*, Department of Prehistory & Research School of Pacific Studies, ANU, Canberra, 1988; JL Kohen, *The Darug and their Neighbours*, Darug link/Bankstown & District Historical Society, Sydney 1993; J Lawrence, *A Pictorial History of the Sutherland Shire*, (captions by P Curbey), Kingsclear Books, Sydney, 1997, ch 2.

5   Smith, *Eora*.

6   Navin Officer Heritage Consultants/PPK, *Proposal for a Second Sydney Airport at Badgerys Creek or Holsworthy Military Area: Technical Paper ~ Aboriginal Cultural Heritage*, vol 11, (C'wth) Dept of Transport and Regional Development, Sydney, 1997; Sydney Prehistory Group, *In Search of the Cobrakall: A Survey of the Aboriginal Sites in the Campbelltown Area South of Sydney*, pt 1, NPWS, Sydney, 1983; FD McCarthy, *Archaeological Reconnaissance of Aboriginal Sites: Port Hacking and the Georges River*, Australian Museum: Archaeological Reconnaissance Reports 1936–1946, AIATSIS, MS 790, 1936; Sutherland Library Local Studies, J Thomas and

B Gunther, *Aboriginal Site Survey Report: Liverpool Weir Fishway*, Gandangara LALC, Liverpool, Liverpool Library Local Studies, 1996. This list is far from exhaustive.

7   These are now buried under 1960s council development works: R Staples, interviewed by H Goodall 27 Oct 2005. Carvings in Rockdale (which were known to local people) were also buried under roadworks in the 1960s: IM Sim, 'Records of the rock engravings of the Sydney district,n 111–37, pt 2, *Mankind*, 6(2), 1963; 'Aboriginal rock carvings, Rocky Point, now under Riverside Drive', nd, photo LH 54/080, Rockdale Library Local Studies.

8   V Attenbrow, *Sydney's Aboriginal Past: Investigating the Archaeological and Historical Records* UNSW Press, Sydney, 2002; G Karskens, *The Colony: A History of Early Sydney*, A&U, Sydney, 2009, ch 12.

9   P Adam, 'Mangroves and saltmarsh communities', in BJ Atwell, PE Kriedemann and CGN Turnbull (eds), *Plants in Action: Adaptation in Nature, Performance in Cultivation*, Macmillan, Melbourne, 1998, pp 563–64; RJ Haworth, 'The shaping of Sydney by its urban geology', *Quaternary International*, 103, 2003, pp 41–55; P Kundstadter, 'Socio-economic and demographic aspects of mangrove settlements', in P Kundstadter, ECF Bird and S Sabhasri (eds), *Man in the Mangroves: The Socio-Economic Situation of Human Settlements in Mangrove Forests*, UN University, New York, 1986, p 3.

10 E Dark, *The Timeless Land*, Collins, London, 1943; *Storm Of Time*, Collins, London, 1948; *No Barrier*, Collins, London, 1954; K Grenville, *The Secret River*, Text Publishing, Melbourne, 2005; *The Lieutenant*, Text Publishing, Melbourne, 2008; D Adelaide, *Serpent Dust*, Vintage, Sydney, 1998; E Willmot, *Pemulwuy the Rainbow Warrior*, Weldons, Sydney, 1987; G Bostock, 'Colebe', *Meanjin*, 53(4), 1994. pp 613–18; and 'Pemulwuy', *Ulitarra*, 6, 1994, pp 93–96.

11 I Clendinnen, *Dancing with Strangers*, Text Publishing, Melbourne, 2003; KV Smith, *Bennelong: The Coming in of the Eora ~ Sydney Cove 1788–1792*, Kangaroo Press, Sydney, 2001; Karskens, *The Colony*, esp chs 2,11, 12 and 14.

12 Willey, *When the Sky Fell Down*, p 46.

13 Karskens, *The Colony*, ch 11.

14 Karskens, *The Colony*, ch 14.

15 JL Kohen, *Daruganora: Darug Country ~ The Place and the People*, Darug Tribal Aboriginal Corporation, Sydney, 2006; Smith, *Eora*.

16 The Sydney Prehistory Group investigated areas to the south of the military reserve (see *In Search of the Cobrakall*, 1983); Navin Officer Heritage Consultants for PPK, *Proposal for a Second Sydney Airport* ch 4 (citing studies of L McMah 'A quantitative analysis of the Aboriginal rock carvings in the district of Sydney and the Hawkesbury River', BA (hons) thesis, University of Sydney, 1965; N Officer, 'From Tuggerah to Dharawal: Variation and function within a regional art style', BA (hons) thesis, Dept Prehistory and Anthropology, ANU, 1984; and J McDonald, 'Dreamtime superhighway: An analysis of Sydney Basin rock art and prehistoric information exchange', PhD thesis, Dept Prehistory and Anthropology, ANU, 1994).

17 JL Smith, 'Gundungurra country', PhD thesis, Indigenous Studies, Macquarie University, 2008; C Illert, *Early Ancestors of Illawarra's Wadi-Wadi People*,

C Illert, Wollongong, 2003; Flynn, 'Place of eels'; Brook and Kohen, *The Parramatta Native Institution*; Kohen, *Daruganora*.

18 S Rosen, *Bankstown: A Sense of Identity*, Hale & Iremonger, Sydney, 1996; C Keating, *On the Frontier: A Social History of Liverpool*, Hale & Iremonger, Sydney, 1996; S Gapps, 'A history of Fairfield City' (working title), Fairfield City Council, Sydney, forthcoming 2009.

19 Nugent, *Botany Bay*.

20 R Langford Ginibi, *Don't Take Your Love to Town*, Penguin, Melbourne, 1988.

21 G Cowlishaw, *The City's Outback*, UNSW Press, Sydney, 2009; Brook and Kohen, *The Parramatta Native Institution;* Kohen, *Daruganora*.

22 K Langloh Parker, *The Euahlayi Tribe: A Study of Aboriginal Life in Australia*, Archibald Constable, London, 1905, p 39; H Goodall, 'Colonialism and catastrophe: contested rememberance of measles and bombs in a Pitjantjatjara community', in K Darian-Smith and P Hamilton (eds), *Memory and History in Twentieth Century Australia*, Oxford University Press, Melbourne, 1994, pp 55–76.

23 Karskens, *The Colony*, chs 11 and 12.

24 Phillip's journal from 1788 to 1792 appears in J Hunter, *An Historical Journal of Events in Sydney and at Sea 1787–1792* (facs edn, J Bach ed, Angus & Robertson/RAHS, Sydney, 1968), p 327.

25 J Hunter, 'Map of the colony of NSW', 1798, *HRNSW*, vol 3, opp p 347.

26 W Tench, *A Complete Account of the Settlement at Port Jackson*, G Nicol & J Sewell, London, 1793, ch 12 (reprinted as *1788: Comprising 'A Narrative of the Expedition to Botany Bay' and 'A Complete Account of the Settlement at Port Jackson'*, ed T Flannery, Text Publishing, Melbourne, 1996, pp 164–176. Bennelong and Colebe refused to disclose Pemulwuy's location.

27 D Collins, *Account of the English Colony of New South Wales*, T Cadell & W Davis, London, 1802 (facs edn, ed B Fletcher, Reed/RAHS, Sydney, 1975, pp 20 and 70).

28 Collins, *Account of the English Colony*, p 24

29 P King, 'Orders', 22 Nov 1801, *HRA*, 1:3, pp 466–67.

30 King, 'Orders'; P King to Lord Hobart, 30 Oct 1802, *HRNSW*, vol 4, p 867.

31 King to Hobart, 30 Oct 1802. The discrepancy echoes the contradictions in stories about the death of Pigeon, a resistance fighter in the Kimberleys in the early twentieth century: see S Muecke, 'Discourse, history, fiction: Language and Aboriginal history', *Australian Journal of Cultural Studies*, 1(1), 1983, pp 71–79. The version of Pemulwuy's shooting and beheading is consistent with narratives of vengeful settlers, although it marginalises the Aboriginal people who may have been active in the conflict on any side.

32 G Caley, in JEB Currey (ed), *Reflections on the Colony of New South Wales: George Caley*, Lansdowne, Sydney, 1966, p 49 (cited in Flynn, 'Place of eels', pp 61–62): see also pp 91, 140.

33 Caley, *Reflections on the Colony*.

34 King to Hobart, 30 Oct 1802.

35 *Sydney Gazette*, 19 Aug 1804, p 3; see also 5 May 1805, p 1; and 9 June 1805, pp 2 and 4.

36 *Sydney Gazette*, 1 and 15 Oct 1809, p 2, in BJ Madden, 'Attack by natives:

Punchbowl 1809', *Bankstown Historical Society Newsletter*, 10(3-4), 1976, p 17.

37 Rosen, *Bankstown*, p 27.

38 *Sydney Gazette*, 24 June 1804, p 2; E Willmot, *Pemulwuy the Rainbow Warrior*, Weldons, Sydney, 1987.

3 Holding on to country: Goggey's river

1 C Liston, 'The Dharawal and Gandangara in colonial Campbelltown', *Aboriginal History*, 12, 1988, pp 49–59.

2 Liverpool Regional Museum, *Sweetgrass and Cohbra*, Liverpool Regional Museum, Sydney, 2001, p 13.

3 L Macquarie, [1810], *Journals of his Tours in New South Wales and Van Diemen's Land 1810–1822*, P Mander Jones (ed), Public Library of NSW, Sydney, 1956, pp 6 and 9.

4 Keating, *On the Frontier: A Social History of Liverpool*, H& I, Sydney, 1996, p 19.

5 Accounts of the following events from Liston, 'The Dharawal and Gandangara'; Brook and Kohen, *The Native Institution*, 1991, pp 21–36; Willey, *When the Sky Fell Down*, 1979, pp 118–216.

6 C Throsby to D'Arcy Wentworth, 5 April 1816, Wentworth Correspondence 1809–1816, ML MS A752, f 183 (cited in Liston, 'Dharawal and Gandangara', p 58); *Sydney Gazette*, 23 Mar 1816, p 2.

7 D d'Urville (1824) in C Dyer, *The French Explorers and the Aboriginal Australians 1722–1839*, UQP, Brisbane, 2005, pp 168–72; KV Smith, *King Bungaree*, Kangaroo Press, Sydney, 1992, pp 170–73.

8 See Evidence of Mahroot, 1845, in *Report from the NSW Select Committee on the Condition of the Aborigines*, Government Printers, Sydney.

9 Karskens emphasises the long-term impacts of the small pox epidemic, but also points out that it was a convenient fallacy for the settlers to believe that Aboriginal people had 'disappeared' after either the epidemic or the Appin Massacre: *The Colony: A History of Early Sydney*, A&U, Sydney, 2009.

10 MH Ellis, *Lachlan Macquarie: His Life, Adventures and Times,* Dymocks, Sydney, 1947, p 358 (cited in Liston, 'Dharawal and Gandangara', p 58).

11 Liverpool Regional Museum, *Sweetgrass and Cohbra*, Liverpool Regional Museum, Sydney, 2001, p 13.

12 Liston, 'Dharawal and the Gandangara', pp 57–58.

13 JL Kohen, *The Aborigines in the West: Prehistory to the Present*, Western Sydney Project, Nepean CAE, Sydney, 1985; Keating, *On the Frontier*, p 19.

14 C Lucas, Stapleton & Partners, *Voyager Point: Assessment of Historical Archaeological Significance*, prepared for Wattle Grove Developments, Sydney, 1996.

15 Keating, *On the Frontier*, p 43.

16 A MacKenzie, 'Australian languages and traditions', *Journal of the Anthropological Institute of Great Britain and Ireland*, 7, 1878, pp 232–74. John Rowley, son of Capt Thomas Rowley from Harris Creek and uncle of the John Rowley who tried to evict Jonathon Goggey from Voyager Point, was a contributor to the same volume (pp 258–62).

17 Keating, *On the Frontier*, p 43.

18 T Rowley jnr's son: family genealogist, 'Thomas Rowley', <www.home. mira.net /~merowley/rowley/thomas.html>. See also MacKenzie, "Australian languages'.

19 J Goggey, Petition to the Governor General, 18 Nov 1857, SRNSW, NRS 7933, Department of Lands and Public Works, Correspondence: letters received 1856–1866, 57/4196, [5/3581] (identified by Terry Kass, consultant historian and researcher in Lands Department history).

20 H Reynolds, *Law of the Land*, 2nd edn, Penguin, Melbourne, 1992 (orig 1987).

21 H Goodall, *Invasion to Embassy: Land in Aboriginal Politics in New South Wales 1770–1972*, A&U, Sydney, 1996, pp 44–56; H Goodall, 'Land in our own country: the Aboriginal Land Rights movement in south eastern Australia 1860–1914', *Aboriginal History*, 14 (1), 1990, pp 1–24.

22 Goodall, *Invasion to Embassy*, pp 29, 82, 89, 99, 145–46; Goodall, 'Land in our own country'. For Burragorang demands for land, see J Smith, 'Gundungurra country', PhD, Macquarie University, 2008, pp 351–456.

23 Surveyors General's Office, 16 Jan 1858, Land and Public Works, Correspondence: letters received 1856–1866, SRNSW, NRS 7933, 57/4196, [5/3581].

24 Keating, *On the Frontier*, p 19; Lucas et al, *Voyager Point*, p 8; Navin Officer Heritage Consultants, *Proposal for a Second Sydney Airport at Badgerys Creek or Holsworthy Military Area: Technical Paper, Aboriginal Cultural Heritage*, vol 11, (C'wealth) Department of Transport and Regional Development, Sydney, 1997, pp 22–23.

25 A McGrath, in P Grimshaw et al (eds), *Creating a Nation*, McPheeGribble, Melbourne, 1994, pp 7–27; I Clendinnen, *Dancing with Strangers*, Text Publishing, Melbourne, 2003; Karskens, *The Colony*, ch 2.

26 Karskens discusses these two breastplates, in *The Colony*, ch 1. For illustrations of Cora Gooseberry's breastplates, see T Cleary, 'Poignant regalia: Nineteenth century Aboriginal breastplates & images: a catalogue of Aboriginal breastplates held in public, regional and private collections', Historic Houses Trust NSW, 1993.

27 J Carruthers, 'Captain Cook and Botany Bay', *JRAHS*, 11, 1925, pp 34–35.

28 Karskens, *The Colony*, ch 2.

29 Surveyor E Knapp to Surveyor General, 30 Sept 1868, SRNSW, Lands and Public Works, Correspondence, MS 68/4452, [2/1045].

30 Throsby was employing Tegg in 1841 at Glenfield: see Keating, *On the Frontier*, p 19.

31 *St George Call*, 30 Mar 1907, p 3.

32 Karskens (*The Colony*, ch 13 and 14) notes the significant number of children taken from the earliest interactions.

33 Dr K Scherzer, 'Journal', Jan–Feb 1858 (transcribed by D Clark, 1995: <www. michaelorgan.org.au/novara2.htm>).

34 NSW Department of Public Instruction, School records 1876–1979, Sandringham Public School, 1884–1898, Admin file, SRNSW, NRS 3829 [5/17590.3]. Karen Maber family history about the relationship between John Malone and his wife Lizzy Walden, their daughter Elizabeth (also known as Elizabeth Timbery after her second marriage to John Timbery) and son Harry.

Harry's widow, Agnes and her daughters, Mary and Eliza, were documented as residents at the Kogarah Bay camp at Ellesmere in 1883 in the campaign to have a public school established in the area: see letter and petition, 29 Oct 1883, also 'Application for the establishment of a public school at Sandringham' & Annex, 29 Dec 1883 also signed by them (details above). A sketch map shows the camp's location: SRNSW, NRS 3829 [5/17590.3]. *Sands Sydney Directory*, 1886–1888, locates it at Vista Street, St Kilda, off Rocky Point Road.

35 Scherzer, 'Journal', 1 Dec.

36 MacKenzie, 'Australian languages and traditions', pp 232–74.

37 This is seen in wages ledgers also in the form of inverted commas around names, and sometimes the generic 'gin' for an Aboriginal woman: Goodall, *Invasion to Embassy*, p 60. Entries like 'Gin, five weeks washing at 7/- per week' are found throughout the ledgers of the Dungalear pastoral property north of Walgett, in the 1910s: see H Goodall, 'A history of Aboriginal communities in NSW 1909–1939', PhD thesis, University of Sydney, 1982, p 53.

38 This account of the persistence of the Malone holding, based on the evidence of the parish maps and SRNSW files, has been discussed extensively (August 2008) with Terry Kass, historian of the NSW Lands Department. While we feel the contextual evidence of continued Malone residence is very strong, Kass is more cautious. He suggests that due to the inaction of Lands Department officials, names may have lingered on parish maps long after any people continued to live on the ground which bore their names.

39 See John Connell to A Macleay, 17 Oct 1831; discussion of readvertisment of land and failure to record James Malones grant, 1 July 1839; and response of Crown Solicitor, 28 Feb 1840 and 25 March 1840, eventually favouring Connell: all Colonial Secretary, Letters from individuals relating to land 1826–1856, 'James Malone 1830–1852', SRNSW, NRS 907, 2/7913.

40 DL, Parish of Sutherland Map, County of Cumberland, [nd], 140664, Pmap MN05, Im Id 14066401.

41 DL, Parish of Sutherland Map, County of Cumberland, [nd], 140393 PmapMN05, Im Id 14039301 and Parish of Sutherland Map, County of Cumberland, no 359, [nd], 140620, Pmap MN05, Im Id 14062001.

42 Mackenzie, 'Australian languages', including John Malone, pp 262–63.

43 *The Propeller*, 31 Jan 1935, p 7.

44 Teacher, Sandringham, to Chief Inspector of Schools, 5 Apr 1897, SRNSW, NRS 3829 (5/17590.3); and M Wyatt (teacher), Sandringham, to Chief Inspector, 'Explanation re report', 3 Apr 1901: NSW Department of Public Instruction, School Files, Sandringham Public School 1898–1923, SRNSW, NRS 3829 [5/17591.1]. Initial reference to the petition and sketch map from B Earnshaw, *The Land Between Two Rivers: The St George District in Federation Times*, Sydney, 2001.

45 *Propeller*, 31 Jan 1935, p 7; M Nugent, *Botany Bay: Where Histories Meet*, A&U, Sydney, 2005, pp 47–49.

46 W Foot, W Rowley, C Edwards, J Dixson and Timberly to G Thornton, 20 Jan 1883, appx A, *Aborigines: Report of the Protector of Aborigines NSW*, 3, p 9.

47 Census Collectors Books, District 80, County of Cumberland, Heathcote,

B Holt Sutherland Estate, 1891, SRNSW NRS 683, [2/8423]. Another Aboriginal man was listed as living at on the property of RP Rush, at the Dolan Estate: NSW Police, Census of Aboriginal people 1891, in APB Report, 1891.

48 Initial reference for Rowley's work with oyster leases from M Larkin, *Sutherland Shire: A History to 1939*, Sutherland History Press, 1998; J Murphy, manager, to W Rowley and F Smidmore, 6 Nov 1893; J Murphy to J Hawkins, H Little and C Hawkins, 23 Jan 1894; J Murphy to F Smidmore and W Rowley, 29 Nov 1894: Holt Sutherland Estate Land Co, Letterbook, no 5, 15 Nov 1892– 2 Mar 1896, Holt Family Papers 1861–1933, ML MS 2170/9.

49 *Propeller*, 31 Jan 1935, p 7.

50 Application for the establishment of a public school at Sandringham, 29 Dec 1883 SRNSW, NRS 3829, [5/17590.3]; Teacher to Chief Inspector, 5 Apr 1897 (to explain poor inspection report), SRNSW, NRS 3829 [5/17590.3].

51 Descendents of the Malones, including Karen Maber, attended this same school, and some relatives continue to live nearby: Karen Maber, pers comm, July 2008.

52 W Pritchard to J H Carruthers, 5 Oct 1889, SRNSW, NRS 3829, [5/17590.3].

53 Keating, *On the Frontier*, pp 123–24; DL, Parish of Holsworthy Map, County of Cumberland, ed 3, 1899, 140414, Pmap MN03, Im Id 14041401.

54 Goodall, 'Land in our own country'; *Invasion to Embassy*, pp 77–78.

55 The first NSW reserve in this period was notified in 1861, at Eurobodalla: see Goodall, *Invasion to Embassy*, p 79.

56 J Smith ('Gundungurra country') asserts that early calls came in 1860s, followed by a cluster of petitions and demands in mid-1870s.

57 Goodall, *Invasion to Embassy*, pp 79–84.

58 Eg William Drew's application at Kempsey, 1880: see Goodall, *Invasion to Embassy*, pp 77–84.

59 Goodall, *Invasion to Embassy*, pp 75–87.

60 Goodall, *Invasion to Embassy*; Smith, 'Gungungurra Country'.

61 See comments by police on the 'continual going to and fro' of people between the Botany and La Perouse camps, and that the Botany camp was frequently visited by Aboriginal people 'from Wollongong, George's River and Burragorang': Snr Constable Byrne to Chief Protector of Aborigines, 17 Jan 1883, 'Report of the Protector', Legislative Assembly, NSW, 1883, p 7. Visitors from the Hunter River as well as Kiama and Illawarra were also in the camp at the Quay, in the Government Boat Sheds: J Nonohoe, Sub Inspector Water Police, to Protector, 1883, 'Report of the Protector', 1883, p 6. See also APB Minutes, 15 Oct 1891 (re Kangaroo Valley families at Port Hacking); 28 Apr 1892 (re J Phillips from Brungle at Weeney Bay): APB Minute Books 1890– 1896, SRNSW, NRS 2 [4/7108-11].

62 Preliminary Report of the Protector of Aborigines, Aug 1882; 'Report of the Protector', 1883, p 2.

63 'Report of the Protector', 1883, pp 1–2 (and appx B contains detailed reports from police in all districts, and reports on many deputations and petitions for land, pp 10–27).

64 W Foot et al to G Thornton, 'Report of the Protector', 1883, Appendix A, p 9.

65   W Saunders, Senr Constable Liverpool Police, 18 Jul 1893, Colonial Secretary
     Correspondence, Main series: letters received 1826–1982, SRNSW, NRS 905,
     5/6135 [93/7210]; see also NSWDL, Parish of Holsworthy Map, County of
     Cumberland, 1899, PMapN03, Im Id 14064901.

66   APB, *Report of the Board for the Protection of Aborigines*, 1892, appx A, p 8.

67   W Saunders to APB, 1893, SRNSW, NRS 905, 5/6135 [93/7210]. The names of
     at least nine of the 13 children born to William and Lucy Leane in Liverpool
     are known: Elizabeth (BDM, 9889/1865), Emma M, (10662/1867), Ellen L
     (12417/1869), Edmund W (11864/1871), George Henry (13319/1875), Albert
     Charles (14015/1877), Ruth (15978/1879) and Thomas (14373/1881). Edmund
     continued to live in the area, and Mary Jane married a neighbour, Salvatore
     Passanisi (BDM, 4630/1887).

68   L Leane, Petition to Colonial Secretary, 31 May 1893, Colonial Secretary, Main
     series: letters received 1826–1982, SRNSW, NRS 905, 5/6135 [93/7210].

69   Death certificate, BDM, 8961/1895.

70   Liverpool Municipal Council, *Sesqui-Centenary Commemoration: One
     Hundred and Fifty Years of Progress*, Liverpool Municipal Council, Sydney,
     1960. 'Falder' (real name R Kaleski, 'State kids', *The Bulletin*, 6 July 1905,
     p 36) mentions an Aboriginal child in the Campbelltown area who frequently
     ran away to the city with his school mates. See also DL, Parish of Holsworthy
     Map, County of Cumberland, 1905, PMapMN03, Im Id 14043201.

4 Travelling Guragurang: Biddy's river

1   *United Aborigines Messenger*, 1 Sept 1941, p 4.

2   J Kohen and J Brook, *The Parramatta Native Institution and the Black Town:
     A History*, UNSW Press, Sydney, 1991.

3   See entries for Billy, Wallace and Johnny, sent to Cartwright in December
     1826: SRNSW, Male Orphan School Admission Books, 1828–1832, vol 3,
     [4/352].

4   See minutes for 5 April 1900 (f 171) and 10 May 1900 (f 223), APB, Minute
     Book 30 Nov 1899–20 Sept 1900, SRNSW, 4/7114.

5   J Kociumbas, *Australian Childhood: A History*, A&U, Sydney 1997; and R van
     Kreiken: *Children and the State*, A&U, Sydney, 1991; H Goodall, *Invasion to
     Embassy: Land in Aboriginal Politics in New South Wales 1770–1972*, A&U,
     Sydney, 1996, pp 115–24.

6   William Macarthur, 'Notes of outrages committed by the blacks at Port
     Macquarie and also memoranda relative to their outrages in the early days of
     the colony', c 1870, Supreme Court: Miscellaneous Correspondence relating to
     Aborigines 1824–1840, SRNSW, COD/294B (thanks to KV Smith for pointing
     out this reference).

7   This was recorded in the 1890s by M Everitt and RH Mathews: C Illert,
     'The centenary of Mary Everitt's "Gundungurra Grammar"', *Journal and
     Proceedings of the Royal Society of New South Wales*, 134, 2001, pp 19–44.

8   P Geeves, 'Thomas Holt', *Australian Dictionary of Biography*, online edn,
     <www.adbonline.anu.edu.au/A040466b.htm>; HE Holt, *An Energetic
     Colonist: A Biographical Account of the Activities of the late Hon Thomas Holt*,

Hawthorne Press, Melbourne, 1972.

9   Jacko Campbell and Ted Thomas, interviews with H Goodall, 1980.

10 *St George Call*, 14 May 1904, p 1.

11 M Nugent, 'Emma Timbery', *Australian Dictionary of Biography*, online edn at <www.adbonline.anu.edu.au/biogs/AS10461b.htm>.

12 APB Reports, appx B, 1883–1892; 'Tabulated expenditure 1887: Kogarah Station', no 33, in Register of Expenditure at Aboriginal Stations 1887-1890, Aborigines Welfare Board papers, SRNSW, NRS 16, 7/3641.

13 Petition, NSW Department of Public Instruction, School records 1876–1979, Sandringham Public School, Admin file 1884–1898, SRNSW, NRS 3829 [5/17590.3].

14 *St George Call*, 23 Jan 1904, p 2; and 22 Nov 1929, p 6. See also recollections of resident J Bowmer *Rockdale Times*, 17 April 1947 (reprod in *St George Historical Society Bulletin*, June 1963); and DJ Hatton, *The English Family of Kogarah 1854–1912*, 1976, p 23; *St George Call*, 14 May 1904, p 1; 22 Nov 1929, p 6.

15 RH Mathews and MM Everitt, 'The organisation, language and initiation ceremonies of the Aborigines of the south-east coast of NSW', *Journal and Proceedings of the Royal Society of New South Wales*, 34, 1900, pp 262–81 (p 265). The language groups referred to here are now spelt Dharug, Gandangara and Dharawal.

16 Ellen Anderson to CW Peck, reported in 'Prelude: A Princess', *Australian Legends: Aboriginal Folk-Lore*, 1933 edn (originally published by Stafford and Company, Sydney, 1925). The 1933 edition is reproduced online at: <www.sacred-texts.com/about.htm> and the 'Prelude' section at <www.sacred-texts.com/aus/peck/peck02.htm>.

17 Kohen, *Daruganora*, p 44.

18 Emma Timbery's use of the surname Lowndes, from her step-father, was confirmed on the marriage certificate of her son, John, in 1910: BDM, 1910/006400 (from copies supplied by the Mabers). The 1916 death certificate of Emma Timbrey (15855: cited in C Illert, Submission by NIAC on various environmental matters, 2006, appendix) indicates she was born at Liverpool. Nugent ('Emma Timbery', *Australian Dictionary of Biography*) identifies her as Jimmy's step-daughter after his marriage to her mother Betsey.

19 Everitt's letter, 24 June 1901 in Illert, *Early Ancestors of the Wadi Wadi*, C Illert, Wollongong, 2003. King Kooma/Cooman may have been the man identified as 'Kourban' in the 1840s drawing by PHF Phelps of the 'Cabramatta tribe' in Bigge Park Liverpool: reproduced in Chris Keating, *On the Frontier*, Hale & Iremonger, Sydney 1996, p18.

20 For the naming of Biddy's husband and Ellen's father as Paddy Davis, see Ellen's death certificate, 14 May 1931, and for Paddy's language name of Burragalung, see his grandson's letter: Joe Anderson/King Burraga to AP Elkin, 16 Jan 1936, in B Attwood and A Markus, *The Struggle for Aboriginal Rights: A Documentary History*, A&U, Sydney, 1999, pp 74–75. Shayne Williams, Ellen Anderson's great-grandson, understands that Paddy Burragalung worked for a white man called Davis and may have been referred to as Paddy 'Davis'.

21 R Longfield, 'Reminiscences', 22 Jan 1905, recorded by W Housten, Archives of Captain Cook's Landing Place Trust, Kurnell, box 12, item 141. Nugent (*Botany Bay: Where Histories Meet*, A&U, Sydney, 2005, p 31) has pointed out the parallels with Cook's own account, which had been widely circulated in popular publications and settler narratives by the early nineteenth century.

22 Illert, *Early Ancestors of the Wadi Wadi*, p 9; see also death certificate for Mary Kearney, Rosie's grand-daughter, 14 Feb 1930, Wollongong, in which J Anderson is the informant and identifies himself as her cousin (p 20). What is not clear is why both Ellen and her sister Rose were recorded with surname 'Russell' in various, quite separate documents, eg all those in which Daniel Matthews refers to Ellen in 1881 and 1882.

23 For the recollections of white men about King Kooma and Biddy, see *St George Call*, 9 Jan 1904, p 7; 23 Jan 1904, p 2; 30 Jan 1904, p 7; 11 May 1907, p 3 (this last is the only reference where Biddy is said to have actually passed on the name of her former husband herself as 'King Kooma').

24 JL Kohen, *Daruganora*, 2006, p 42, citing the correspondence of Mary Everitt (24 June 1901) on the details of Emma Timbrey's account.

25 Kohen, *Daruganora*; Illert, *Early Ancestors*; C Illert and NIAC, NIAC, Submission to Department of Environment and Heritage on various environmental matters, 2006, appx ; J Smith, 'Gundungurra country', PhD thesis, Indigenous Studies, Macquarie University, 2008; K Vincent Smith, pers comm, 2008.

26 *St George Call*, 17 Aug 1907, p 3A later and much less direct reference suggests Biddy had originally 'come from' Broughton Creek, somewhere on the south coast, but the source is not specific: *St George Call*, 22 Nov 1929, p 6.

27 Illert (*Early Ancestors*) p 13 suggests Mrs Timbery believed Biddy began her fourth relationship here, living with a Holt Estate overseer, Mr Holdsworth, until his death.

28 Ellen Anderson, d 14 May 1931, aged 76 [ie b 1855], BDM 1931/07672 (her son, J Anderson, informant); but see *Illawarra Mercury*, 23 Feb 1857: 'Birth: On the 9th ultimo, at the Encampment, near Tom Thumb's Lagoon, the lady of Mr Paddy Burrangalong, of a daughter', cited in M Organ *Illawarra and the South Coast Aborigines*, Aboriginal Education Unit, University of Wollongong, 1990, p 303For other reports of Kooma: *St George Call*, 9 Jan 1904,p7; 23 Jan 1904,p2; 30 Jan 1904,p7; 23 Mar 1907, p 7, and 11 May 1907, p 3; and death certificate for Ellen, 14 May 1931(7672/1931).

29 Illert, 'The centenary of Mary Everitt's "Gundungurra Grammar"', p 25.

30 See above, ch 3, n 37.

31 *St George Call*, 14 May 1904, p 1.

32 S Rosen, *Bankstown: A Sense of Identity*, Hale & Iremonger, Sydney, 1996.

33 Karskens, *The Colony*, ch 14.

34 *St George Call* (17 Aug 1907, p 3) called them 'half cast waifs' who had found a home under Billy's hospitable roof.

35 *St George Call*, 14 May 1904, p 1; 17 Aug 1907, p 3, 6 Apr 1907, p 3; 8 Apr 1911, p 6

36 *St George Call*, 8 April, 1911, p 6

37 *St George Call*, 27 Apr 1907, p 3.

38 *St George Call*, 8 April 1911, p 6.
39 *St George Call*, 17 August 1907, p 3.
40 His account in the *St George Call*, 23 Mar, 6 April, 13 April, 20 April, 27 April,
    11 May and 18 May 1907, all pp 3, with references to Biddy in each article.
41 *St George Call*, 18 May 1907, p 3
42 *St George Call*, 11 May 1907, p 3.
43 *St George Call*, 27 April 1907, p 3. The rock fall is described in a number of
    publications, and is associated directly with Simpson's property in this 1907
    article, and in two articles associated with the Simpson family: an obituary
    in *St George Call* (26 Jan 1918, p 2) and *Dubbo Dispatch and Wellington
    Independent* (20 Sept 1918, p 5). This is consistent with Biddy's focus
    on Jibbon Point in her explanation of rock engravings and also with the
    geography of this trip as it was described by 'One of the Old Sort'. See also
    F Cridland, *Port Hacking, Cronulla and Sutherland Shire*, Sydney, A&R,
    1924, pp 15–16, although he suggests the location of the rock fall is further
    upstream at Little Turriel Point, near Lilli Pilli on the northern shore of Port
    Hacking.
44 Various versions of this story are in circulation today, including that told by
    Fran Bodkin in Darwala-Lia Archaeological Services for NSW Dept Urban
    Affairs and Planning, *Draft Georges River Foreshore Improvement Program:
    Cultural Heritage Study ~ Aboriginal Culture and Heritage Study of the Georges
    River and Catchment*, DUAP, Sydney, 2002, appx F, pp 142–43
45 Karskens (*The Colony*, ch 11) has speculated on the massive psychological
    impact this trauma must have left. Similarly K Langloh Parker recorded that
    as late as the 1890s there persisted memories of terrible illness and lingering
    guilt over failure to bury the dead after the small pox epidemic in 1830
    in north-western NSW: *The Euahlayi Trive: A Study of Aboriginal Life in
    Australia*, Archibald Constable, London, 1905.
46 *St George Call*, 11 May 1907; <www.wadgogerly.com/new_page_1.htm>.
47 *St George Call*, 13 April 1907, p 3
48 *St George Call*, 20 April 1907, p 3.
49 *St George Call*, 8 April 1911, p 6; M Nugent, 'Historical encounters: Aboriginal
    testimony and colonial forms of commemoration', *Aboriginal History*, 30,
    2006, pp 33–47.
50 *St George Call*, 30 Mar 1907, p 3; 6 Apr 1907, p 3; 13 Apr 1907, p 3; 27 Apr 1907,
    p 3.
51 Nugent, *Botany Bay*, p 49. James Bundong and George Timbery are listed as La
    Perouse fishermen in *Sands Directory* of 1882: pp 168 and 170.
52 SRNSW, Census Collectors Books, District 80, Heathcote, B Holt Sutherland
    Estate, 1891, 2/8423.
53 J Murphy to W Rowley, 28 Feb 1893, 29 May 1893 and 6 Nov 1893; Murphy
    to F Smidmore, 6 Nov 1893; Murphy to Smidmore and Rowley, 29 Nov 1894:
    Holt Sutherland Estate Land Co, Letterbook no 5, 15 Nov 1892–2 March 1896,
    ML MS, 2170/9
54 Mrs Timbrey, from Mary Everitt's 1901 letter cited in Illert, 'The centenary of
    Mary Everitt's "Gundungurra Grammar"'.
55 *St George Call*, 22 Nov 1929, p 6.

56 There are two photographs of the same group of people on the Holt Estate in the same clothes, but they are dated differently: 'Last of the Georges River Tribe, NSW, 1880', Australian Indigenous Ministries: Pictorial Collection, no 42 (identifying Jim Brown, Joe Brown, Joey [Biddy's brother], Biddy Giles, Jimmy Lowndes), ML PXA 773, box 6; and J Robinson, nd [c 1884], Rockdale Library, (also published, *St George Call*, 14 May 1904, p 1).

57 22 Nov 1929, p6.

58 23 Jan 1904, p 2. This is probably the same Albert listed at Sans Souci: Census Collectors book, district 99, Kogarah Rockdale, Subdistrict C, 1891, SRNSW, NRS 683, 2/8428; see also J Troy, *King Plates: A History of Aboriginal Gorgets*, Aboriginal Studies Press, Canberra, 1993, pp 122–23.

59 NSW Dept of Public Instruction, School records 1876–1979, Sandringham Public School, Admin file 1884–1898, SRNSW, NRS 3829, 5/17590.3; B Earnshaw, *The Land Between Two Rivers: The St George District in Federation Times*, Sydney, 2001, pp 84–85.

60 Minutes, 15 Oct 1891 and 28 Apr 1892, APB Minute Books 1890–1896, SRNSW, NRS 2 4/7108-11.

61 Discussed by J Smith ('Gundungurra country') as the many Aboriginal people who had by this stage demanded and won land as reserve or permissive occupancy in the Burragorang and related valleys.

62 Jean Stewart (née Simms), 'The Story of the Littlest Gundungaras and their great walk to La Perouse', ed C Illert, 2005, in Submission by NIAC to Dept of Environment and Heritage on various environmental matters, 2006, appx 1, p 3. Note that Smith ('Gundungurra country') argues that Simms was a Dharawal man. There is no dispute however that he was living in the Burragorang country and so his very presence, and that of his abandoned family, is a strong demonstration of the continued and active east–west movement of Aboriginal people in the period.

5 River of flowers: Ellen's river

1 NSW Protector of Aborigines, *Report of Protector of the Aborigines*, 31 Dec 1882, Legislative Assembly, NSW, 1883, p 7.

2 M Nugent, *Botany Bay: Where Histories Meet*, A&U, Sydney, 2005, pp 49, 53

3 Rev Matthews, diary, cited by Illert, *Early Ancestors of Illawarra's Wadi-Wadi*, C Illert, Wollongong 2003.

4 C Illert, *Early Ancestors*.

5 H Goodall, *Invasion to Embassy: Land in Aboriginal Politics in New South Wales 1770–1972*, A&U, Sydney, 1996.pp 129–30

6 *Riverine Herald*, 29 Jan 1889.

7 APB, Register of Reserves, f 25, rev 1899, WA Bayley, *Shoalhaven: A History of the Shire*, Shoalhaven Council, Nowra, originally published 1965/, repub 1985, pp 122–23, cited in Illert 2003, *Early Ancestors of the Wadi Wadi*, p 20; EE Morris (ed), *Cassell's Picturesque Australia*, Cassell & Co, Melbourne, vol 4, 1889, p 224; J Griffith, *A History of Kangaroo Valley, Australia*, Kangaroo Valley Historical Society, 1978, p 11.

8 APB, Minutes, 9 Feb 1899, APB Minute Books 1898–1899, SRNSW, NRS 2,

4/7113.

9   Illert, *Early Ancestors of the Wadi Wadi*, interpreting CW Peck, *Australian Legends: Tales Handed Down from the Remotest Times*, 1933.
10 Title Deed, lot 126, transferred to Ellen Anderson, 1925: copy held by Shayne Williams.
11 *The Propeller*, 1935, p 7.
12 See photos of site visit, 30 Nov 2008, held by H Goodall.
13 See L McLoughlin, 'Mangroves and grass swamps: Changes in the shoreline vegetation of the middle Lane Cove River, Sydney 1780s–1880s', *Wetlands*, 7(1), 1987, pp 13–24; G Barhnam, *Riverside Reflections: Memories of Lugarno*, self published, 2003; S Rosen, *Bankstown: A Sense of Identity*, Hale &Iremonger, Sydney, 1996; A Molloy, *The History of Padstow*, Australian Media, Sydney, 2004; B Earnshaw, *The Land Between Two Rivers: The St George District in Federation Times*, Sydney, 2001, ch 6.
14 J Lawrence, *Pictorial Memories of St George*, Kingsclear Books, Crows Nest, 1996.
15 Robert Haworth, interview with Heather Goodall, 17 Nov 2005.
16 Title Deed, lot 126.
17 *The Propeller*, 24 July 1928.
18 Title Deed, lot 127, transferred to William Rowley, 1929: copy held by Shayne Williams.
19 Molloy's *History of Padstow* (pp 34 and 163) includes Bankstown and District Historical Society photographs of a Salt Pan Creek Progress Association working bee on the river banks in 1914, showing open space and lack of mangroves.
20 E Dickinson, 'Salt Pan Creek about 1913', *Bankstown Historical Society Journal*, Dec 1984.
21 Jacko Campbell and Ted Thomas, interview with Kevin Cook and Heather Goodall, 24 Sept 1980; Ellen James (née Williams), interview with Heather Goodall, 21 Oct 2005.
22 G Peake, Annual Ward Havard Memorial Lecture, Hurstville Historical Society, 8 Aug 1981.
23 M Porter, 'Some reminiscences of Hurstville in the 1930s', *Hurstville Historical Society Newsletter*, 2(1) 1977, pp 3–4.
24 Jacko Campbell and Ted Thomas, interview 24 Sept 1980; Ellen James, interview 21 Oct 2005.
25 *St George Call*, 30 Dec 1927, p 2.
26 Kel Connell, interview with Heather Goodall, 5 May 2006.
27 *Our Aim*, 17(6), 1924, p 8, 22 Dec 1930, p 11.
28 Ellen James, interview with Heather Goodall and Shayne Williams, 21 Oct 2005; one such photo appears in *Randwick: A Social History*, Randwick Municipal Council/UNSW Press, Sydney, 1985, p 106 (no source noted).
29 Ellen James, interview, 21 Oct 2005; Robert Haworth, interview 17 Nov 2005.
30 Photographs from the 1920s to 1950s in the AIM Pictorial Collection (ML, PXA 773, Box 1, no 78) show Aboriginal people at various places including Salt Pan Creek. Location of the photo confirmed by a number of people who grew up there, including Ellen Williams and Ern Blewitt (a non-Aboriginal friend of the Williams children).

31 *St George Call*, 30 Dec 1927, p 2 ; *Propeller*, 3 Jan 1930, p 1; G Blewett, 'Salt Pan Creek Aborigines', *Hurstville Historical Society Newsletter*, 2(49), July 1981, p 4.

32 *St George Call*, 7 May 1926, p 1; *Sydney Morning Herald*, 30 Dec 1927, p 9; 31 Dec 1927, p 10; *Propeller*, 14 Feb, p 2 and 30 May 1930, p 1; Jacko Campbell and Ted Thomas, interview, 24 Sept 1980.

33 DJ Hatton, 'Salt Pan Creek Aborigines', *Hurstville Historical Society Newsletter*, 2(48), 1981 pp 3–4 and 2(79), April 1984, pp 3–4. He was, however, denied a prize, as one school mate, 'still burning with rage' angry after many years, recalled to local historian Brian Shaw: pers comm, Feb 2008.

34 Photo of Joe Anderson buying bread, *Sydney Sun*, 23 Jan 1931 and in *St George and Sutherland Shire Leader*, 3 Aug 2000, p 13.

35 DJ Hatton, *Peakhurst in the early days*, Hurstville Historical Society, Sydney 1981, p 32.

36 Hatton, 'Salt Pan Creek Aborigines', April 1984.

37 Ern and Ettie Blewett, interview with Heather Goodall, Peakhurst, 10 Nov 2005.

38 Joe Timbery, interviewed by Jeff Carter, *People*, 5 June 1963, p 14, cited in P McKenzie and A Stephen, 'La Perouse: An urban Aboriginal community', in M Kelly (ed), *Sydney: City of Suburbs*, UNSW Press/Sydney History Group, Sydney, 1987, pp 179–80.

39 McKenzie and Stephen, 'La Perouse', p 180; see also Lee-Anne Mason and Gloria Ardler's memories of boomerang-makers and mangrove wood sources (Weeney Bay) in Individual Heritage Group, *La Perouse: The Place, the People and the Sea ~ A Collection of Writing by Members of the Aboriginal Community*, Sydney, 1987, pp 14–15.

40 Mavis Longbottom, quoted in McKenzie and Stephen, 'La Perouse', p 189.

41 Ellen James, interview, 21 Oct 2005.

42 M Organ, 'CW Peck's *Australian Legends*':<www.michaelorgan.org.au/peck1.htm>.

43 J Smith, 'Gundungurra country', PhD thesis, Indigenous Studies, Macquarie University, 2008, has a valuable discussion of the role Charles Peck took, as well as an assessment of Ellen's contribution and ongoing relationship with the writer. Smith differs from the interpretation developed in Illert, *Early Ancestors of the Wadi Wadi* – that Ellen was Peck's only or main source – although he concurs with Illert on Ellen's importance in shaping some of the stories.

44 See comments by the anonymous republisher of Peck's 1933 edition in digital form at The Internet Sacred Text Archive, Santa Cruz, California, 1999, <www.sacred-texts.com/aus/peck/index.htm>.

6 A free community: King Burraga's river

1 H Goodall, *Invasion to Embassy*: *Land in Aboriginal Politics in New South Wales 1770–1972*, A&U, Sydney, 1996, pp 126–36; *The Aborigines Protection Act* 1909. Once the APB decided on new policy, around 1906, it began to pursue it by a variety of means, and so evictions and 'dispersal'

activities actually began before the Act was passed, as had the Cumeragunja intervention.

2   H Goodall, 'King Burraga and local history: Writing Aborigines back into the story', *Bridging the Gap: National Issues in Local History*, Proceedings of the RAHS Annual Conference, 1988; Goodall, *Invasion to Embassy*, pp 145–46.

3   M Nugent, *Botany Bay: Where Histories Meet*, A&U, Sydney, 2005, p 79, J Smith, 'Gundungurra country', PhD thesis, Indigenous Studies, Macquarie University, 2008, pp 413–55.

4   G Blewett, 'Salt Pan Creek Aborigines', *Hurstville Historical Society Newsletter*, 2(49), Jul 1981, p 4.

5   Jacko Campbell and Ted Thomas, interview with Heather Goodall, 24 Sept 1980.

6   These photographs, now held by NIAC and published here with their permission, may have been taken at Hill 60, a long-standing Aboriginal camp near Wollongong. They show not only the interaction of Ellen and other members of her family with Peck and his family, but also show the Andersons with their relations who lived in and around Wollongong.

7   C Illert, *Early Ancestors of the Wadi Wadi People*, C Illert, Wollongong, 2003.

8   *Our Aim*, 20 Feb 1924, p 8; 22 Dec 1930, p 11.

9   J Maynard, *Fight for Liberty and Freedom: The Origins of Australian Aboriginal Activism*, Aboriginal Studies Press, Canberra, 2007, pp 16-39. Garvey's movement was interested in promoting the value of African traditional cultural heritage, but was also strongly assertive of contemporary African-American cultures. This mixture of tradition and current cultures was strongly evident in all of the statements made by Fred Maynard on behalf of the AAPA.

10 J Maynard, 'Aboriginal people and Newcastle', paper delivered at 'Cities, Nature, Justice' symposium, UTS, Dec 2008.

11 Goodall, *Invasion to Embassy*, pp 115–72; Maynard, *Fight for Liberty and Freedom*.

12 *Our Aim*, 20 Mar 1925, cited in Maynard, *Fight for Liberty and Freedom*, p 48.

13 *Daily Guardian*, 24 Apr 1925; J Maynard, '"Light in the Darkness": Elizabeth McKenzie Hatton', in A Cole, V Haskins and F Paisley (eds), *Uncommon Ground: White Women in Aboriginal History*, Aboriginal Studies Press, Canberra, 2005, pp 3–27.

14 *Daily Guardian*, 7 May 1925.

15 See later discussion of the details of the Campbell family's conflict with the APB at Kempsey.

16 Jacko Campbell and Ted Thomas, interview, 24 Sept 1980. Jack Lang was premier 1925–1927 and 1930–1932.

17 Charlie Leon, interview with Faith Bandler, in F Bandler and L Fox, *The Time Was Ripe*, Alternative Publishing Cooperative, Chippendale, 1983, pp 21–25.

18 Goodall, *Invasion to Embassy*, pp 147–48; JJ Fletcher, *Documents in the History of Aboriginal Education in NSW*, self published, Sydney, 1989, pp 125–26 (the letter is reproduced p 125).

19 Goodall, *Invasion to Embassy*, p 160.

20 Goodall, *Invasion to Embassy*, pp 166–68.

21 Ted was born 1909 and so was around 15 or 16 when he came to Sydney: Jack Campbell and Ted Thomas, interview, 24 Sept 1980. All the following account of Jacko and Ted is drawn from these interviews.

22 N Wheatley, 'Meeting them at the door: Radicalism, militancy, and the Sydney anti-eviction campaign of 1931', in J Roe (ed), *Twentieth Century Sydney: Studies in Urban and Social History*, Hale & Iremonger/Sydney History Group, Sydney, 1980; D Cottle and A Keys, 'Danger from below: Anti-eviction struggles in Sydney, January–July 1931', paper presented to Australian Historical Association, Melbourne, 2008; Pat Eatock, interview with Heather Goodall July 2008.

23 Charlie Leon, interview with Faith Bandler, *The Time was Ripe*, p 21.

24 Discussion of this 1980 interview was originally published in H Goodall: 'Cryin' out for land rights', in V Burgmann and J Lee (eds), *Staining The Wattle*, vol 4, *The People's History of Australia,* Penguin/McPhee-Gribble, 1988, pp 181–97. Attwood and Markus (*The Struggle for Aboriginal Rights*, A&U, Sydney, 1999, pp 5–6) suggest the terminology was anachronistic, but do not locate Jacko Campbell's usage in the context of interwar land politics, as discussed in this chapter.

25 This newspaper has not been located. Jacko was however insistent that it was not the 1938 *Abo Call*, and that it was associated with a religious group. This may have related to support the Andersons gained from the AIM, with whom Ellen was closely associated. However, it seems from Jacko's account of its content that it would have been more consistent with the campaigns of the AAPA in the 1920s, and the alliance between the north coast nationalists like John Maloney and the Aboriginal farmer-land owners at Kempsey, whom Jacko knew, like John and Percy Mosely, and with which the AAPA was able to form strong links from 1925 to 1927.

26 Goodall, *Invasion to Embassy*, pp 335–51; and see below ch 8 and 9.

27 'Salt Pan Creek Aborigines', *Hurstville Historical Society Newsletter*, 2(48), June 1981 and 2(79), April 1984, p 4.

28 M Garside, *Padstow Park Progress Association History 1913–2001*, Padstow Park Progress Association, Sydney, 2001, p 9.

29 Garside, *Padstow Park*; L Singleman, *Secrets of Sandy Point: A History of Sandy Point*, Sandy Point Progress Association, Sydney, 2002, p 63; DJ Hatton, *The Kogarah Bay Progress Association 1921–1981*, Hurstville Historical Society, Sydney, 1981.

30 Not only were these Progress Associations objecting to Aboriginal residents (eg Lugarno 1926; Herne Bay, 1930) but also to gypsies (Padstow Progress Association, 1941): A Molloy, *The History of Padstow*, Australian Media, Sydney, 2004, p 24 (citing Padstow Progress Association Minutes of request to Bankstown Council). See also Hurstville Council, Minutes, 15 April 1926 (p 161), 15 Jan 1931 (p 24), Hurstville Library Local Studies.

31 *St George Call*, 7 May 1926, p 1.

32 *The Propeller*, 21 Nov 1930, p 4; 15 May 1931, p 7; Hurstville Council, Minutes, 15 Jan 1931, p 24, Hurstville Library Local Studies.

33 The original is *The Sun*, 23 Jan 1931; copy held by Shayne Williams. A misleading report in the *Leader* (3 Aug 2000, pp 15, 17) reproduces the photos

of Anderson, correctly sourced from *Sydney Sun*, but alters the caption to 'Moved on: the Dharawal "king" at his bush camp'.

34 '*The Propeller*, 16 Jan, 1931, p 3.

35 As discussed in chapter 5, Jacky had developed connections with Jack Price and this had led to the images showing Ellen and Hugh with their family as well as their links to Charles Peck. See also photographs held by the James Studio: Illert, *Early Ancestors of Illawarra's Wadi-Wadi*.

36 The precise location for this filming is not known but Jacko Campbell and Ted Thomas both identified the setting as being among the tea trees at Salt Pan Creek and close to the camp where Joe had lived.

37 'Australian royalty pleads for his people: Burraga, chief of Aboriginal Thirroul tribe, to petition King for blacks' representation in Federal Parliament',*Cinesound Review*, no 100, 29 Sept 1933.

38 'Evicting a King', *Daily Telegraph*, 28 Aug 1936, p 7. The text discussed the content of the letter to the governor general. This is confirmed in Joe Anderson/King Burraga to AP Elkin, 16 Jan 1936, University of Sydney archives, AP Elkin papers, P130, 12/88/144; reprod in B Attwood and A Markus, *The Struggle for Aboriginal Rights: A Documentary History*, A&U, Sydney, 1999, pp 74–75.

39 Joe Anderson/King Burraga to Elkin, 16 Jan 1936.

40 VK Haskins, *One Bright Spot*, Palgrave Macmillan, Basingstoke, 2005, pp 170–71.

41 *The Propeller*, 23 Feb 1939, p 1; *St George Call*, 3 March 1939, p 1. Jean Carter (née Mackenzie), who was born at Salt Pan Creek remembers that when she was a young girl her family had to move suddenly from Salt Pan Creek to La Perouse: 'A big dose of social justice', in Older Women's Network *Steppin' Out and Speakin' Up*, Older Women's Network, Sydney, 2003, pp 45–47; C Edwards and P Read (eds), *The Lost Children*, 2nd edn, Doubleday, 1997, p 3.

42 *Man*, Jan 1938, p 101.

43 Robert Haworth, interview with Heather Goodall, 17 Nov 2005.

44 Anderson family accounts: pers comm Shayne Williams.

45 Denis Foley, pers comm 30 Nov 2008, born at Manly Vale but resident at Chester Hill through the 1950s and 1960s, quoted in S Gapps, 'A history of Fairfield City' (working title), Fairfield City Council, Sydney, forthcoming (2009).

46 Robyn Young and Fran Bodkin (both née Perry), interview with Heather Goodall, 23 Mar 2008. Robyn is Mr Hannah's grand-daughter, and has many records of her grandfather's role in establishing the Georges Hall Public School in 1942.

47 N Stanyi and M Bishop, *The Dom*, exhibition catalogue, 2 June–30 July 2000, Liverpool Regional Museum, Sydney, 2000; see the report on 'Dom Syme: A remarkable life', in 'Cultural dissent', *Green Left Weekly*, 410, 28 June 2000.

7 The river under challenge: defending Goggey's victory

1 Memories about Aboriginal families at Doctors' Bush (identified as the 'southern end of Stuart St Reserve on the banks of Salt Pan Creek'), the camp

at Salt Pan and Padstow Park school by Allan Smith and Bobby Clarke, in A Molloy, *The History of Padstow*, 2nd edn, Australian Media, Sydney, 2004, p 7.

2   Allan Smith, in Molloy, *History of Padstow*.

3   Jacko Campbell and Ted Thomas, interview with Kevin Cook and Heather Goodall, 24 Sept 1980; photograph of Anderson family with family members and in-laws, probably at Hill 60 (c 1926) in C Illert and NIAC, *Early Ancestors of Illawarra's Wadi-Wadi People*, C Illert, Wollongong, 2003. Allan Carriage (pers comm) recalls being at the Hill 60 protests as a child with his mother.

4   Kevin Cook, interview with Heather Goodall, 13 Mar 1992; NIAC and EC Eklund, *Steel Town: The Making and Breaking of Port Kembla*, Melbourne University Press, Melbourne, 2002, cited in M Organ, 'The fight to save Illowra', chronology: <www.michaelorgan.org.au/hill60.htm>

5   Organ, 'The fight to save Illowra'.

6   Roy Burns (senior Aboriginal man) to Department of Defence, 1942: 'I was living on Hill 60 Port Kembla, which is now a Naval Fort and fully controlled by your Department. The Officer in charge there gave us six days to move from Hill 60 and he informed me that if I left my place there it would be cared for and I could return to it after the war.' quoted by his grandson Allan Carriage, and cited in Organ, 'The fight to save Illowra'.

7   D Winston, *Sydney's Great Experiment: The Progress of the Cumberland County Plan*, A&R, Sydney, 1957.

8   Winston, *Sydney's Great Experiment*, pp 15–16; P Spearritt, *Sydney's Century: A History*, UNSW Press, Sydney, 1999, pp 91–92.

9   C Allport, 'Castles of security: The New South Wales Housing Commission and home ownership 1941–67', in M Kelly (ed), *Sydney: City of Suburbs*, UNSW Press/Sydney History Group, Sydney, 1987, pp 95–124.

10 Spearritt, *Sydney's Century*, ch 5.

11 Winston, *Sydney's Great Experiment*, p 83; Molloy, *History of Padstow*, p 115; see also the President's report, Padstow Park Progress Association, 1957 (quoted in M Garside, *Padstow Park Progress Association History 1913–2001*, PPPA, Sydney, 2001, p 26), celebrating 'the lifting of the Green Belt restrictions on development … allowing valuable subdivisions to be opened up for residential purposes'.

12 DH Coward, *Out of Sight: Sydney's Environmental History 1851–1981*, Department of Economic History, ANU, Canberra, 1988, pp 240–42.

13 Coward, *Out of Sight*, pp 245–52; NG Butlin (ed), *Sydney's Environmental Amenity 1970–1975*, ANU Press, Canberra, 1976, pp 133, 140–49, 176–83. Butlin demonstrates both the disproportionate historical pressure on the Georges River and that it had continued until this survey in the early 1970s.

14 *Leader*, 12 Oct 1961, p 7; 3 Apr 1963, p 3; 8 May 1963, p 9.

15 Winston, *Sydney's Great Experiment*, p 43 on housing in relation to new industrial areas; Allport, 'Castles of security', p 103; Coward, *Out of Sight*, p 250; Molloy, *History of Padstow*, p 152; see also D Powell, *Out West: Perceptions of Sydney's Western Suburbs*, A&U, Sydney, 1993, ch 4.

16 Coward , *Out of Sight*, p 251; figures drawn from NSW Statistical Register, cited in Metropolitan Water Sewage and Drainage Board, 1960.

17 Even by 1957, Winston (*Sydney's Great Experiment*) demonstrates the tensions

arising from very different perceptions of planners and working-class residents.

18 I Flick and H Goodall, *Isabel Flick: The Many Lives of an Extraordinary Aboriginal Woman*, A&U, Sydney, 2004.

19 G Morgan, *Unsettled Places: Aboriginal People and Urbanisation in New South Wales*, Wakefield Press, Adelaide, 2006.

20 H Goodall, *Invasion to Embassy: Land in Aboriginal Politics in New South Wales 1770–1972*, A&U, Sydney, 1996.

21 Ironically, it was the much more recent pressure for conversion of former defence land for the proposed Voyager Point housing development in the 1990s which has gathered some of the files to allow the re-examination of Aboriginal people's presence near Goggey's land: C Lucas, Stapleton & Partners, *Voyager Point: Assessment of Historical Archaeological Significance*, prepared for Wattle Grove Developments, Sydney, 1996. This report was completed as a heritage requirement, before construction could take place.

22 WA Pert, Depy Comm Taxation, to Surveyor and Property Officer, Dept of the Interior, 3 May 1949, re assessment of Portion 53: NAA, SP857/1, item PA/123 East Hills migrants' hostel site.

23 Edmund W Leane married Ellen Pike, 1895 (BDM, 3337/1895).

24 Lucas et al, *Voyager Point*, contains historical and archival information about Portion 53 and brief consideration of why the area may have been considered an Aboriginal reserve.

25 C Keating, *On the Frontier: A Social History of Liverpool*, Hale & Iremonger, Sydney, 1996.

26 Ted Trainer, interview with Heather Goodall, 23 Aug 2008.

27 Pert to Surveyor and Property Officer, 3 May 1949.

28 W Funnell, Secy Dept Labour and National Service, to Secy Dept of Immigration, 2 Feb 1949: NAA SP857/1, PA/123 East Hills migrants' hostel site.

29 Pert to Surveyor and Property Officer, 3 May 1949.

30 Leslie Leane b 1905 at Liverpool (BDM, 24571/1905), m E Kennedy at Chatswood in 1927 (12095/1927).

31 Pike stayed at 11 Bedford St,Willoughby: Joseph Pike to Dept of the Interior, 29 May 1951: NAA, PA/2465.

32 Notes from informal interview with Heather Goodall, 23 May 2008.

33 G A Watson,Depy Crown Solicitor to Surveyor and Property Officer, Dept of the Interior, 7 Dec 1949; and WE Davidson, Surveyor and Property Officer, to JH Pike, 24 May 1950: NAA, SP857/1, item PA/123 East Hills migrants' hostel site.

34 Compare plan PR 49/1917 (enclosed in Pert to Surveyor and Property Office, 3 May 1949) and sketch map of fence line of migrant workers' hostel (enclosed in R Snellgrove, Dept of the Interior to Manager, Ray Fitzpatrick Quarries, 5 Nov 1964, granting right of way to access commercial quarry lease: both NAA, SP857/1, item PA/123 East Hills migrants' hostel) with Pike's own sketch map, 19 June 1951 (NAA, SP857/10, item PR/2465, East Hills NSW: Application for purchase of land).

35 JH Pike to Property Officer, Dept of the Interior,19 June 1951: NAA, SP857/10, item PR/2465, East Hills NSW: Application for purchase of land.

36 Depy Comm Taxation to Surveyor and Property Office, Dept of the Interior, 24 Aug 1951; WE Davidson, Surveyor and Property Officer to JH Pike, 3 Dec 1951: NAA, SP857/10, item PR/2465, East Hills NSW: Application for purchase of land.

37 JH Pike to Property Officer, 8 May 1954: NAA, SP857/10, item PR/2465, East Hills NSW: Application for purchase of land.

38 R Snellgrove, Chief Property Officer, Dept of the Interior, to JH Pike, 18 June 1954: NAA, SP857/10, item PR/2465, East Hills NSW: Application for purchase of land.

8 Herne Bay to Green Valley: Judy's river

1   This chapter's account of the Smith family's experiences is based on the family photo album and a series of interviews with Judy Chester and Janny Ely (née Smith): Judy, Janny and Robyn Williams, interviews with H Goodall, 13 March 1992, 8 Aug 1999 and 24 Feb 2002; Judy and Janny, interview with H Goodall, 12 Oct 2006. All quotations from these interviews unless otherwise noted.

2   *The Dawn*,1 March 1954, p 7.

3   S Rosen, *Bankstown: A Sense of Identity*, Hale & Iremonger, Sydney, 1996, p 129.

4   DH Coward, *Out of Sight: Sydney's Environmental History 1851–1981*, Department of Economic History, ANU, Canberra, 1988, pp 250–51; NG Butlin (ed), *Sydney's Environmental Amenity 1970–1975*, ANU Press, Canberra, 1976, p 151; see also D Powell, *Out West: Perceptions of Sydney's Western Suburbs*, A&U, Sydney, 1993, ch 4.

5   Rosen, Bankstown, p 129.

6   Robyn Williams, interview with Heather Goodall, 30 Aug 2006.

7   John Lennis(Indigenous Liaison Officer, Hawkesbury-Nepean CMA), interview with Allison Cadzow, 12 Sept 2006.

8   Jason Groves, interview with Allison Cadzow, 29 Aug 2006.

9   *New Dawn*, August 1970, p 13.

10 One of the authors, Heather Goodall, was growing up with her brothers just a few kilometres away at exactly the same time. The boys in the Goodall family were particularly familiar with the tunnels, but none of the family were aware of the by-then large Aboriginal population just across the creek.

11 C Allport, 'Castles of security: The New South Wales Housing Commission and home ownership 1941–67', in M Kelly (ed), *Sydney: City of Suburbs*, UNSW Press/Sydney History Group, Sydney, 1987, p 114.

12 Kel Connell and Frances Seitch, interview with Heather Goodall, 5 May 2006; Robert Haworth, interview, 17 Nov 2005.

13 M Garside, *Padstow Park Progress Association History 1913–2001*, PPPA, Sydney, 2001.

14 Examples are some of the central figures in these chapters, Janny Ely and Robyn Williams, who remained living on the middle Georges River until the later years of their lives, but have now moved further upstream towards Campbelltown and Picton.

15 H Goodall, *Invasion to Embassy*: *Land in Aboriginal Politics in New South Wales 1770–1972*, A&U, Sydney, 1996, ch 20.

16 G Morgan,'The moral surveillance of Aboriginal applicants for public housing in NSW in the 1970s', *Australian Aboriginal Studies*, 2, 1999, pp 3–14; 'Assimilation and resistance: Housing Indigenous Australians in the 1970s', *Journal of Sociology*, 36(3), 2000, pp 187–204; *Unsettled Places: Aboriginal People and Urbanisation in New South Wales*, Wakefield Press, Adelaide, 2006; P Read (ed), *Settlement: A History of Australian Indigenous Housing*, Aboriginal Studies Press, Canberra, 2000.

17 Judy Chester, interviews 1992, 2005 and 2006; Morgan, *Unsettled Places*, pp 59, 70–71, 87, 91, 118.

18 *The Dawn*, Sept 1962, p 5.

19 *The Dawn*, Sept 1962, p 5.

20 Goodall, *Invasion to Embassy*, ch 20.

21 Robyn Williams, interview with Heather Goodall, 30 Aug 2006.

22 This quote and those following are from interviews with Judy with Heather Goodall on 25 Mar 2005, 4 Sept 2005 and 12 Oct 2006.

23 Morgan, 'The moral surveillance', pp 3–14; *Unsettled Places*, pp 116–119.

24 R Langford, *Don't Take Your Love to Town*, Penguin, Ringwood, 1988, pp 174–76; *Real Deadly*, A&R, Sydney, 1992, pp 23–32and see also similar reflections by Langford, 'The Koori way': Belongin places', in D Modjeska (ed), *Inner Cities: Women's Memory of Place*, Penguin, Melbourne, 1989. Powell, *Out West*, pp 66–67 discusses Langford's account of Green Valley.

25 C Allport, 'Women and public housing in Sydney 1930–1961', PhD thesis, Macquarie University,1990, p 360 notes: 'the vitality that arose in these communities came from a strong commitment made by individuals towards community goals, their willingness to harass authorities for proper provision and their commitment to finance facilities from their own resources'.

26 Charlie Leon, interview with Faith Bandler, 1981, in F Bandler and L Fox, *The Time Was Ripe*, Alternative Publishing Cooperative, Chippendale, 1983, p 23.

27 J Maynard, *Fight for Liberty and Freedom: The Origins of Australian Aboriginal Activism*, Aboriginal Studies Press, Canberra, 2007; J Horner, *Vote Ferguson for Aboriginal Freedom: A Biography*, Australian and New Zealand Book Company, Sydney, 1974.

28 Helen Hambly, interviews with Heather Goodall, 15 and 22 Aug, and 10 Oct 1989; Leon interview with Bandler, *The Time Was Ripe*, p 21; *AAF Bulletin*, Oct 1961, report of rural trip by Leon, Helen Hambly and Ray Peckham, cited in *The Time Was Ripe*, p 79.

29 Leon, interview with Bandler, *The Time Was Ripe*, p 21.

30 C Leon to Groves, 11 Dec 1957, ML MS, AAF correspondence files 1957–1967, file G, 4057/11. Groves was AAF president from 1958 to 1966, then again on its closing in 1969.

31 Leon, interview with Bandler, *The Time Was Ripe*, p 22.

32 J Horner to Ald TF Lewin, Moorebank, 19 July 1963, ML MS, AAF correspondence files, file L, 1957–1967, 4057/11.

33 *The Dawn*, Mar 1964, p 3.

34 Bandler and Fox, *The Time Was Ripe*, p 126.

35 C Leon, press release to country media, 4 Feb 1961, ML MS, AAF correspondence file 1957–67, file L, 4057/11.
36 Jean Horner to Peggy Leon, 22 Nov 1962, ML MS, AAF correspondence files 1957–1967, file L 4057/11.
37 *The Dawn*, Dec 1963.
38 Bandler and Fox, *The Time Was Ripe*, pp 130–31.
39 Leon, undated speech, ML MS, AAF correspondence files 1957–1967, file L, 4057/11; (dated from brief quote in *The Time Was Ripe*, p 193).
40 Judy Chester, interviews 25 Mar and 4 Sept 2005.
41 *The Dawn*, Aug 1963, p 1 (ML holds the negatives: GP02–21472, GPO 2-21630, 1963).
42 Robyn Williams, interview, 30 Aug 2006.
43 Robyn Williams, interview, 30 Aug 2006.
44 Judy Chester, interview, 4 Sept 2005.
45 Robyn Williams tells similar stories from her past, in conversation with Janny Ely and Allison Cadzow, 7 Oct 2004.

9 Finding Guragurang: caring for country

1 Mrs Jean Stewart (née Simms) recorded account of her family history in C Illert (ed),'The Story of the Littlest Gundungaras and their great walk to La Perouse', 2005, attachment 1, in C Illert and NIAC, Submission to Dept of Environment and Heritage on various environmental matters, 2006.
2 Brad Steadman, interview, 20 Nov 2005; H Goodall, 'Main streets and riverbanks: the politics of place in an Australian country town', in R Washington and H Goodall (eds), *Echoes from the Poisoned Well: Global Memories of Environmental Injustice*, Lexington, 2006.
3 C Leon, undated speech, ML MS, AAF correspondence files, file L, 4057/11; (dated from brief quote in *The Time Was Ripe*, p 193).
4 IS Mitchell and JE Cawte, 'The Aboriginal family voluntary resettlement scheme: an approach to Aboriginal adaptation', *Australian and New Zealand Journal of Psychiatry*, 11, 1977, pp 29–35; I McLeod, *Shade and Shelter: The Story of Aboriginal Family Resettlement*, illust B Reid, Jacaranda Press, Brisbane, 1982; G Morgan,'The moral surveillance of Aboriginal applicants for public housing in NSW in the 1970s', *Australian Aboriginal Studies*, 2, 1999, pp 3–14.
5 Bitumen and Oil Refineries (Aust) Ltd.
6 J Kijas, '"From obscurity into the fierce light of amazing popularity": Internal migration on the far north coast' in H Wilson (ed), *Belonging in the Rainbow Region*, Southern Cross University Press, Lismore, 2003; J Kijas, 'A place at the coast: Internal migration and the shift to the coastal countryside', in *Transformations: Region, Culture, Society*, 2002, <www.ahs.cqu.edu.au/transfonTiations/ioumal/pdf/Ro2/1cijas.pdf>.
7 H Goodall, *Invasion to Embassy*: *Land in Aboriginal Politics in New South Wales 1770–1972*, A&U, Sydney, 1996, pp 288–302; H Goodall, 'Evans Head and area: Research in respect of the application for a determination of native title, Federal Court of Australia, number NG 6034 of 1998: Lawrence Wilson

v Minister for Lands and Conservation. Prepared for the Native Title Services NSW, Oct 2003, unpublished.

8 Kijas, 'From obscurity'; 'A place at the coast'.

9 See chapter 8, n 1 for the main interviews conducted with these women.

10 E Ross, *Of Storm and Struggle: Pages from Labour History*, Alternative Publishing/New Age, Sydney, 1982, p 176; C Sullivan, *Castles in the Air: Ideology, Myth and the Australian Folk Revival*, National Film and Sound Archive, Canberra, 2006, p l7.

11 M and V Burgmann, *Green Bans, Red Union: Environmental Activism and the New South Wales Builders Labourers' Federation*, UNSW Press, Sydney, 1998.

12 *Herstory*, Liverpool Women's Health Centre, <www.liverpoolwomens health. org.au/aboutUs/herstory.html>.

13 K Cook and H Goodall (eds), *Yarning with Cookie: Key Activists Talk with Kevin Cook about Tranby, Land Rights and the Struggle for Change*, Aboriginal Studies Press, forthcoming, 2010. The Aboriginal Education Consultative Group was a wholly Aboriginal advisory group recently set up to review all Aboriginal-related education initiatives.

14 Cook and Goodall, *Yarning with Cookie*.

15 J Kijas, *Revival, Renewal & Return: Ray Kelly & the NSW Sites of Significance Survey*, DECC, NSW, 2005; MA Hamilton and S Andersen, 'A commemorative history of the National Parks and Wildlife Service', draft, DECC, Sydney, 2008.

16 It became law only when the Aboriginal groups were forced into accepting a concurrent bill, the *Crown Lands Validation of Revocations Act, No 55*, 1983. This was a piece of retrospective legislation, validating what had been the illegal revocation of thousands of hectares of Aboriginal reserve land between 1913 and 1966. Aboriginal people universally condemned this retrospective legislation but had little choice but to accept it if they wanted any Land Rights at all to be recognised by the State: see L Behrendt, *Achieving Social Justice: Indigenous Rights and Australia's Future*, Federation Press, 2003.

17 M Wilkie, *Aboriginal Land Rights in NSW*, Alternative Publishing/Black Books, Sydney, 1985; J Terry, Review of Wilkie in, *Aboriginal Law Bulletin*, 50, 1985.

18 Wayne Dargan, interview with Heather Goodall 10 Sept 2008.

19 Wayne Dargan, interview, with Heather Goodall 10 Sept 2008.

20 Sydney Prehistory Group, *In Search of the Cobrakall: A Survey of the Aboriginal Sites in the Campbelltown Area South of Sydney*, NPWS, Sydney, 1983, pt 1. This important survey investigated areas to the south of the military reserve.

21 AXIS Environmental/AMBS Consulting, for the Dept of Defence, *Holsworthy Training Area Environmental Audit: Main Report*, 1996, pp 91–111; Evidence of Ms Glenda Chalker, of the Cubbitch Barta Native Title Claimants Group, Minutes of evidence to Joint Committee of Public Works, 12 Dec 2005: <www.aph.gov.au/hansard/joint/commttee/J8900.pdf> (viewed 8 Feb 2009).

22 (C'wlth) Dept of Environment, Water, Heritage and the Arts, Australian Heritage Database, 'Cubbitch Barta', <www.environment.gov.au/cgibin/ahdb /search.pl?mode=place_detail;place_id=100633>,

23 The spelling of the Tharawal Land Council's name, which uses the unvoiced

'T' for the first consonant, is one of the well accepted variants of 'Dharawal', and was chosen by that Land Council's members at the time of its formation.

24 Tharawal LALC, 're Relocation of 171st Aviation Squadron to Holsworthy Barracks', submission to the C'wlth Parliamentary Standing Committee on Public Works, 9 Nov 2005. He was citing the National Estate Statement of Significance, written with much involvement by the Aboriginal organisations, in which Cubbitch Barta was nominated for the National Estate in 1998: see its inventory entry, Australian Heritage Database (as above n 22).

25 C Foley (Secy Tharawal LALC) to Navin Officer (consultants mediating Trans-port and Regional Development and Aboriginal communities), statement, 16 July 1997, in Navin Officer/PPK, 'Technical paper: Aboriginal cultural heritage proposal for a second Sydney airport at Badgery's Creek or Holsworthy', Commonwealth Dept Transport and Recreation, Dec 1997, appx J.

10 Resilience on a city river today

1 M Wilke, *Aboriginal Land Rights in NSW*, Alternative Publishing Co, Sydney, 1985 is a useful overview of the Land Rights structure established in 1983.

2 For example, a shire in far north-western NSW argued that land on the outskirts of a tiny town could not be claimed because it was 'wanted for future urban expansion'. Such assertions did not have to be proven, only stated, to obstruct any land claim.

3 H Goodall, *Invasion to Embassy: Land in Aboriginal Politics in New South Wales 1770–1972*, A&U, Sydney, 1996, ch 11, 12, 22 and 24.

4 *The Leader*, 12 Mar 1991, pp 1–2, showing internal debates within the Land Council over sale of land vs anxiety about housing. There were 30–40 families in Gandangara LALC who needed housing, yet many within the Land Council did not agree to sales or land swaps to meet those needs.

5 'Residents in shock', *The Leader*, 12 March 1991, pp 1–2.

6 *The Leader*, 6 Sept 1999, pp 3 and 21.

7 *The Leader*, 25 May 2000, p 19.

8 *The Koori Mail*, 23 Jan 2002, p 14.

9 *Aboriginal People Protecting Country: Environmental Sustainability Success Stories ~ Our Environment*, Cultural Heritage Division, DECC, Sydney, 2004, 2006, pp 2–6.

10 G Peacock, '"Aboriginal dreaming": Aboriginal Land Councils and sustainable land development projects in Sydney', paper to the Royal Australian Planning Institute conference, 2001.

11 Notes from informal interviews and conversations with Fred Malone, John Lennis, Lew Solberg, Janny Ely, Robyn Williams, Glenda Chalker.

12 Evidence of Glenda Chalker (Cubbitch Barta Native Title Claimants Group), Minutes of evidence to Joint Committee of Public Works, 12 Dec 2005, <www.aph.gov.au/hansard/joint/commttee/J8900.pdf>.

13 Gandangara Local Aboriginal Land Council Achievements, <www.gandangara.org.au/Achievements/tabid/54/Default.aspx>.

14 *Liverpool Leader*, 21 July 2004, p 12.
15 Known as the 'stolen generations': see A Haebich, *Broken Circles: Fragmenting Indigenous Families 1800–2000*, Fremantle Arts Centre Press, Fremantle, 2000. The restoration of family links for the people removed from their families by government policies has been undertaken by the pioneering body Link-Up, founded by Coral Edwards and Peter Read in 1980 as a voluntary research and support service: <www.linkupnsw.org.au>.
16 G Cowlishaw, *The City's Outback*, UNSW Press, Sydney, 2009.
17 Lew Solberg, interviews with Allison Cadzow, 29 Sept 2004; 4 May 2007.
18 B Donald, *Hargrave Park? Never Heard of It ~ The Story of a Forgotten Suburb*, Casula Powerhouse Arts Centre, Sydney, 2007, p 93.
19 Combined NSW Catchment Management Authorities, Annual report 2003–04, vol 1, CMA Activities and Acheivements, p 29: <http://www.cma.nsw.gov.au/pdf/cma_ar_vol01.pdf >; Donald, *Hargrave Park?*, pp 82–84.
20 CMA, 'Catchment Management Authorities: An overview', <http://www.cma.nsw.gov.au>, 2007.
21 Combined NSW CMAs, Annual Report 2003-4, p 29; Sydney Coastal Councils Group, Minutes, 18 Dec 2004, p B438; Botany Bay Coastal Councils Initiative, reference committee, <www.sydney.cma.nsw.gov.au/bbcci/ReferenceCommittee.html>; CMA, Annual Report 2004-5, p 11.
22 Sydney Metropolitan CMA, Annual report 2006–07, p 11 discusses partnerships with Aboriginal Communities.
23 VK Haskins, *One Bright Spot*, Palgrave Macmillan, Basingstoke, 2005, p 171.
24 T Banivanua-Mar, 'Carving wilderness: Queensland's National Parks and the unsettling of emptied lands 1890–1910', forthcoming.
25 See M Harper and R White, 'The "nationalisms" of the first National Parks: Was Australia's model different?', AHA conference, Melbourne, 2008; on exclusivity and parks generally, see M Rangarajan and G Shahabuddin, 'Displacement and relocation from protected areas: Towards a biological and historical synthesis', *Conservation and Society*, 4(3), 2006, pp 359–78; M Adams, 'Foundational myths: Country and conservation in Australia', *Landscapes of Meaning: Transforming Cultures eJournal*, 3(1), 2008, pp 291–317: <http://epress.lib.uts.edu.au/ojs/index.php/TfC>. See also J Huggins and J Jacobs, 'Kooramindanjie Place', in L Johnson, J Huggins and J Jacobs (eds), *Placebound: Australian Feminist Geographies*, Oxford University Press, Melbourne, 2000, on the presumed absence of contemporary Aboriginal visitors to National Parks.
26 The most recent extension, in 2007, including land all the way from Mill Creek up river to Pleasure Point on the southern bank.
27 Y Stewart, 'Living on country', *Landscapes of Meaning: Transforming Cultures eJournal*, 3(1), 2008, pp 353–76; and in the same volume P Thompson, 'From movement to management: Aboriginal assertion, government and environmentalist responses and some ways forward regarding conservation and social justice', pp 323–47; and Adams, 'Foundational myths', pp 291–317: <www.epress.lib.uts.edu.au/ojs/index.php/TfC>.
28 One National Park covers the northern point, where the French explorer La Perouse landed in 1788 and close to the home of the La Perouse Aboriginal

community, the other is at Kurnell on the southern point, where Captain Cook had landed in 1770.

29 D Kelly, paper on the Towra initiative, 'Cities, nature, justice' symposium, UTS, 10 Dec 2008.

11 Reflections in the river

1   VK Haskins, *One Bright Spot*, Palgrave Macmillan, Basingstoke, 2005, describes Joan Kingsley-Strack's encounter with Joe Anderson, as well as outlining his continuing involvement with the Day of Mourning and surrounding events.

2   H Goodall, *Invasion to Embassy*: *Land in Aboriginal Politics in New South Wales 1770–1972*, A&U, Sydney, 1996, pp 358–60; P Fiske (director), *Australia Daze*, 1989 (a documentary on Australia's bicentennial celebrations on 26 Jan 1988).

3   The following, unless otherwise noted, is drawn from these submissions: Evidence of members of Tharawal LALC, Glenda Chalker (Cubbitch Barta Native Title Claimants Group), Cliff Foley (chair), and Charlie Mundine, Minutes of Evidence, Joint Committee of Public Works, 12 Dec 2005, <www.aph.gov.au/hansard/joint/commttee/J8900.pdf> (viewed 8 Feb 2009).

4   Heather Goodall was the coordinator for the UTS subject, Applying Aboriginal History, part of the Graduate Certificate in Applied History offered by the School of Humanities in 1990. Our photographs of the field trip to Sandy Point show Cliff and Robyn with both Aboriginal and non-Aboriginal students, along with the extraordinary artwork and prolific artifact scatters along the southern bank of the river.

5   Cliff Foley, interview with Heather Goodall, 18 Sept 2006.

6   Tharawal LALC (Cliff Foley chair), submission to Parliamentary Committee on expansion of military activities at Cubbitch Barta, Holsworthy, 9 Nov 2005, <www.aph.gov.au/House/committee/pwc/holsworthy171/subs/sub2.pdf>.

Index

Page numbers in **bold** refer to illustrations.

48–49, 53, 286
Perkins, Charlie 217
Perry family 162–63
petitions 56, 58–59, 70, 72, 73–75,
    77–78, 85, 149, 155, 175, 201
Phillip, Arthur 35, 41–42, 44, 48, 82,
    279
Phillips, Clara 91
Picnic Point 171
Pike family 163
Pike, Ellen 176
Pike, Joe 179–84
Pitman, Paddy 148
pleasure grounds 118, 152
Pleasure Point 271
Pigface Point 177
pollution 3, 10, 169, 171–72, 189, 192–
    93, 194, 212, 213, 218, 265
Port Hacking 33, 67, 71, 84, 94–95,
    97–98, 100–101
Port Kembla 167–68
Portion 53: 56, 58–59, 61, 72, 78, 175–
    77, 178–79, 180–84, **181**, 193
Price, John 139
Progress Associations 146, 152–57, 170,
    192, 254
Prospect Creek 28, 36, 43, 135, 162
Protection policy 29, 82, 151

Racklin, Robert 91
Red Jack 101
Redfern 173, 186–87, 195, 204, 260
RSL 126
reserves, Aboriginal 56, 59–60, 74–75,
    114–115, 173, 176, 178, 186, 197, 231
    revocation of 60, 136, 142, 145, 168,
    208, 220, 231, 252
resilience 4, 11, 87, 108, 132, 161–62,
    249–50, 278–88
    see also locality; mobility; networks;
    travelling
Revesby 194
Ridgeway, Sid 142–43, 144
River Keeper 264
Riverwood *see* Herne Bay
Robinson, J 102
Robinson, SBJ 94–96, 99–100

Roma 18–19
Roseby Park 5, 148, 220
Rowley, Evelyn 126, **128**
Rowley, John (I) 58
Rowley, John (II) 58, 61
Rowley, Thomas 56, 58
Rowley, William 69–72, 76, 81, 102,
    105, **107**, 112, 115, 116, 119, 125,
    148, 249, 273

St Clair 115
St Johns Park women's group 225–26,
    228, 229, 232, 233, 235–36, 242,
    244, 245
St Marys 198
salt marsh 34
Salt Pan Creek 1–4, **2**, 5, 21, 26, 28, 29,
    31, 33, 49, **117**, 119, 126, **127**, **138**,
    185, 194, 195–96, 248, 272
Salt Pan Creek community 4, 10, 72,
    85, 109, 112, 115, 119, 122–29, **123**,
    125–26, 135–36, 147–53, 161, 165,
    166, 205, 248–49
    activism of 145, 147–49, 157–58, 184,
    248–49, 279
    and white neighbours 49–50, 153,
    254
Salt Pan Creek Progress Association
    152
    see also Padstow Park PA
Sandy Point 33, 272
Sandy Point Progress Association 152
Sans Souci 33
Saunders, Kate 91
Scherzer, Karl 66, 105
schools 64, 65, 72, 82, 85, 105, 146,
    152, 186, 194, 201–203, 204, 216,
    225, 247
segregation policy 10, 111–112, 146,
    151, 172, 216
Shepherd family 136–37
Sherrit family 137, 199–203
Simms family 215
Simms, Henry 106
Simpson, George 97
smallpox 33, 37, 39, 42, 54, 98
Smith family 199, 215

www.ingramcontent.com/pod-product-compliance
Lightning Source LLC
Chambersburg PA
CBHW020455270326
41926CB00008B/616